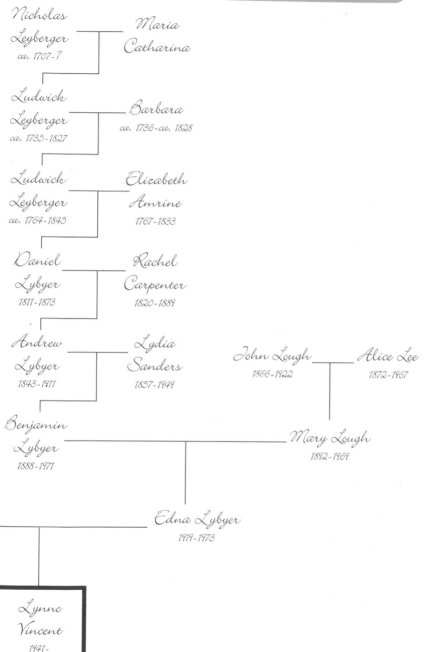

Nicholas
Leyberger
ca. 1707-?

Maria
Catharina

Ludwick
Leyberger
ca. 1735-1827

Barbara
ca. 1736-ca. 1828

Ludwick
Leyberger
ca. 1764-1845

Elizabeth
Amrine
1767-1833

Daniel
Lybyer
1811-1873

Rachel
Carpenter
1820-1889

Andrew
Lybyer
1843-1911

Lydia
Sanders
1857-1949

John Lough
1866-1922

Alice Lee
1872-1967

Benjamin
Lybyer
1888-1971

Mary Lough
1892-1969

Edna Lybyer
1919-1973

Lynne
Vincent
1941-

Blue Skies,
No Fences

For:
Henry Delfiner —

Lynne Cheney

Casper, Wyoming, 1945.

Blue Skies, No Fences

A Memoir of Childhood and Family

LYNNE CHENEY

Threshold Editions

New York London Toronto Sydney

This work is a memoir. It reflects the author's present recollections
of her experience over a period of years.

Threshold Editions
A Division of Simon & Schuster, Inc.
1230 Avenue of the Americas
New York, NY 10020

First Threshold Editions hardcover edition October 2007

THRESHOLD EDITIONS and colophon are
trademarks of Simon & Schuster, Inc.

For information about special discounts for bulk purchases,
please contact Simon & Schuster Special Sales at
1-800-456-6798 or business@simonandschuster.com.

Designed by Joy O'Meara

Manufactured in the United States of America

1   3   5   7   9   10   8   6   4   2

Library of Congress Cataloging-in-Publication Data
Cheney, Lynne V.
Blue skies, no fences: a memoir of childhood and family /
Lynne Cheney. — 1st Threshold Editions hardcover ed.
p. cm.
Includes bibliographical references and index.
1. Cheney, Lynne V.—Childhood and youth.   2. Cheney, Lynne V.—Family.
3. Vice-Presidents' spouses—United States—Biography.
4. Cheney, Richard B.—Childhood and youth.   5. Cheney, Richard B.—Family.
6. Vice-Presidents—United States—Biography.   7. Wyoming—Biography.
I. Title.
E840.8.C4335A3 2007
352.23'90922—dc22
[B]   2007022279
ISBN-13: 978-1-4165-3288-0 (alk. paper)
ISBN-10:   1-4165-3288-9 (alk. paper)

To my family

ACKNOWLEDGMENTS

M Y THANKS FIRST of all to Chris DeMuth, president of the
American Enterprise Institute, for creating a setting that
fosters intellectual exchange and encourages wide-ranging research on a variety of subjects. Those of us who are AEI scholars
are very fortunate, not least because of the fine young people who
are drawn to AEI and help in our work. Kathryn Duryea, my assistant on this book, brought intelligence, patience, and persis-
tence to a multitude of research tasks, and I am grateful to her as
well as to Elisabeth Irwin, who helped when this book was in its
beginning stages, and to Cristina Allegretti, my assistant as I
finished it. My gratitude as well to AEI interns Amanda Fritsch,
Danny Laurence, Kate Majeski, and Meredith Slater.

I'd like to thank my dear friend Mary Matalin, under whose
Threshold imprint this book is being published. Her unflagging
energy and clear insight lift the spirits and guide the way, and I
feel lucky to have her in my life. I'm grateful to the entire team
at Simon and Schuster, beginning at the top with president and
CEO Jack Romanos and president of the Adult Publishing
Group, Carolyn Reidy. Editorial Director Alice Mayhew read the
manuscript and made many wise suggestions, for which I am
most appreciative. Louise Burke, publisher of Pocket Books, is
an inspirational and enthusiastic leader, and I would like to thank

her for her advice and assistance and to acknowledge the terrific group she has working with her, including Anthony Ziccardi, Sally Franklin, Lisa Litwack, Johanna Farrand, and Min Choi.

I would also like to express my gratitude to Robert Barnett, who has cheerfully and with unfailingly good judgment guided me yet one more time through the publishing process.

In the notes to this book, I thank the many librarians, archivists, curators, and researchers on whom I have relied, but there are two leaders I would particularly like to acknowledge: Archivist of the United States Allen Weinstein and Librarian of Congress James Billington. During their tenures, the vast holdings of the National Archives and Record Administration and the Library of Congress have become increasingly accessible to people all across America who want to know more about history. That is an accomplishment of which they—and all of us—can be very proud.

Blue Skies,
No Fences

PROLOGUE

IN THE YEARS right after World War II, the Vincent family spent Saturday afternoons watching people go by. The three of us—my mother, my father, and I—would get into the front seat of our 1940 cream-colored Oldsmobile and head toward Second and Center, an intersection in downtown Casper that my father considered prime for people watching. As soon as we saw the Rialto Theater, a Second and Center landmark, we'd start looking for cars backing out, sometimes circling the block until one of us, usually my mother, spotted something. "There, right there, Wayne," she'd say, whereupon my father would slam on the brakes, prompting honking behind us, which in turn led to profanity from him and ensured as certainly as anything could that he wasn't budging, not until the departing car was out of the way and he could pull into the parking place—very, very slowly if the cars behind him were still honking.

Once we had secured our spot, my mother would get out, stick a nickel in the meter, then get back in and light a cigarette. My father would light one, too, and they'd settle back while I got on my knees so I could see the passing scene. "There's Mary Stuckenhoff," my mother might say. "She worked for the paper before she married Doc." Or one day: "There's Anne Marie Spencer. She's on the radio, Lynnie. The new show on KVOC about the Stuart Shop?"

"Where style knows no size," I replied, repeating the slogan I'd learned listening to the radio with my mother while she ironed.

She smiled at this cleverness, but my father saw it as occasion for a nudge. "And what grade are you going to be in, Lynnie?" he asked.

"First grade," I told him.

"Only *first grade?*" he asked in mock dismay. "Little girl smart as you ought to be in second grade at least."

I pretended to ignore him and watched the people passing by, the women in dresses, the men in shirtsleeves and hats. All walked with heads high, giving even strangers hospitable glances, stopping for friends, moving over to the side if a long conversation was in order, into the Leed's Shoe Store alcove or under the Ayres Jewelry clock, mounted high above the sidewalk on a cast-iron pedestal.

My mother had the most to say. "There's Nick Brattis," she might observe. "He's starting a grocery store down on the Sand-bar." Or "There's Willocine. You remember Willocine, Lynnie?" I certainly did remember Willocine, a plump and pretty redhead who had plans to open a beauty shop but was meanwhile tending to customers out of her apartment on North Beech. Earlier in the summer, she had enticed my mother into letting her give me a permanent wave, a procedure that involved wrapping my hair around rollers, applying a foul-smelling liquid, and attaching the rollers to clamps hanging down from a large machine. I sat there forever while the machine heated my hair, to be rewarded when the process was over with frizz standing straight out from my head. "The child's hair doesn't look so thin!" Willocine announced, proud of the result. My mother didn't say a word but undertook to disguise Willocine's handiwork as soon as we got home—and for weeks thereafter—by braiding my hair into pigtails.

I was related to Willocine somehow, as I was to many of the people my mother called to my attention. One Saturday, she identified a handsome gray-haired woman who seemed vaguely familiar as Alma, one of my grandpa's sisters, and she repeated a fact so amazing that I never tired of hearing it: my grandfather was one of *eighteen* children, most of them boys and most back in Missouri. "Alma's married to Ulysses," she said, "but everybody calls him Ulyss." "Useless is more like it," my father added.

Although my mother was more adept at narrating the passing scene, my father had a keen eye for the unusual. One day, he pointed out a man wearing two-tone shoes, something not often seen in Casper, Wyoming, in the mid-1940s. The shoe wearer was Harry Yesness, whose haberdashery had a fountain out front that every kid in town clamored to drink from. It was a bronze likeness of Yesness himself, dressed in a barrel, water burbling out of his head. "He's got more money than Carter has liver pills," observed my father as the two-tone shoes went by.

Sooner than I wished, it was time to go home. My father would back out of our parking place, and we'd head for our white frame house on South David Street. Later, my mother would fix supper, and then sometimes one of my aunts would come over to take care of me while my parents went dancing. They loved to dance, and I loved to watch them practice in the dining room, which they'd never furnished, my pretty mother being whirled around by my handsome, curly-haired father.

My favorite Saturday nights, though, were the ones they stayed home. If it was summer, we'd go outside after the dishes were done, move the painted metal chairs off the front porch, and put them on the grass. There were only two chairs, so I'd sit on my mother's lap and then my father's and maybe my mother's again. We'd watch the stars come out, more and more of them as the night grew darker. My father would go inside and fix a drink for himself and bring one out for my mother. They would smoke, and I would follow the patterns that the glowing ends of their cigarettes made in the dark.

When it got too cool to sit outside, as it often does on summer evenings in Wyoming, one of them would take me upstairs to my room. My dog, Boy, a female despite her name, would follow, and when I was tucked in, she would jump onto the bed and lie down next to me. I would fall asleep and dream, often that I could fly. It's easy to do, just a matter of will, of closing your eyes and lifting yourself off the ground. Just want to fly and try very hard to fly, and you will find yourself soaring above the earth.

IT'S BEEN SIXTY YEARS since I sat on Second Street watching people go by. My memories come in bits and pieces, and I turn to old newspapers and photo albums to fit the fragments together. I talk to friends and relatives, prevail upon my husband for his memories, and the clearer the picture of that time after World War II becomes, the more I realize how lucky we were to grow up then. America had come through the Depression; we had triumphed in war; and the people of Casper, walking heads high down Second Street, reflected the mood of much of the nation. The country seemed in control of its destiny and individual Americans in charge of theirs. No doubt, there were kids from California to Maine dreaming at night that if they just tried hard enough, they could fly, and during their waking hours, they were thinking that life was like that. If you were determined, the sky was the limit.

To grow up in those years and in the place that I did was to be twice fortunate. Casper, Wyoming, population 18,000 when I was born, was large enough to hold the surprises of civilization but small enough that the prairie was close by, for some in our town right out the front door, stretching on forever under the great curving sky. It didn't rain much in Wyoming, so green was a color we saw mostly in spring, but there were endless days when a brilliant blue stretched from horizon to horizon.

The prairie defined not only the surrounding landscape but the place we lived, making the identity of Casper clear. There were no suburbs rolling on and on into other towns that rolled into still more suburbs and other towns. There was Casper, and then there wasn't, so that kids had no doubt about where they were from. You could encompass Casper in your mind, begin to see the forces at work in it, and imagine that you yourself might have an impact on them. You could see yourself creating your own future rather than having one handed to you.

And it never occurred to me that my chances of doing this were diminished because I was a girl. My first-grade readers might show mothers at home and fathers off at work, but I saw my mother working and my grandmother, too. My female teachers, many of whom had known Wyoming in its horse-and-buckboard days, were role models of amazing strength. And while the girls I knew had few opportunities to shine on athletic fields, they were always finding skills they could perfect. Jacks, spelling bees, and baton twirling are period pieces, to be sure, but they were also ways in which we learned how much fun it is to win and how losing should make you try harder.

Casper was a place where girls could thrive, and it was heaven for boys, particularly those who played sports and enjoyed the adulation of small-town fans. The boy I knew best—and would later marry—played baseball and football and also hunted the prairies, fished the streams, and, with his more daring friends, used the five-hundred-foot spillway of one of the dams near Casper as a water slide—an adventure that is in its own way a period piece, impossible to re-create in our safer days, when the great dams of central Wyoming are surrounded by fences.

The town in which we grew up was not a perfect place, not some sin-and-crime-free Pleasantville. Alcohol flowed freely, as signified by a lineup of drinking establishments, the most famous of which was the Wonder Bar, right in the center of town. Patrons who drank too much staggered out onto the sidewalk at all hours of the day, leading mothers to caution their daughters to walk on the other side of the street. One of my friends, whose parents ran a hardware store located next to the lineup of bars, remembers her mother teaching her to jaywalk so she wouldn't have to walk past the saloons on her way to the family store.

Behind the county courthouse, stretching out to the west, was the Sandbar, a district known for gambling, bootleg liquor, and prostitution. Many an honest citizen went there for fried chicken at Fannie Bell's or steak at Shirley's Café, but violence was common in the Sandbar, and it reached other places as well. One summer right after the war, Casper police were kept busy trying to track down the murderer of a woman whose charred body was found in a burnt-out car on a dirt road east of town.

Still, children grew up feeling safe. Adults issued standard warnings ("Don't get into cars with strangers") and made us memorize our phone numbers ("Tell the operator 2069-W"), but they didn't see any need to frighten us. In their view, crime had to do with criminals, not with ordinary people. The murdered woman was an out-of-towner, and, according to rumor, the mob had something to do with her demise. There was no great cause for worry, our parents thought, no need to lock the doors or call the kids in early. And for the most part, they were right.

Casper had this advantage as well: a belief in a bright future was in the gene pool. Many residents of the town either were themselves or were recent descendents of people who had persevered through harrowing circumstances to get to the high plains of the West. One of my Mormon foremothers, who came from Wales in 1849, lost husband and child on the journey west but kept going, convinced that ahead lay the New Zion. Others whom my husband and I count among our forebears arrived in America earlier: tough-minded Puritans, hardworking Germans, Scots-Irish tenant farmers who immigrated in clans. Their families made the westward journey over the course of generations, coming through the struggles and calamities that are part of the American story with belief intact that over the next river or the next mountain range, they would find a better life.

And they usually did, but even when they didn't, they were sure their children would. In the years of my growing up, the adults closest to me, beginning with my parents, had no intention of leaving this to chance. My mother was constantly on the lookout for opportunities for me to learn, whether from teachers, the parents of friends, or an instructor who might make me a world-class tap dancer. My father's self-assigned job was to make sure I understood how much was expected of me, and he did this by letting me know that no matter how well I was doing, I could do better. For all the years of my growing up, he ran variations on the theme he struck when I was in first grade. "Little girl smart as you ought to be in second grade at least."

It was a powerful mix, particularly when combined with the reinforcement that a small town can offer. If you won an award in junior high, your picture would be in the paper. Everyone you knew would read about you at the same time they were reading about Secretary of State John Foster Dulles. The fellow behind the counter at Bluebird Grocery would congratulate you. All your parents' friends would know what you had done.

The passing years bring you face to face with certain realities, of course. We experience turmoil and sadness, see our faults and failings, and come to realize that our destiny is not entirely in our control. We cannot fly, no matter how hard we try. But to start out with utter confidence in the future is a very good thing, and I am grateful beyond measure to those who made it possible for me—my parents, first and foremost, but also the determined men and women stretching back generations, who pinned their hopes on America and kept heading west.

PART ONE

CHAPTER ONE

I AM WRAPPED UP, lying on a bed near a window where white curtains stir. A small boy comes into the room and picks me up. And he drops me.

I have been told that I cannot possibly remember this, but if it happened, and I believe it did, it occurred in a duplex apartment at 630 West 11th in Casper, Wyoming, where my parents brought me after I was born. My mother, the most vigilant of souls, would never under normal circumstances have left me where a child might pick me up, but about the time I turned two months old, my father, a surveyor, had a terrible accident, and I can imagine her being distracted. He fell into the canyon below Seminoe Dam, and although he caught himself on the canyon wall about twenty feet down, he was still badly injured. Rescuers lowered him with ropes and carried him two miles on a makeshift litter to an ambulance. When he arrived in Casper, doctors determined he had broken a leg, both ankles, and every bone in his right foot. My twenty-one-year-old mother was told that my twenty-five-year-old father would be "a cripple for life."

She brought him home from the hospital, took care of him as well as me, and one unseasonably warm winter day pushed his wheelchair out onto the stoop in front of our apartment, where someone took his picture. I've looked at this photograph for

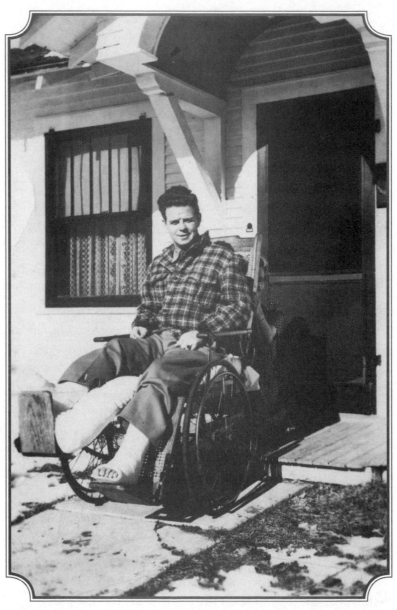

My father, who took a terrible fall in 1941 while working as a surveyor.
I looked at this photo for years before I realized that my mother, trying to
stay out of camera range, is behind his wheelchair.

years, noting patches of snow on the ground and my father in his shirtsleeves squinting into the sun, and then one day not long ago, I discovered my mother, bare-armed, hiding behind his wheelchair. Apparently not wanting her picture taken, she has tried to crouch out of sight. And where am I? Could this be the moment when my contemplation of the white curtains was rudely interrupted?

The date on the photograph is December 1941. The Germans have taken most of Europe, and the Japanese may at this moment be winging their way to Pearl Harbor. A great conflagration is sweeping the world, and in Casper, Wyoming, a small boy drops an even smaller baby on the floor. He is my half-brother, Leon, who is not yet two.

My father's first wife, Tracy Schryer, died giving birth to Leon on March 6, 1940. My father's Mormon mother, Anna Vincent, a beautiful, red-haired woman of legendary will, was so determined that Tracy's Catholic relatives not raise Leon that as soon as the funeral was over, she boarded a train with him and headed for La Junta, Colorado, where she and my grandfather lived. My father, blaming Catholic teaching for Tracy's death, fully supported Anna's leaving with his son. Tracy had hemorrhaged while giving birth, and my father was convinced that her Catholic doctor, believing her soul was safe, had neglected her to focus on the baby, who had to survive and be baptized to avoid eternity in Limbo. Grieving and bitter, my father wanted every bit as much as my grandmother to keep Leon away from the Catholic church.

The trip to La Junta was long and caring for a newborn hard. I imagine Anna holding him close against the spring chill, trying to persuade him to nurse from a bottle, trying to keep the bottle and the baby clean. The milk supply on the train was unreliable and once ran out entirely, whereupon my indomitable grandmother bullied the conductor into wiring ahead so that milk would be waiting at the next stop. By the time she had cared for the baby for five days on the train, she loved him as though he were her own.

My mother and father must have met not long after Tracy Schryer died, because they were married ten months later. Photographs show my mother pretty and stylish, her hair rolled back from her face. My father, with a head of black curls, looks as if he knows how to enjoy himself, and, according to those who knew him then, he did. He loved pool halls and poker games, and he was good at starting fights. Although not a big man, five foot ten perhaps, he had a large temper, and when he felt offended, he would go after the offender, never pausing to consider the other person's size or how many friends he might bring to a fight. In a memorable dance-hall brawl in Cheyenne, Vince, as his friends called him, took on a half-dozen soldiers from Fort Warren and ended up with his jaw so swollen he couldn't eat for days.

In a photograph dated 1940, my father has on a wool overcoat, belted at the waist. In another photo taken at the same time, he has his coat off, revealing a double-breasted pinstripe suit. My mother is the photographer, it's a bright winter day, and you can see her shadow on the snow. And you can understand why she fell for him. As he stands by his new Oldsmobile coupe, hands in his pockets, he looks positively dashing.

I suspect that this picture was taken on December 28, the day my parents eloped to Harrison, Nebraska. I would be born on August 14, 1941, seven and a half months later, so they no doubt suspected I was on the way. But my father may have had another reason for wanting to marry quickly, and that was to create a home for Leon. There were trips between Colorado and Wyoming, with my parents going there and Anna bringing Leon

*My mother and father probably took these pictures of each other
as they were eloping to Nebraska.*

*My beautiful grandmother
Anna Vincent, with me
and my half-brother,
Leon.*

to Casper, and it may have been on a visit to see his father, newly home from the hospital, that the little boy succumbed to the temptation to pick up the baby he found lying on the bed. His effort to carry me was no more successful than my father's attempts to convince Anna that Leon should live with him. She was determined to raise the little boy she had cared for since his birth, the little boy who by this time was calling her Momma. When he was three years old, my grandmother and grandfather officially adopted him.

One might have expected Tracy's family to be up in arms, but sorrow piled upon sorrow for them, leaving little room for indignation. Tracy's father, Paul, died in 1943, and her mother, Theresa, in 1944, at age fifty. According to her obituary, Theresa died of a heart attack, but I remember visiting the house she lived in on David Street and seeing her, rosary in her hands, weeping for her husband, lost so soon after her daughter, and I wonder, did she die of a broken heart? Six months later, there was another death. Tracy's brother, Technical Sergeant Russell Schryer, who had survived thirty months of service in the China-Burma-India theater, was killed when a cargo plane he was aboard crashed into a hangar at Wright Field in Dayton, Ohio.

At war's end, when Betty Schryer, Tracy's sister, got married, she healed whatever rifts there were by inviting the Vincents to her wedding and even asking me to preside over the guest book. In a photo in our family album, I'm standing solemnly in front of the dark-haired bridegroom, wearing a long dress with puffed sleeves. Betty, beautiful in white satin, smiles from the center of the picture—beams, really, as does her sister Doris, the maid of honor, a lovely brunette in taffeta, holding a bouquet of carnations. They have lost parents, a sister, and a brother, but there is still happiness in the world, and in this moment, they have found it.

CHAPTER TWO

IN THE SUMMER after Pearl Harbor, the Army built an air base west of town and began to bring thousands of pilots to Casper to train on the B-24 Liberator Bomber, a workhorse of a plane that was beginning to roll off the nation's wartime production lines. My father, defying dire warnings from doctors, was up and getting around on crutches, unable to return to work as a surveyor at the Bureau of Reclamation but newly employed as an engineering aide at the air base. He and my mother were eager to move out of their crowded apartment, but the arrival of the pilots in town had created a severe housing shortage. They couldn't find a larger place, not until one day when my grandmother Mary Lybyer telephoned. A seamstress at H & G Cleaners, she had heard that a small stucco house hidden behind the H & G was coming up for rent. In 1943, we moved in.

My mother took dozens and dozens of photos of me in front of the stucco house, or the half house, as we sometimes called it, since its address was 1236½ South Walnut. In all of her pictures, I am dressed to the nines. I wear little suits she has made, often with matching coats and hats. There are tiny pleated skirts with suspenders and puffed-sleeve blouses underneath. One photograph shows me squatting in our Victory garden digging for worms. I am wearing a velvet dress.

My mother dressed me up
but didn't worry about
what I did in nice clothes.
Here, in velvet, I'm looking
for worms.

*Being at the center of my mother's
universe was very pleasant, and I
figured out ways to keep her attention.*

My mother regularly took me to Johnson Studio for profes-
sional portraits. Here I am, at one month, not in control of my
head; here at six months, my hair brushed up into a point. When
I was about a year old, my mother had our picture taken together.
I am in a highly starched dress and pinafore, with bangs swirled
onto my forehead; my pretty mother, wearing a dress with beaded
patterns, looks young but exhausted.

Once, with many tears, she began to fill packing boxes in
the little half house. My father had accepted a job in Denver, and
she did not want to move. Her parents, Ben and Mary Lybyer,
were in Casper, as were her three sisters—Maxine, Norma, and
Marion—and her ties to her family were strong. The Lybyers
were close in the way people often are when they have known
hard times, and the Lybyers had seen their share of those for many
generations.

THE FAMILY'S TIME in America dated back to 1739, when Nicholas Leyberger, possibly accompanied by his wife and son, arrived
in Philadelphia aboard a ship called the *Snow Betsey*. Nicholas
had come from the Palatinate, a region in southwest Germany
through which warring factions had been marching for more
than a century, leaving ruined crops and poverty in their wake.
Along with thousands of others, Nicholas left to find a new life,
traveling the Rhine to Holland, sailing to England, and thence
to America. According to a story passed down from his great-
grandson Elijah to Elijah's grandson William, Nicholas sold himself into servitude for three years to pay for his passage.

Within fifteen years, Nicholas and his family were across the
Susquehanna River, farming the rich soil of the Appalachian
Piedmont. Twenty years after that, at the time of the American
Revolution, Nicholas's sons and grandsons were in the Alleghe-

nies, defending the Pennsylvania frontier against Indian attacks, murderous raids that settlers firmly believed were incited by the British, although the Indians certainly had reasons of their own for wanting to drive frontiersmen away. The newcomers were farming on what were hunting lands; they had burned Indian villages; they had murdered Indian women and children. There was violence on both sides, but it was when settlers were killed that the Leybergers left their farms and spent one or two months "scouting the country . . . in protection of the inhabitants," as Nicholas Leyberger, grandson of the immigrant Nicholas, described it many years later. Testifying to his Revolutionary War experience in order to prove that he was a veteran, he reported on a raid in 1776, in which "the Indians made an incursion into Morrison's Cove in Bedford County and burnt Ulrick's Mill and killed all Ulrick's family." Militia and volunteer forces manned a garrison in the area and for five weeks "kept sentry in the country and look[ed] out for the Indians." The next year, "in the time of harvest," a boy hunting cows discovered an Indian trail. According to Nicholas: "The alarm was given and the volunteers were called out. . . . We went in pursuit of the Indians. Our company went along on a ridge of the mountain. The [other] scouts went into a gap of the mountains and were ambushed by the Indians and the captain and all the men belonging to the company except four were killed at the first fire." One of the survivors directed Nicholas's company to where the militiamen had fallen. "Thirty men were killed," Nicholas reported. "We buried the dead."

There were times during the war when settlers left their fields untilled rather than go outside. Only the heavy snows of winter gave relief from raids, and when spring came, only the militias, operating without sufficient arms, provided protection. Concerned about safety, so many settlers fled that wolves moved into the area, and the remaining inhabitants organized an association to encourage their destruction, offering a bounty of two shillings a wolf scalp. Those who stayed sent pleas for assistance to the state and to counties farther east, but although promises were made, no help came, and the list of the dead grew: five near Dunnings Creek; some children by Frankstown; the Tull family, mother, father, and nine daughters; the Peck family, mother, father, and two children. Volunteers and militiamen continued to patrol, but they could not begin to cover all the hills and valleys of the Allegheny frontier.

Finally, the end of the war brought an end to the raids. The Indians moved farther west, and the farmers of Bedford County planted their crops, tended to their cattle, and had time for occasional lightheartedness, as when Ludwick Leyberger, a man who would be remembered for being strong well into old age, demonstrated the soundness of his teeth by using them to pick up a sack of grain and throw it over his shoulder.

Family members who came of age after the Revolutionary War began to move west, most to Ohio, though a few went farther. One of them was the immigrant Nicholas's great-grandson Daniel, who changed his last name to Lybyer and moved to western Indiana, probably traveling on the National Road. By 1835, it provided a graveled route to the Valley of the Wabash, where Daniel, like his ancestors, worked the land.

His son, Andrew Simon Peter, part of the fifth generation in America, grew up as a farmer, but in his nineteenth year, he enlisted in the Union Army, perhaps convinced that if he did not, he would be drafted. Northern governors, trying to meet President Lincoln's call for troops, were using the threat of conscription to persuade men to volunteer, and on March 1, 1863, in Greencastle, Indiana, Andrew signed up for a three-year term of service. Enlistment papers show that he was "free from all bodily defects and mental infirmities." Captain James H. Sands described him as "six feet high," with dark hair, dark eyes, and a light complexion, and testified that he "was entirely sober when enlisted."

As a private in the Sixth Indiana Cavalry, Andrew soon found that sickness was at least as great a threat as the enemy. Sent to Tennessee to defend Knoxville, under siege by Confederate forces in late 1863, he became very ill after the men in his company, surprised by Confederate forces, were driven into the mountains, where they had to survive in freezing weather without tents, blankets, or rations. Carried to a hospital on the second floor of the Masonic Temple in Tazewell, Tennessee, Andrew lapsed into a coma and seemed certain to die, prompting the commander of his company to dispatch Salem Lybyer, Andrew's brother and company mate, to care for him.

By spring 1864, Andrew had rejoined his unit, which participated in the Atlanta campaign, then moved to Tennessee, where the Sixth Indiana helped protect Union supply lines against the cavalry raids of Confederate General Joseph Wheeler. Andrew served to war's end, but when he mustered out, he was still feeling the effects of his time in the mountains. Particularly in cold weather, his limbs and joints swelled painfully and made it difficult for him to move. His brother Salem, similarly afflicted but even more disabled, blamed his ills on his duties at Tazewell. As a condition of caring for Andrew, he had agreed to nurse all the soldiers on the second floor of the Masonic Temple, and the punishing climbs up and down the stairs in cold weather carrying food, medicine, and wood for a ward of the sick and wounded had been, Salem believed, accomplished at a terrible cost to his health.

Andrew got on with his life, marrying when he returned from the war, becoming the father of three, losing his wife, and marrying again, this time to Lydia Candacy Sanders, a woman of remarkable vitality who would bear fifteen children and live to be ninety-two. Before she died in 1949, Lydia, born four years before the start of the Civil War, would take a ride in a small propeller-driven airplane.

In the early 1880s, Andrew and Lydia moved west to Missouri to take advantage of a law passed during the Civil War, the Homestead Act, which allowed citizens to claim one-hundred-sixty-acre parcels of public land and make them their own by living on them and improving them. Andrew filed for land in the rolling uplands of the Ozarks, built a five-hundred-square-foot farmhouse with a sleeping loft above, and there on August 4, 1888, my grandfather, Andrew and Lydia's eighth child, came into the world. The Republican Party had just selected a United States senator and Civil War hero from Indiana as its nominee for president, and the Lybyers named their son after the candidate— and future president—Benjamin Harrison. They were no doubt influenced by the fact that the senator had championed the rights of homesteaders like themselves. He was also a supporter of veterans' pensions, a cause favored by Andrew, who because of his ailments received a payment of six dollars a month. Convinced it should be more, he regularly—and unsuccessfully—petitioned the government for an increase.

Fifteen of the eighteen Lybyer children were sons, and they would long remember how Andrew got them up early and sent them into the fields before they walked to school and sent them out again after they returned home until late at night. "Not too much for schooling and hard on work," one of them described him, which was probably true of the way Andrew had himself

My great-grandfather Andrew Simon Peter Lybyer, whose forebears came from Germany, with his wife, Lydia, and twelve of his eighteen children. My grandfather, standing, is second from the left.

My grandfather Ben, on the right, with his brother Leonard, in what served as cowboy clothes in Wyoming in 1910.

My grandfather and grandmother, Ben and Mary Lybyer, about the time of their 1913 wedding.

been raised and his forefathers before him. Nicholas, the first of the family to come to America, signed his name with an X; his grandson Nicholas was able to write in German, but barely; his great-great-grandson Andrew struggled to write in English. But their world did not depend on literacy. If a pension form needed to be filled out, there were clerks and lawyers to do that, and similarly with homestead applications. What their success—indeed, their survival—depended on was the farm, and from the time the first German immigrants plowed American soil, the hard work of farm life was undertaken not by hired hands or slaves but by family members. A contemporary of the early German arrivals in America observed that they raised their children to fear God, love labor, and respect patriarchal authority, exactly as Andrew was doing when he required his boys to walk five miles to church on Sunday and sent them to shovel manure, grind corn, and slaughter hogs the other days of the week.

As Andrew no doubt saw it, he was building habits in his boys that would ensure their welfare in this world and the next. He also may have depended on his sons to do work that he couldn't manage as the years advanced and his ailments grew worse. Although he is a handsome man in old photographs and appears strong and vital, he has the stiff, too-erect posture one often sees in people whose backs are troubling them, as Andrew's had begun to in his late fifties. One doctor diagnosed his condition as lumbago, but it may have been the beginning of Bright's disease, a kidney affliction that would kill him when he was sixty-six. Youngsters are not apt to think of adult woes, however, and to his sons, Andrew, old enough to be a grandfather to most of them, seemed a tyrant, and he did little to encourage their sympathy. Late in their lives, they would remember how he rode the farm on Kaiser, a big white horse, overseeing their work and whipping them if it didn't satisfy him. They also remembered that Lydia often joined in their chores, trying to help them avoid Andrew's wrath.

The farmhouse grew until it had five big rooms on the first floor, two large bedrooms upstairs, and a porch across the front. There were also outbuildings: a woodshed, a wash house, a well house, a spring house, and a large barn. A long split-rail fence neatly separated the Lybyer property from the road, and chrysanthemums brightened the front of the farmhouse well into the fall every year, protected from frost by the salt barrels that the boys put over them every night.

But a prosperous, well-maintained farm was not enough to reconcile the Lybyer boys with what seemed to them servitude, and one day when Ben was thirteen, he packed a bag and ran away. He worked on another farm in Missouri for a time, then got a job in the lead mines in the southeastern part of the state. In 1907, he traveled to Lost Cabin, Wyoming, with his older brother Clarence, and soon two younger brothers, Leonard and Clyde, joined them. They worked as ranch hands, sometimes for Charlie Bader, who had a houseful of daughters, one of whom Leonard would marry, and sometimes at George Davis's, where Clyde met his wife. Ben also worked for J. B. Okie, whose holdings in sheep, cattle, and general stores had made him so rich that he had built a chandeliered mansion along Badwater Creek near Lost Cabin. Indians passing through called the grand ranch house Big Teepee, the name it's still known by today.

Ben had been courting Mary Lough, a pretty brown-eyed girl who'd grown up on a farm near the Lybyer homestead in Missouri. As a teenager, she had moved with her family to Colorado, and early in 1913, she found herself facing a crisis. She wrote to Ben asking for help, and in a return letter, he instructed:

"Pack your trunk and set the night you want me to meet
you . . . at your uncle's house. You name the night and I will
meet you there with an auto . . . about the right time to get the
11:00 train out of there. You get ready and I will be there any-
time. The quicker you do this, the quicker your troubles will be
over with and mine also." In his letter, my grandfather confesses
he has been "so nervous I could not write." He tells my grandmother that he has consulted her older sister Macy and that the
two of them "will go the limit for you." He also tries to allay her
concerns that he will abandon her in her hour of need. "I will
stay with you," he writes. "Don't worry about that one minute."
And in another place, "You said something about me going back
on you. I never will. Death is the only thing that will get me
away from you."

My grandparents married in March 1913, and their oldest
child, Maxine, was born in 1914, a respectable time later, throwing doubt on the most obvious interpretation of the letter. But it
is clear from it that he loves her. "Oh, Mary, please don't forget
me," he writes, "or I will not know what to do." Whatever the
crisis, she long treasured his words, carrying the letter with her
as they moved from place to place. When death took her from
him after more than a half-century of marriage, my aunts found
the letter tucked away in one of her drawers.

The newlyweds set out for Wyoming to begin their life together, and after a night at a hotel in Arminto, they headed for
Salt Creek, an expanse of treeless hills some fifty miles north of
Casper. The area had been booming since a Dutch company,
looking for oil there in 1908, had hit it big. Salt Creek Number
One had sent a gusher of oil a hundred feet into the sky, setting
off a frenzy of development and drilling.

Ben got a job as a mule skinner, hauling oil-field equipment from Casper to Salt Creek, but three days after he had hired on, a tool dresser who was tired of working in the oil fields offered to trade him positions. Ben handed over the reins, took up the dresser's sixteen-pound sledge, and started working at the anvil, completing one of the first of many job changes. Perhaps because of the way his father had dictated his life, Ben didn't take kindly to people telling him what to do. He'd regularly get fed up with his boss, walk off the rig, and sign on with somebody else. For a while, he worked as a line rider in the Salt Creek Field, patrolling leases against claim jumpers, but when he got mad at his boss, he quit, got himself a spring-pole drilling outfit, and jumped a claim or two himself.

Oil-field workers, even ones who changed jobs a lot, made twice as much as ranch hands, two dollars a day rather than one dollar, but it was a tough work, twelve-hour shifts on the rigs with the band-wheel drills going full blast, laboring on through spring mud, summer dust storms, and winter blizzards. There was danger, as when one of the "nitro wagons"—cars hauling nitroglycerin—would explode or when a spark would ignite the gas coming out of a well, causing the whole thing to blow up and burn. There were also times of just plain misery, like the cold January day that Leonard Lybyer, my grandfather's younger brother, put a casing down a well. "The well would flow about every hour and go about twenty feet in the air," he wrote his wife-to-be. "I was wet to the skin with oil."

But there were also plenty of good times, such as the Fourth of July celebrations with patriotic orations and a bucking bronco or two. One of the first buildings in Salt Creek was an amusement hall, and the workers had some riotous dances there. Malcolm Campbell, a friend of my grandfather, recalled in a letter the night when "Jodie Gantz shot the fellow through the middle." The victim survived, and his assailant escaped, as Campbell remembered it, by hiding out with "that bunch that lived in the two-story bunk house across from the machine shop. [They fed] him out of their lunch pails until Francis Brown, who was a deputy sheriff, got through looking for him."

Campbell also recalled that he and his wife were at the dance on the night in 1914 when my grandfather walked outside the amusement hall and fell over a fifty-foot bank nearby. Ben's friends realized he had broken his back but, knowing nothing about the importance of keeping him immobile, made a bed of hay for him in the backseat of a Cadillac touring car and drove him over rough roads to the hospital in Casper. Only twenty-five years old, he was resilient and recovered somehow, but it was months before he was back with my grandmother, who was twenty-one and caring for her first baby.

The Lybyers lived in an oil-field "ragtown," a place defined by the fact that its dwellings had canvas roofs. Ragtown houses were a little like sheep wagons, with wood partway up the sides and a tent for a top, but instead of wheels, ragtown houses had skids so they could be moved from place to place. Late in 1916, a second Lybyer child, Wilbur, was born in one of the ragtown houses, and shortly thereafter, the Lybyers left the oil fields, possibly because Ben had grown angry with one of his bosses. A family story explains their departure that way, but Ben and Mary moved to northwest Colorado, near Mary's family, and they may have been attracted to the area by hearing about the high prices farmers were getting for their crops in the boom market created by the Great War.

Upon their arrival, Ben, following a time-honored pioneer practice, created a shelter for his wife and children by digging a cave in the side of a hill and framing in the opening. Then he filed on a homestead near Price Creek, began work on a house, and started dryland farming—growing small grain crops such as wheat and oats on arid land with no irrigation.

In the spring of 1919, Mary, in labor with her third child, asked Ben to drive her to town, probably to a midwife, but a spring storm had left the roads deeply rutted, and the going was slow. When it became clear that the baby was going to arrive before they reached town, they stopped in a barn alongside the road, and there, on the eighth of April, my mother was born. My grandparents bundled her up against the chilly weather, took her home, and, having accomplished her birth on their own, saw no particular need to inform the authorities of her arrival. Years later, when she was an adult and in need of a birth certificate, she would find, to her embarrassment, that there was no official record of her having been born.

Ben proved up his homestead, but farming without irrigation on Colorado's arid western slope was a chancy enterprise, and when the end of the war brought falling crop prices, the Lybyers returned to Salt Creek, moving back into a ragtown house. A photograph from 1921 shows Ben, Mary, several children, and a dog at the front door of a canvas-roofed dwelling that my grandmother has labeled "Lybyer Mansion." She no doubt meant the name sarcastically, but this ragtown house seems in fact to be unusually large, two rooms instead of one, a good thing, without doubt, since Ben's brother Clyde had now moved in with the family.

Salt Creek was booming when my grandparents moved back. One observer described "cars, trucks, and teams going and coming in every direction; crews building wooden rigs, drilling crews working, gushers spouting in the air, gangs connecting lines, tank batteries and pump stations springing up." The field

My grandparents, four children, and a dog outside the oil-field home my grandma labeled "Lybyer Mansion." Uncle Clyde was also living with them.

My mother, on the right, and three of her siblings, Wilbur, Maxine, and baby Norma, all scrubbed and curled for the camera.

became even busier when Mammoth Oil Company began to build an oil camp, erect storage tanks, and start a pipeline at Teapot Dome, a naval oil reserve next to Salt Creek that was named after a teapot-shaped outcropping in the area. The reserve had been intended to ensure an emergency supply of oil for Navy ships, but President Warren G. Harding's colorful, mustachioed secretary of the interior, Albert Fall, had taken control of it and leased it to oilman Harry Sinclair, the head of Mammoth Oil.

Over the next several years, the activity at Teapot Dome came under suspicion as Senate investigators looked into reports that Secretary Fall had suddenly become wealthy. Eventually convicted of accepting bribes, including bonds and cattle from Harry Sinclair, Fall would serve a year in prison. Salt Creek was drawn into the scandal when Teapot Dome investigators began to look into a deal involving Sinclair and Henry Blackmer, head of Midwest Refining, the company that controlled Salt Creek. The two men, it turned out, were part of an oil-trading deal involving kickbacks, and when some of the profits from their scheme were found to have gone to the disgraced Albert Fall, Blackmer, rather than testify before Congress, left for France, where he led quite a pleasant life until he bargained his way back into the United States in 1949.

Week in and week out for a decade, Teapot Dome was in national headlines. The *Midwest Review*, the official publication for oil-field employees, ignored the scandal, but my grandfather knew all about it. Years later, still indignant, he would tell any grandchild who would listen about the perfidies of Fall, Sinclair, and especially Blackmer, who my grandfather felt had paid no price at all.

At the same time that scandal was keeping Wyoming's oil fields in the headlines, there was genuine improvement in the way oil-field families lived. In later years, my grandfather's friend Malcolm Campbell opined in a letter to him that the field just wasn't the same once Midwest Refining started building houses and schools, but the women and children no doubt appreciated both. The houses—or shacks, as the workers called them—might not have had indoor plumbing, but they had walls, windows, and hard roofs and offered some privacy. Instead of a single room, there were multiple rooms, usually four. The company built bath houses where you could get a shower, opened a hospital, started a recreation center, and gave the main oil camp an official town name: Midwest. By the time my mother was ready to go to school in 1924, the town boasted classrooms for hundreds of elementary-school kids. By the time she entered high school in 1932, there was a gymnasium, where girls as well as boys played basketball, and a lighted field for the football team. Students could join the Glee Club, the Etiquette Club, or the Nutrition Club, and they were encouraged to participate in civilizing events such as drama productions. The year my mother was a freshman, her class put on a play entitled *The Dearest Thing in Boots*.

But the oil fields were still a rough place. Drinking was a near-universal form of recreation, and fighting and prostitution were common. Kids learned a lot about the unsavory side of life at a pretty young age and picked up the language to go with it. At ball games against Casper, eight- and nine-year-olds from Salt Creek were known to yell, "Beat 'em once! Beat 'em twice! Holy, jumping Jesus Christ!"

My grandmother left no doubt about where she stood on matters such as foul language. Although she was small, she could wrestle a bar of soap inside an offending child's mouth almost before the offending word had left that child's lips. But she relied on more than discipline to raise her children's sights. She dressed them up in clothes she had sewn and took them for studio photographs that memorialized them at their combed and scrubbed best. She bartered her dressmaking skills for piano lessons, though there was no piano in their company shack to practice on. She tried to make a comfortable home, even while they were living in ragtown. An old photograph shows a baby in a shiny wooden chair propped up by homemade pillows with freshly pressed ruffled edges, and behind the baby another ruffle has been hung for decoration. I think of how the wind blows at Salt Creek and how little plant life there was in the early days to hold down the dust. I think of hauling water, using a washboard, heating an iron on a wood stove. I look at the gleaming chair, the pressed ruffles, the baby all in white, and I am breathless with admiration.

ACCORDING TO FAMILY genealogies, my grandmother's family, the Lees, had been in America since 1714, and some of her early ancestors, Protestants from Ireland, had become wealthy enough to own land and have servants. By the time she was born, however, even the memory of prosperity had faded. Her father, John, and mother, Alice, after struggling to make a go of it in Missouri, had moved to Colorado to improve their luck, and for a time they did, but after the Great War, commodity prices dropped, and in 1922, grasshoppers attacked their crops. John took a wagon team out to poison the insects, and when he came back and was unhitching the horses, one of them wheeled suddenly and kicked him in the chest, opening a fearful wound. A son carried him to a nearby creek, where he frantically tried to staunch the bleeding with cold water, but John's lungs had collapsed, and by the time a doctor arrived, he was dead. Alice, who had broken her right arm in a fall from a horse a few days before John's accident, reinjured it on that frantic day. When the cast came off, her elbow was immobile, and it remained fixed at a right angle for the rest of her life.

For my grandmother, living in the oil fields and raising her children, these sad events no doubt played into the somber view she generally took of the world. She saw the importance of working hard and improving life for her children but not of enjoying it with them. She once succumbed to a beautiful spring day and, accompanied by her oldest, Maxine, went wading in a reservoir with some other women from the oil field, but as though to reinforce the idea that such an outing was folly, one of the women, Carmen Glenn, slipped into a hole beyond her depth. As the *Midwest Review* reported, "None of the party could swim, and the screams of the other women brought help and when rescued Mrs. Glenn was apparently lifeless." A doctor at Midwest Hospital managed to revive her, but the event was traumatic for all who witnessed it and others as well. Describing the accident at the reservoir, my grandmother communicated a fear of drowning to her children, particularly to my mother, that lasted for a lifetime.

In the Salt Creek oil field, the Lybyer family grew very close, which is not the same as saying that they always saw eye-to-eye. Both my mother's older sister and my mother hated the names my grandmother had given them, Wyoma and Lutie, and from practically the time they could talk, insisted on going by their middle names, Maxine and Edna. My mother and her younger sister Norma were forever convinced that Maxine had had a privileged childhood, and, relatively speaking, she may have. When the Lybyers moved from their ragtown home to a four-room company house, Ben and Mary took one room for themselves, and Wilbur, the family's only boy, got another. That much was fine with Edna and Norma, but they never got over Maxine's getting a third room while they were consigned to sleeping in the common area. Maxine added to her younger siblings' consternation then and for decades by freely offering her unvarnished assessments on every aspect of their lives. In my observation, she never intended her opinions on her sisters' hairdos or children to hurt their feelings; she was just convinced that if she didn't point out failings, nobody would notice them, and they might go unremedied.

WHATEVER THEIR DISAGREEMENTS, the Lybyers took comfort from one another, and in 1944, when my father came home to our house on Walnut Street and told my mother he had taken a job in Denver, she was stricken at the idea of leaving Casper. She could walk a few steps and visit her mother at the H & G Cleaners, a few blocks and see her sisters, and how would she manage even the simplest things in a big city like Denver? In Casper, if you needed a loaf of bread, you walked to one of the little stores scattered around, like Christiansen's, Edgington's, or CY Grocery, all of which were within a couple of blocks. In Denver, you'd have to drive everywhere, and how could she do that, since Wayne would take the car to work? And how would she find a doctor who knew her or friends she could drop in on? My mother filled up the wooden packing crates, crying all the while, until finally, my father gave in. He came home one night and told her we could stay.

Not long after this reprieve, she went to work behind the soda fountain at Lloyd's Confectionery, which took up the point of a narrow triangular building less than a block from our house. She took me with her, holding my hand as we crossed 13th Street, steering me past the mahogany magazine stands and display cases inside the drugstore, then lifting me up onto one of the black leather and metal stools at the soda counter. "You stay here, Lynnie," she would say, and I would, scribbling on paper napkins with a Crayola or playing with straws from the round-domed holder that sat on the counter. "Say hi, Lynnie," she'd tell me when someone she knew came in for a malt or a cherry phosphate. And on the rare occasion when there was a customer she didn't know, I would be introduced right after she had introduced herself: "This is my little girl, Lynnie."

Being at the center of the universe was very pleasant, and I did my best to stay there. When I was about three, my mother lined up her sister Norma and some friends to take their picture in the yard of our stucco house. No sooner were they posed than I skipped in front of them, smiling and waving my skirt until my mother focused the camera on me, chopping off the teenagers' heads. Looking through boxes and photo albums, I find so many copies of this photo that I imagine my mother showing it to everyone she came across. "Here's Lynnie," I can hear her saying, shaking her head as though there were no accounting for my behavior. "She didn't want me taking anybody's picture but hers."

In the winter of 1945, my father had a chance to buy a house—the one at 906 South David that the Schryers had lived in. My mother must have objected. Perhaps she pointed out that the house was in sad condition, with cracked linoleum on the floors and windows that sat crooked in their frames so that winter winds whistled through, but her real point would have been that my father and Tracy, his first wife, had once lived there with Tracy's parents. Still, housing was tight, and however run-down it was, whatever ghosts it held, the David Street house was a prize. My father bought it from the Schryer heirs for $3,500 and, for another $500, got a few sofas, some chairs, a couple of beds, and a white kitchen table with a chipped enamel top.

On August 14, 1946, I celebrated my fifth birthday in the yard of the South David Street house. We played Statues, a game particularly exhilirating because one of the party guests was Diane Gardner, an older girl whose father, Harold, ran Gardner's Food Store, the one-room grocery across the street. Taller and stronger than the rest of us, Diane would whirl us around and send us flying across the yard, our arms pinwheeling as we struggled to get our footing so we could freeze and try to stay that way. As we ran and stumbled, there were narrow misses with the big cottonwoods that stood in our front yard and more than a few bruises as we collided with one another or tripped over the dog. The adults present, talking in low voices on the porch, seemed oblivious to our screams and laughter.

When we were so exhausted that we sought them out, they bestirred themselves to bring out party hats and cake, and as the shadows grew long, we listened to church bells ring. They were marking an anniversary, my mother said. It had been a year since the Japanese had surrendered, a year since the end of World War II.

CHAPTER THREE

HOLDING A PLACE of honor in the front room of our house on South David was a Zenith floor radio. In the summer, I would sit cross-legged in front of it, waiting for the momentous question to be asked: "Would you like to be queen for a day?" Broadcast from the El Capitan Theater at the corner of Hollywood and Vine, the *Queen for a Day* show starred Jack Bailey and featured contestants who had a wish of some sort, maybe to put their feet in cement in front of Grauman's Chinese Theater, to send orchids to much-deserving in-laws, or to buy new clothes for a youngest child who had never had anything but hand-me-downs. After the women told their stories, the audience would applaud to select a winner. The one chosen queen would get not only her wish but a head-to-toe outfit, red roses, and a solid silver scepter.

I loved *Queen for a Day*. The stories that the contestants told were pretty compelling, but just as interesting was figuring out who would win. Would it be the contestant with the saddest story? Or the one who was trying to do something kind for someone else? And what was the winning demeanor? Was it better to be shy or sassy? Or, since the winner was the one who got the most applause, was the real key to winning to come to the show with a large group of friends?

I listened to Jack Bailey and his contestants every day during the summer, and I was dismayed when the 1948 Republican convention took over the radio waves and there was no *Queen for a Day* for nearly a week. Hardly had I gotten through that when the Democrats gathered and knocked the program off again. In my estimation, neither Tom Dewey nor Harry Truman could hold a candle to Jack Bailey. At least, that was my assessment until a few years later, when I actually got to see President Truman. He came to Wyoming to dedicate a dam, but before he headed out to the Platte River canyon, he made a speech in the auditorium of the high school, which was right across the street from my friend Linda Bowman's house. We waited on her front porch for hours, and although we caught only a glimpse of him as he drove by in an open car, we were thrilled.

The Zenith floor radio had a record player inside, and my father played the Ink Spots over and over. "If I Didn't Care," "I Don't Want to Set the World on Fire," "I'll Never Smile Again." I learned the words to them all. But the most beautiful song ever written, according to my father, was "Ave Maria," and he played a recording of it from time to time. It never failed to bring tears to his eyes, perhaps because it made him think of Tracy. I know he loved my mother. I saw them dancing in the empty dining room. But maybe Tracy's ghost was in this house.

I can't be sure why my father cried, but I do know this was a side of him that few suspected. His round face, twinkling eyes, and curly hair made people think of him as jolly. He was the one they would choose to play Santa for the kids at the Christmas party. He was also, his friends learned, the one you didn't want to be around when he was provoked. If someone cut him off on the road, he'd follow them, honking his horn and cursing. If a waiter took too long, he would erupt. As far as most people who knew

My father dressed as Santa Claus for the
Bureau of Reclamation's children's party.

him were concerned, he was a jovial fellow given to exploding from time to time, particularly if he had been drinking. They would have been astounded to know that he wept when listening to a song.

The house on South David had what was called an unfinished basement, and my father decided it was his civic duty to finish it. In the years right after the war, the local newspapers ran ads showing frantic people trying to find housing. "Convert an attic, basement, or garage into living quarters," the ads urged. And so my father bought some wallboard and started hammering away. Since he was not an experienced carpenter, the project involved many mistakes and much cursing. Deciding that something had to be done about the profanity, I got a pencil and tablet and announced that I would be keeping track of his foul language and charging him a nickel for each instance. For several evenings, I sat on the basement floor, back against the wall, keeping tally. He would miss a nail and hit the wallboard with his hammer, leaving a mark in it. "Oh, shit!" he would say, and I would draw a line in my notebook. Standing back to admire his work, he'd knock over his bourbon and coke. "Goddamit!" he would say, and I would draw a line in my notebook.

One might reasonably have expected him to put an end to my project. I was, after all, behaving disrespectfully, doing exactly what he suspected the aggressive driver or slow waiter of doing. He blew his top at them, but in my case, he handed over the money. The fact that I was a child was no doubt the difference, but there was also this: he thought the aggressive driver and the lazy waiter didn't think he mattered. That's what he couldn't stand. And he knew he mattered to me.

The first residents of our basement were my mother's younger sister, Norma, and her new husband, Cork Brown. My mother's best friend, Norma was movie-star beautiful in a blond, sweet way. When she was a little girl, one of her teachers, Violet Hovey, had written home, "She is as near perfect as any child I ever saw," an appraisal that I am sure was about not only her appearance but also her generous heart. Norma would give you the clothes off her back and literally did this for me once when I fell into a teenage funk and she thought a dress she had just made for herself would cheer me up. She became a top-notch court reporter, much in demand because of her fast and accurate shorthand, and she was creative as well, perhaps the best seamstress of the Lybyer daughters and later in life an accomplished potter. She numbered many local artists among her friends.

Her husband, Cork, newly discharged from the Navy, would sometimes say he was part Indian, and with his dark hair and high cheekbones, he might well have been, but he had been raised by his maternal grandmother, Anna Bergstrom, an immigrant from Sweden who had arrived in America as a mail-order bride. Bergie, as everyone called this wonderful, ever-cheerful woman, had raised Cork and his brother, Arthur, after their mother, Florence, died under circumstances about as sad as it is possible to imagine. Florence's husband, a ne'er-do-well, had been institutionalized in the state hospital in Evanston, Wyoming, after late-stage syphilis infected his brain. Florence had struggled on but in a few years became pregnant. Alone, trying to raise two small boys in an isolated house on the prairie outside Casper, she tried to abort the baby and died.

Bergie, then seventy years old, left her home in Leadville, Colorado, came to Casper and found a house in North Casper, where she cared for Cork and Arthur through the years of the Depression. Right after Pearl Harbor, Cork enlisted, following Arthur into the Navy and to the Pacific. Arthur, after surviving the sinking of the USS *Lexington,* was selected for pilot training and killed in a plane crash in Vero Beach, Florida. Cork came home at war's end to marry Norma. With my mother as matron of honor, they said their vows at the Casper Women's Clubhouse, a graceful brick building that Standard Oil of Indiana had built in the 1920s so their executives would have a place to stay and then sold in the 1930s to a number of women's groups. After the ceremony, the bride and groom had their wedding picture taken in front of the clubhouse fireplace, decorated for the occasion with pink gladioli and snapdragons.

After their stay in our basement, the Browns went to Fort Collins, Colorado, where Cork, using the G. I. Bill, enrolled at Colorado State University, attended classes as often as he thought necessary, and spent a significant amount of time drinking with his buddies. After one hard evening, he returned home and collapsed on the couch, provoking a response from Norma that would enter family lore. Because she worked during the day at a clerical job to support them, she had been catching up on housework when he arrived. At first, she continued sweeping, ignoring him, but then the sight of him sleeping off his evening got to be too much, and she went after him with her broom, poking at his face and arms until he was covered with scratches. Having to explain his appearance the next day, he leveled with his buddies about what had happened, spurring them to present Norma with a trophy: a new broom to replace the one she had destroyed. She interpreted the prize—correctly, I think—as their acknowledgment that Cork had gotten what he deserved.

Cork earned his degree and spent most of his life as an organizer for the International Brotherhood of Electrical Workers. He was a responsible husband and a good father but never entirely gave up the wild ways of his youth. Every year on his birthday, December 18, he would disappear at about four P.M., returning only after he had caroused his way through most of Casper's nightspots. Many a Christmas was celebrated with no one in the family speaking to him.

My mother's older sister, Maxine, and her husband, Bub Lockwood, also got caught up in Casper's postwar housing shortage. My grandparents had moved to town by this time, into a white frame house at 637 West 11th, and when Bub got a job at the Texaco refinery, the Lybyers' dirt-floored garage was the only place he and Maxine could find for themselves and their two children to live. Bub, tall and handsome, was a gentle, easygoing man, despite having emerged from a Depression experience that might have left him embittered. His father, William, had been well off, the owner of two farms, one near Philip, South Dakota, and the other near Verdel, Nebraska. Burning trash one day, William had poured kerosene on the fire to make it burn faster. Flames had traveled back up the kerosene stream, set William's clothes alight, and he had burned to death. His widow, Karene, who had come to South Dakota from Norway as a sixteen-year-old, sought help managing the family's farms and finances, but the banker she turned to was unscrupulous. When Karene made mortgage payments, he pocketed them rather than putting them against the note, and then he foreclosed. Eventually, the banker would serve time for fraud, but not before the Lockwoods lost everything.

On her last day on the Nebraska farm, Karene went into a field to pick crabapples, carrying along a blanket, thinking she might sit awhile, but when she whipped it into the air to spread it out on the prairie, a young bull that she had raised from a calf charged, goring her in the stomach. Bub got her on a train for Omaha, but the bull's horn had pierced her intestine, and in those days before penicillin was in use, she died.

After he buried his mother, Bub got a job shoveling snowdrifts in front of trains and thus worked his way to the Salt Creek Field, where he managed to scrape together enough money to buy a small dairy. Making his daily milk deliveries, he attracted the notice of many young women, but it was Maxine, quick and tiny, who caught his eye. They married, and he signed on for a job with Texaco that took him first to Texas and then to the refinery in Casper. Living with Maxine and their two children, Ron and Karen, in my grandmother's dirt-floored garage, he searched in vain for a house, then finally bought a lot west of town. He dug a large hole in his lot, found an abandoned house at Teapot Dome, then moved the house to the lot, where he put it over the hole, creating an instant basement. He made all the utility connections on his own.

My mother swore she could smell natural gas every time she stepped into Bub and Maxine's house, but they lived safely in it for nearly fifty years, Bub working at the refinery and Maxine exhausting everyone who came near her, except possibly the laid-back Bub. Perhaps because of the startling number of Coca-Colas she drank, Maxine ran on a very fast motor. Once when my mother was sick, she came over to take care of me and, in the blink of an eye, scrubbed the kitchen floor, ran the Bissell sweeper around the house, and dusted everything in sight. Maxine would preside at a church rummage sale in the morning and hook three rugs in the afternoon. She would eventually work her way to the pinnacle of the Masonic sisterhood of Eastern Star in Casper, while at the same time knitting blankets for the needy, crocheting potholders for every occasion, and providing daily advice to her younger sisters on how they ought to live.

CHAPTER FOUR

P ARK SCHOOL KINDERGARTEN teacher Persis Goddard let her students nap wherever they liked, and I usually chose to stretch out in the playhouse beside a small blond boy called Buster, though his name was really Clyde. No one paid much attention to us when we were stacking blocks or pasting May baskets, but when we napped together, we got noticed. The adults probably thought we were oblivious to their whispers and smiles, but I got the drift right away and began churning out pictures of a wedding featuring me, "the bride," in a long veil, and Buster, "the greum," in a carefully balanced top hat.

In my small town, it was easy to imagine being a bride, but you could also imagine being Desert Dust, a wild palomino that had been captured in the Red Desert of Wyoming by a rancher from Glenrock, a town about twenty-five miles away. The horse had become a local celebrity, appearing on a calendar and having a movie made about him, and he became central to an ongoing game that I played with my friend and schoolmate Linda Bowman, whose father was my father's boss, now that my father had returned to work at the Bureau of Reclamation. No matter that Desert Dust was a stallion, he was the prototype for the wild and noble steeds we imagined ourselves to be. We ran and neighed, sometimes during recess, though the dresses that we wore to school in combination with a gravel-covered playground meant that all galloping had to be done on hind legs. After school or on weekends, we concocted scenarios starring Desert Dust as we tore around on all fours on the grass in our yards.

Wonder Woman was another favorite game, one I would play with friends like Linda or sometimes by myself. It involved running, leaping, and flying through the air. I'd pump my tree swing as high as it would go, then bail out at the top, ready to deflect bullets with my magic bracelets upon landing. I read every Wonder Woman comic book I could get my hands on and knew not only about her magic lasso and invisible plane but also the back story, how she had been born on Paradise Island to Queen Hippolyta, and how Steve Trevor, who had crash-landed on Paradise Island, had persuaded her to come to the United States. Once here, she disguised herself as Diana Prince but speedily turned into Wonder Woman when evil villains (many of whom were female) appeared on the scene.

I have read that the creator of Wonder Woman, psychologist William Moulton Marston, was a great admirer of women, such a fan, in fact, that he lived with two of them in a ménage à trois. He apparently believed that his comic books would help usher in an American matriarchy, a utopia in which women would dominate men and rid the world of male aggression. Whatever his motives, he surely succeeded in providing little girls a chance to imagine the exhilaration of being strong and powerful. Wonder Woman was a heroine we could relate to, different from any heroine that earlier female generations might have admired, and she cast a wide spell, with followers not only in Casper, Wyoming, but in Toledo, Ohio, where Gloria Steinem was growing up, and in Queens, New York, home of Letty Pogrebin. In 1972, when Steinem and Pogrebin put Wonder Woman on the cover of the first issue of *Ms.* magazine, I had a moment of complete empathy with the feminist movement.

The kids at Park School came from a variety of backgrounds. Their fathers were doctors (who prospered) and sheep ranchers (who usually didn't). There were a few people flying high in the oil business and a lot more working hard at the other end of it. At Park School, you could find kids whose fathers were real estate speculators, truckers, butchers, store managers, government workers, salesmen, and clerks. If you went home with somebody, you got an idea how well off that person's family was, but at school, you didn't know—except maybe on stamp day, a weekly event in which we were encouraged to buy stamps to put in a book that would, when filled up, become a U.S. savings bond. Most of us bought red stamps (which were actually pink). Decorated with a minuteman's picture, they cost ten cents each. But a few kids marched to the front of the room and bought a fistful of green stamps, a king's ransom's worth, it seemed, since green stamps went for a quarter apiece.

One of the green-stamp regulars was my friend Karen Whitlock, a bright-eyed little girl with long dark curls. Her father, Oscar Whitlock, owned several businesses, including the Wigwam Bakery and the Mission Auto Court, a white stucco, one-story motel where Ernest Hemingway and his wife Mary had once stayed. Karen's mother had died when she was born, Oscar had remarried, and Karen and her brother, Jim, lived with their aunt and uncle, Anna and Charles Tweedy, in a turreted brick house that Oscar had built on Wolcott Street in the center of Casper's prettiest neighborhood.

Both Karen and I were fans of the Bobbsey Twins, Nancy Drew, and board games. We'd walk to her house after school and play Clue, Sorry, and Parcheesi while lying on the wall-to-wall carpet in her living room—the first wall-to-wall carpet I'd ever seen. Karen collected Storybook Dolls as I did, she had wonderful costumes we could dress up in, and, best of all, she wore braces. This meant that every six weeks or so, her aunt would drive her to Denver, three hundred miles away, to see an orthodontist, and Karen would return home with hints of the amazements that a city could offer. Once she brought back a Slinky, a wire creation that seemed to take on a life of its own as it walked down her basement stairs. Another time, she returned with red rubber molds of Disney characters and a plaster-of-paris mix for pouring into them and creating a Snow White or a Pluto that you could paint. A few times, Anna Tweedy, a warm and generous woman, took me with them on the Denver trip, and I got to see city wonders for myself. We went to Denver Dry Goods, which had an escalator. We visited Elitch Gardens, an amusement park with a lake, acres of flower beds, and a carved and painted carousel. We saw first-run movies such as *Easter Parade* and *Little Women* that wouldn't come to Casper for months or even years.

Karen's long dark curls worried my mother. Hair that hung to your waist and beyond sapped your strength, she believed. "They should cut that girl's hair," she would say, though Karen showed not the least sign of enervation and looked quite glamorous, I thought, in the costumes we wore for the various pageants that marked the school year. A photograph in an old *Park Ranger*, Park School's student newsletter, shows Karen and me and a half-dozen other girls wearing bonnets and long dresses. The boys in the picture are in overalls and straw hats, garden tools are scattered around, and we are apparently celebrating spring, probably by acting out a nursery rhyme, since in one of the pictures, Linda Bowman appears dressed as Mother Goose.

At Christmas, we created "living tableaux," which required rushing into position while the stage curtains were drawn, then standing very still for several minutes when they opened. A *Park Ranger* shows that in 1947, I and a half-dozen or so of my classmates were assigned to the crèche scene, where we did something my grandchildren will no doubt find remarkable: right there on the school stage, we prayed, some of us actually kneeling, beside Baby Jesus in the manger.

The adults in charge of our education had no hesitation about inculcating us with certain ideas, among them that what we did with our early years was important—and not just to us but to the whole country. In 1948, a seventh-grader wrote in the *Park Ranger*, "Remember, that the nation that has the schools has the future." In 1949, a student used the *Park Ranger* to warn classmates who were throwing candy wrappers on the playground that they were "tearing down what others have put up." They needed to remember, he told them, that they were "future citizens of these United States" and should ask themselves how they would like their children "tearing down some things we have built."

We were to consider the consequences of our actions, to think how they would reverberate in years ahead. Judging from an art project I undertook in first grade, I was much impressed by this message. I decorated my last name with red and blue pencils and wrote underneath it in painfully neat cursive, "I will make the name of Vincent a proud one. I'll make sure that I will not bring disrespect to my name. I am going to plan ahead for the future and hope it will be a good one."

The fact that I still have this art project speaks to the interest our teachers took in us. In 1967, some twenty years after I labored over my high-minded sentiments, my creation arrived in

My first-grade class. I'm fourth from the right in the front row.
Buster, my boyfriend, is on the far left, next to my best friend, Mary Grant.

Praying onstage at the Christmas concert. I'm to the right of Joseph. My friend Mary Grant is Mary.

the mail. At the time, I was a graduate student at the University of Wisconsin, married for three years, mother of a one-year-old. Harriet Smith, my first-grade teacher, had married and moved to Longmont, Colorado, but she still managed to track me down so that she could send me art and photographs from my time in her classroom. She enclosed a note: "I'm so happy for you that you have a grand husband (I'm sure he is) and a baby daughter. Give your parents my greeting and love to my little girl." Many years later, when I told this story to one of my Park School classmates, Karen Romans Randolph, she reminded me of the affection that Miss Smith had regularly shown us when we were in her care. A returned spelling paper, star on it or not, was usually accompanied by a hug and kiss.

We celebrated heroes at Park School, putting on plays about Columbus in October and writing poems about Washington and Lincoln in February. In a 1948 *Park Ranger*, fourth-grader Sharon Knight portrayed the first and sixteenth presidents as "two great men" whose "glory never ends." Lee Ann Best, another fourth-grader, wrote:

Abraham Lincoln—so brave and bold,
Made this country free.
He loved mankind and worked for them
And gave them liberty.

I can't be sure that I read these poems, but I remember revering Lincoln, in particular, the rail splitter, the savior of the Union, who had persisted against disadvantage and would not give up in the face of war. He was a person to admire, a person whose greatness could inspire us to be better.

Like the vast majority of schoolchildren in the 1940s, those of us growing up in Casper learned to read with Dick and Jane. Or at least, that was the intent. The idea was that if you saw the word *look* again and again (as in "Look, Jane, look") and it was paired with pictures that showed you its meaning, pretty soon you could read it. As Rudolf Flesch would point out in his 1955 book, *Why Johnny Can't Read*, there were many children for whom this method simply didn't work. Fortunately for us, our Park School teachers knew this long before Flesch's best seller and taught us phonics. We'd slide our fingers along the letters, sounding them out, putting the sounds together faster and faster until they ran together, and behold, there was a word. Our teachers read to us every day, books like *The Wind in the Willows* that helped us grow in what we knew and gave us words with which to describe our knowledge. They also encouraged us to listen to storybook records, my favorite being one about a boy named Sparky who heard words in the sounds that trains make. I could hear the whistles of Chicago and Northwestern engines from our house on David Street and tried to imagine the stories they might tell of distant places.

Dick and Jane had been around for some fifteen years when I encountered them in 1947, and it's hard to imagine what children in the Depression made of their cheerful, sunny lives. In postwar Casper, we certainly didn't mistake their world for the real one, in which kids regularly got dirty, skinned their knees, and threw up, but there was still much in the books that was familiar. They emphasized the values our parents did: sharing with siblings, being respectful to elders, and working hard. A 1996 book by Carole Kismaric and Marvin Heiferman, *Growing Up with Dick and Jane*, notes that *work* was the eighteenth word introduced in the books, a statistic that's actually surprising. How were the authors able to hold off so long, with children, parents, and neighbors busy most of the time, sweeping, mowing, doing school assignments, making repairs and deliveries? Even Spot, the dog, keeps an eye out for jobs he can do—like retrieving stuffed animals when baby Sally abandons them.

Dick and Jane's mother worked at home, cooking, sewing, washing, shopping, which wasn't far from how my life was. My mother did all those things and worked behind the soda fountain at Lloyd's Confectionary besides. Dick and Jane's father went out to his job, though exactly what he did there wasn't clear. And that was also pretty much like my life. I knew that my father worked for the Bureau of Reclamation. I loved saying the long name. But it was years before I understood that the great dams of central Wyoming—Pathfinder, Alcova, Seminoe—were part of his work and even longer before I understood that the purpose of the dams was to generate electricity and make it possible for farmers to irrigate arid lands.

Everyone in Dick and Jane was white, which didn't strike me or my classmates as noteworthy. Everyone in our school was white. There were so few African Americans in Casper in the 1940s that I can remember riding a bus with my mother when an African American man got on. No doubt to prevent me from asking a loud and tactless question, she whispered fiercely in my ear, "It's just like clouds, Lynnie. Some are light, and some are dark." I was silent, partly because my mother so clearly wanted me to be and partly because this was such startling information. What did people have to do with clouds?

Looking back, I realize my mother was trying to say that no matter their color, people are just people, a notion that was fairly widely held in Casper. We cringed when we heard about the mechanisms of discrimination in the South—separate schools, restrooms, drinking fountains, and seating areas in theaters. Particularly among those whose lives had been a struggle, there was little inclination to look down on black people, whose lot they knew also had been hard. Aunt Norma had a long friendship with Shirley Williams, an African American woman who was working in a laundry in North Casper when they first met in the 1940s. Shirley started a café in North Casper, and then, after she married the handsome John Gray in the mid-fifties, they opened the Cozy Club, an after-hours place where you were supposed to bring your own liquor but where you could usually get a drink in any case. Norma and Cork went to Shirley's Café for the steaks Shirley was famous for and stopped at the Cozy Club with friends. After the Browns' youngest child, Tina, was born, Shirley and John, who had no children of their own and doted on the little girl, often visited the Brown home.

The friendship survived the fact that Norma, as a court reporter, was often keeping the official record when Shirley appeared for violating liquor laws or was brought up on morals charges. In a videotaped interview she did toward the end of her life, my aunt recalls meeting Shirley's "nieces" on occasion, young women who she knew were not related to Williams. The fact that Shirley was a madam did not make her unworthy in my aunt's eyes. "They were great friends," she says of Shirley and John in the interview. "What they did in their business was not my affair. I loved them very much."

My aunt mourned with Shirley on an April day in 1972, when John was found dead on Bolton Creek Road southwest of Casper. Authorities speculated that his car had gotten stuck in mud and that he had lost his way trying to find help in a spring snowstorm. Tracking him had been difficult, authorities said, because of numerous hoofprints in the area. Norma always thought that more sinister forces had been at work, that John had been forced from his car and chased by men on horseback until he collapsed. It was her suspicion that John had been killed for extorting one of the men who visited Shirley's nieces.

There weren't many who went as far as my aunt in separating what people did from who they were. My mother, knowing, as did anyone who read the papers, about Shirley's nieces, certainly raised her eyebrows when Norma let Shirley and John take Tina, then a preschooler, out to lunch or to the park. But Norma's refusal to relate race to human worth was fairly common— although that's not to say there was no prejudice in Casper. A small, well-established black middle class with its own churches, businesses, and social clubs was largely invisible to the rest of the town, in part because it was concentrated in three places: the Sandbar and two other tiny neighborhoods north of Second Street. Many white people, including many in the middle class, also lived in neighborhoods north of Second Street, but for some it was easier to move than for others. Except in the case of live-in help—a cook in the home of drilling company owner Zack Brinkerhoff, a domestic worker in the home of scrap dealer turned oilman Fred Goodstein—African Americans did not live south of Second Street until the 1950s. And while white-owned enterprises, including banks, clothing stores, movie theaters, and mortuaries, welcomed black business by advertising in directories published by the African American community in 1948–49 and 1955, the only white-owned eating establishment that took out an ad was a drive-in, Rex's In and Out.

Like kids in most parts of the nation, we learned very little about African Americans when we studied history. Had someone suggested teaching us black history, the idea would no doubt have been rejected under the "people are just people" rule. It would be unseemly, rude even, to single out a group because of race, or so the argument would have gone, without the thought ever occurring to anyone that black people and others of color already had been singled out by being ignored in the historical record. Names that are classroom staples today—Frederick Douglass, Booker T. Washington, Harriet Tubman, and W. E. B. DuBois—did not appear in our textbooks. Nor did Sitting Bull and Crazy Horse. Despite the fact that the Battle of the Little Bighorn had occurred just over the state line in Montana, most of what we knew—or thought we knew—about the Indians in that battle probably came from Hollywood. There was a highly popular (and inaccurate) movie in the 1940s called *They Died with Their Boots On*, and when we thought of Crazy Horse, I suspect in our mind's eye, we saw Anthony Quinn, who played Crazy Horse, charging across the prairie at the end of that movie and running General George Armstrong Custer, as played by Errol Flynn, right into the ground.

Several thousand members of the Shoshone and Arapaho tribes lived on the Wind River Reservation, some 150 miles from Casper, but it might as well have been a thousand miles, for all I knew of their lives. We did see Arapaho dancers once a year at fair and rodeo time, but only because of an incident right after the war, when some members of the Arapaho tribe ran up a hotel bill they couldn't pay. The hotel owner confiscated a much-valued ceremonial drum and refused to return it until the Arapahos paid up—which they couldn't do. Into the impasse came Waldo Hurley, the local Coca-Cola bottler, with a suggestion that the street in front of the hotel be shut off, the Indians dance, and Casper citizens pay to watch the performance. The dance drew the crowd Hurley thought it would, the Arapaho drum was returned, and Hurley became lifelong friends with Charley White Man, the Arapaho chief. Every summer, at Hurley's invitation, the Arapahos came to Casper for the fair and rodeo and performed in full ceremonial dress. Although we didn't understand how fortunate we were to witness the dances, we knew they were a marvelous spectacle, made all the more wondrous one summer, when the Arapahos made Hurley's eighteen-year-old daughter, Pat, a princess of their tribe, naming her Plume Woman and presenting her with a long and lovely white buckskin dress.

We did learn in school about Sacajawea, who had guided Lewis and Clark. In fact, she was one of only two women I remember reading about, the other being Red Cross founder Clara Barton. No doubt, we learned that in 1869, Wyoming had become the first government in the world to grant women full voting rights, but I would be grown before I understood how significant this was. Forty-seven years would pass after Wyoming's grant of full suffrage before any state east of the Mississippi extended this right, and in the interval, women would gain the vote in ten Western states and one territory besides Wyoming. Something in the Western experience made political equality for women come more easily, and I suspect it was that life in pioneer days made it clear that they weren't hothouse flowers. They could drive a team of oxen across the Mormon Trail, help work the fields, bear and raise children under astonishingly harsh circumstances. Of course, they should vote. Earlier in the East, colonial women and the women of the early republic had shown strength and resilience in dealing with life in a newly settled land, but in seventeenth- and eighteenth-century America, female suffrage was inconceivable. In the last half of the nineteenth century it was on the agenda, and Western women made it seem an obvious right. Perhaps it was so obvious that no one thought that Wyoming's historic role in gaining female suffrage was worth making a fuss about in the schools.

It's also possible that the event wasn't considered worthy of much notice because it had to do with women. Although we didn't yet have a word for it, sexism abounded in the late forties. A syndicated cartoon called *Modest Maidens* that ran in the *Casper Tribune-Herald* featured gorgeous young women saying things like, "Look at all her books! She must never have a date." One cartoon shows a lovely sitting on the lap of an older man. "We always sit like this," she says. "I used to be his secretary."

I didn't find the cartoons funny, lumping them together with another series in the paper, "They'll Do It Every Time," which also apparently made people laugh, although why was beyond me. It featured husbands who messed up the entire kitchen in the process of making a sandwich or wives who went to the grocery store for milk and bought the place out. What was so funny about that? Or about one Modest Maiden telling another that college was a bad idea since half the men in college were married? But I loved the way Modest Maidens looked, the confident lines with which the women were drawn, and I tried copying the cartoons. The Modest Maidens all had a certain turn to the cheek right by the eyes that I tried for months on end to imitate, but the girls I drew simply looked as if they didn't have noses.

I also spent a lot of time with comic strips, preferring the ones that were light and airy: *Blondie* was that way, and so was *Brenda Breeze*. *Orphan Annie* and *Terry and the Pirates* were entirely too crowded and dark for my taste, and *Dick Tracy* was, too, but I read it from time to time, largely because of Sparkle Plenty. She was the gorgeous baby daughter of Gravel Gertie and B. O. Plenty, a couple one would not have expected to produce a beautiful child. Sparkle had a dear round face and long blond hair that waved all the way to her knees. I got a Sparkle Plenty doll for Christmas one year, and though her yellow yarn hair did not live up to expectations (I had expected something silky and shiny, like the hair on the Toni doll I got a few years later), she was otherwise adorable.

Sparkle had twenty-seven tunes she could play on her ukulele, from "Nobody's Darling but Your'n" to "Way Down upon the Sewanee River." She could play "Two Sons for Tucson" standing on her head and "Bury Me Not on the Lone Pray-ree" behind her back. Watching a talent show on TV with her daddy, B.O., she declared, "I can do that," and she did, performing on Ted Tellum's talent show and not only winning but receiving so many cards and letters that she was called back for a second performance. "I'm as good as Arthur Goshfry!" she exulted.

For a nine-year-old girl, Sparkle could be nearly as motivating as Wonder Woman. Here was female ambition and independence that could not have been further removed from the world of the Modest Maidens. When T. V. Wiggles, a creepy, constantly undulating character, offers to advance Sparkle's career and invites her to sit on his lap, she exclaims, "No! I don't set on strangers' laps, dadburn it!"

There was no Ted Tellum's talent show in Casper, but there was the Bainbrich School of Dance. Located in a small pink stucco building near the railroad tracks, it was run by Eddie and Clay Bainbrich, a hardworking and colorful couple. Eddie, the wife, had red hair and spectacularly well-muscled legs, and she wore short satin skirts and high-heeled tap shoes. Clay, the husband, wore his hair slicked back and his T-shirts tight. Their building's front windows advertised tap dance, acrobatics, ballet, baton twirling. Clay and Eddie Bainbrich would teach whatever your heart desired.

Some Casper mothers did not think the Bainbrich School of Dance an entirely wholesome influence. A childhood friend told me not long ago that her mother made one visit and decided her daughter would have no part of it. But my mother and many others took us to our weekly lessons, watched us practice in the chalk circles that Clay Bainbrich drew on the studio floor, and spent hours sewing up the costumes we needed for the annual recitals. We were bunnies one time, hopping onto the stage at the Elks Club with white ears and cottontails, soft-shoeing to the tune of "Glow, little glow worm, glimmer, glimmer." Our parents clapped and cheered, thrilled in those buoyant postwar years to have produced children who were such stars.

CHAPTER FIVE

O N AN APRIL NIGHT in 1949, about a week after my brother Mark was born, my father came home from the hospital to tell me my mother was very sick. Pulling up a chair beside my bed, he said that the doctors had given her a blood transfusion, but instead of making her better, it had made her worse. He was rubbing his forehead, clearly worried, and as soon as he left, I knelt down beside my bed and prayed furiously that she would be all right. I could not imagine life without her.

Some days later, she was better, though not well enough to come home, so my father took me to the hospital, and I waved to her as she stood at her window. Even from a distance, I could tell that her skin was yellow. She had jaundice, my father said, and it had turned even the whites of her eyes yellow.

Mark came home from the hospital before my mother, and my grandmother, Mary Lybyer, took care of him in an old wood-frame apartment house at 526 West 10th that she and my grand-father had purchased. Called Glendale Apartments, it had three units up and three in the basement, each with a living room (which we called a front room), a single bedroom, a small kitchen, and a bath. My grandmother kept the apartments rented and cleaned, painted them between tenants, and took care of the grass. She would come home from her job doing repairs and alterations at the H & G Cleaners, haul out the lawn mower, and push it over the lawn, wearing the same flowered housedress, knee-length hose, and sensible lace-up shoes she wore to work. A cousin reminded me recently that this was Grandma's outfit no matter what she was doing. She once shot a pronghorn antelope while wearing her flowered housedress.

My grandfather, now in his sixties and pretty bent over from the fifty-foot fall he'd taken when he was working at Salt Creek, started out most days in his brown Naugahyde rocker, chewing tobacco and spitting into an old coffee can. He kept a slingshot close by, and when he'd spot a dog on the grass out front, he would load a ball bearing into it and make the offending animal truly sorry it had ever wandered onto Lybyer property. He also kept an eye on kids from the nearby high school. Some of them ate lunch in cars they parked in front of the Glendale Apartments, and if they threw trash on the lawn, Grandpa would wait until they left, pick up the trash, and throw it into their cars. On the rare occasion when he found they'd locked their car doors, he would lift the car hoods and tuck the trash in around the engines.

I do not remember my grandfather driving, but on occasion he would manage to make his way downtown to the bars. When my grandmother returned from work and found him missing, she would call my uncles to go find him, an assignment to which they assented but grudgingly. Making the rounds of the bars lost much of its charm when your goal was to find your father-in-law and deliver him to your mother-in-law. Deep down, I think, Ben's sons-in-law rather admired his forays onto the wild side.

The garage behind the apartment house, where he kept a few tools, was Grandpa's domain. He always had a project going, usually something just offbeat enough to fascinate his thirteen grandchildren. Once he converted an old oak pump organ to electricity. For mysterious reasons, a working light bulb was necessary to the running of the motor that he put inside the organ, so when the organ would quit, he would produce a screw driver, take off the organ front, and replace the bulb. He polished pieces of jade and agate that he found on the prairie and was forever inventing gadgets such as a surefire fish hook that would spring open when the fish took it, implanting itself in a way that ensured the fish's doom. Once when I was in high school, I asked him to help me drill holes in a dozen foot-long two-by-twos so I could string them together for a science project. The idea was to let them hang loose and then twist the bottom piece of wood so that the whole structure would undulate and the ends of the two-by-twos create a sine wave. It never occurred to me to sand and varnish the two-by-twos, but it did to Grandpa, and for good measure, he painted the ends of the two-by-twos black so that the sine wave was unmistakable.

As he tinkered, I don't believe he was trying to teach us a lesson, but it was impossible not to admire his ingenuity and to think that a good mind and a willing heart could solve almost any problem. I never heard him deride people who gained expertise through long schooling, but with his sixth-grade education, he was testimony that lack of formal training was no hindrance to thinking about the way things worked and trying to improve them.

He often talked about an oil and gas separator he had invented when he was working at Salt Creek. He patented it in 1929, in 1944, and again in 1961, and over these years, there were moments when it seemed it might make money. In 1950, a California company began to market it, giving my grandfather occasion to tell a local newspaper that he had conceived his de-

vice while cleaning out oil wells and readying them for pump-
ing. "The separator," he explained, "is actually a bypass. Oil
being heavier drops back into the packer and is pumped in
through the tubing, while the gas comes out through a different
passage between the tubing and the casing."

Grandpa was supposed to get $22 each time one of the $250
separators was sold, but the royalty checks he hoped for never
arrived, although he was convinced the separator was selling
well. The same thing happened a few years later, when another
company began marketing the separator in the Rocky Mountain
region. In response to a letter from J. J. Larkin, executive vice
president of the Larkin Packer Company, an oil equipment
supplier in Texas, my grandfather wrote that he had read in
brochures that the company selling his invention was grossing
$16,000 in yearly sales from it, but he couldn't be sure, since
they had never been willing to produce their records.

He bought a Geiger counter and began exploring north of
town, but his hopes that uranium would be his big break were
also disappointed. Meanwhile, Grandma was the chief breadwin-
ner, and when Mark came home from the hospital before my
mother, she added him to her responsibilities. He was an exceed-
ingly difficult baby, screaming through the night, and Grandma
decided it must be the milk he was drinking. She began to feed
him Carnation evaporated, and that worked wonders. He became
a smiling, thoroughly dear little boy. By the time my mother
came home, he was also, no doubt as a result of the condensed
milk, a pretty chubby fellow. Walking didn't appeal to him, but
at about eighteen months, he began to run, careening across the
lawn at a fabulous pace, unable to slow down or he would fall. As
we watched him and laughed, my mother would say, "What did
we do before he came?"

Although I feel certain the word *matriarch* never passed my grandmother's lips, that's exactly what she was. Her daughters were expected to call her daily, though visiting was preferred. And on holidays, particularly Thanksgiving, they were expected to show up, families in tow, at her small apartment. We would have a time when we were supposed to arrive, say 4:00, but inevitably the phone would ring at 3:00, and it would be Grandma wanting to know where we were. While my father groaned about my grandmother's ways, my mother would rush around to get us out the door and over to the Glendale Apartments, where she'd take off our coats and head for the kitchen, a room at the back of the apartment that was maybe eight feet by ten. All Lybyer daughters were expected to be in there helping, although there was barely room for one person to turn around. The only time any of the women emerged was to put out plates and silverware, which was no easy feat, since the table, a special plywood creation, took up the entire front room. If you wanted to set a place near the front door, the easiest way to get there was to go out the back door, walk around the apartment building, and come in the front.

While the women worked in the kitchen, the sons-in-law, seated cheek-by-jowl on the couch, discussed exactly two subjects, fishing and hunting, with a slight variation sometimes thrown in, which was how much better my grandfather could hear when he had a rod or a gun in his hand. Although he missed much of what my grandmother had to say, he never failed to respond, or so the sons-in-law told it, to the sound of fish jumping.

One Thanksgiving, Cork did the unthinkable and wandered into the kitchen, and before the women cleared him out, he spotted a bottle of Mogen David wine under the cupboard. None of

Our house on South David Street.

My aunt Marion, Grandma, me, and my mother, at Christmas dinner in my grandmother's apartment. The table took up her entire front room.

the sons-in-law drank wine as a rule, beer and bourbon being more to their tastes, but Mogen David was alcohol, which sounded pretty good in any form as the afternoon grew long, the temperature in the apartment reached eighty, and the children underfoot began to fight. "Mary, you ought to serve that wine with the turkey," Cork advised as he departed the kitchen. "Yeh, Mary, it might be good," Bub joined in. "Better let us drink it, or Ben will," my father added for good measure. They kept up their clamor until my grandmother emerged from the kitchen, Mogen David in hand, and slammed it down on the table. She set out jam jars, used for drinking glasses when there was a crowd, and when everyone was seated, she supervised the division of the bottle—or three-quarters of a bottle, actually. It had been opened sometime in the distant past, perhaps even the prehistoric past, and as the sons-in-law tossed back their Mogen David, you could see their shock. Nothing was supposed to taste this bad! Meanwhile, my grandmother, who had surprisingly served some to herself, sipped away, an expression of total equanimity on her face. Of course, it was bad. Alcohol was supposed to taste rotten. Wine that made tears run down your face was no surprise to her at all.

My father found himself in a financial pinch as 1949 drew to a close. As people who were around then remember it, his mother, Anna Vincent, became so concerned about his financial state that she took it upon herself to ask family members to send him a few dollars for Christmas. I had no idea that we had money trouble, but I knew it was not a happy time. My father and mother had begun to argue late at night. He would shout, she would cry, and he would slam out the door, not to return for hours. I would crawl into bed with my mother, try to get her to stop sobbing, and wonder where he had gone. Thinking back on it now, I suspect it was to the Sandbar. Despite repeated efforts to close it down, including the election of a reform mayor, Robert Rose, it was still a place that provided numerous opportunities to lose money—card games probably being the fastest.

Whatever caused his financial difficulties, the result was that he sold the house on South David, and we took up residence in the Glendale Apartments. Even a nine-year-old could figure out we had come down in the world, a situation I coped with by telling my friends that we lived in the middle upstairs apartment instead of the end unit where we had actually moved. I had some thought that if they believed we were in the middle upstairs unit, where my grandparents lived, my friends would think we owned the building, which was better than having them think we were tenants. I also had a comforting fantasy that I really lived in the high school, half a block away. Built in a style I have since learned is called "collegiate gothic," it looked like a castle, and I imagined myself living there as a queen.

The move to the Glendale Apartments did have this advantage: I could be close to my youngest aunt, Marion, who was still living with my grandparents. Fair-haired and porcelain-skinned, she was Girls League president, the highest office girls generally aspired to at Natrona County High School. She had been chosen the outstanding girl by the students and faculty and regularly appeared in the local newspapers modeling the clothes of local department stores, although in real life, none of her dresses came from a store. My grandmother made them all.

I loved exploring Marion's basement room, especially when she wasn't there. A kidney-shaped dressing table to which she had thumbtacked a ruffled, polka-dotted skirt contained all manner of mysteries. One day, under a white ceramic doll that sat on top of the table, I found nail polish and lipstick. Another time, in a drawer, I discovered a two-dollar bill. Never having seen such a thing before (and having read a lot of *Dick Tracy*), I concluded that my aunt was involved in a counterfeiting ring and waited with dread—and some anticipation—for the police to haul her off. Would they handcuff her before they put her in the police car?

Marion was a homecoming princess her senior year in high school, and my grandmother and I went to watch her at the homecoming dance. As we stood in the balcony of the high school gym, one of Marion's friends, dark-haired Sue Holley, who was homecoming queen, whirled by below, wearing the most amazing formal, as we called it: red, strapless, the skirt lined with ruffle after ruffle. Sue's mother, Ruth, had made the dress, Grandma told me, modeling it after a gown she had seen in *Gone with the Wind*. My grandmother knew this because, while she did repairs and alterations at H & G Cleaners, Ruth, who together with her husband was a part owner of the H & G, worked the counter. An adept seamstress, Ruth was proud of her creation, as well she should have been, but I had seen my grandmother at work on her treadle sewing machine and knew Ruth had nothing on her. From that night forward, when I thought of being a teenager, I imagined myself in red crinoline. Grandma would make the dress, and I would whirl around in the high school gym.

CHAPTER SIX

L IVING IN A ONE-BEDROOM apartment wasn't great for any of us, but I suspect the most miserable member of my family was my father. Thanksgiving, Christmas, and an occasional Sunday were one thing, but now he was subjected to the Lybyer drive for togetherness on a daily basis, which must have driven him crazy. Whatever financial situation had caused us to move to the Glendale Apartments, he fixed it fast, probably paying off debt with the proceeds from the house on David Street and then saving mightily from his government salary for a down payment on another place. Before the summer of 1950 was out, we were moving into Westridge, a new development built on an alfalfa field west of town that had until recently been owned by sharp-dressing haberdasher Harry Yesness. It had been part of the historic CY Ranch, which Yesness had purchased before the war from the heirs of Joseph M. Carey, judge, senator, governor, and all-around luminary of Wyoming's early days.

Like Levittown, the famous development started in 1947 on a potato field on Long Island, Westridge had been built using concrete slabs and assembly-line techniques. Like Levittown, where you could get four rooms and a bath for $8,000, Westridge was cheap: five rooms and a bath for $9,000. Government programs such as VA and FHA meant easy mortgages: no money down for veterans and just 5 percent for others, like my father.

But this was Wyoming, which meant that Westridge was a lot smaller than Levittown, 177 houses as opposed to 17,000. And no matter that in both places people lived in rows of look-alike homes built on former farmland, Westridge was not Levittown once you stepped out the front door. At 5,000 feet above sea level, the sky above was blue of a brilliance never seen at lower elevations, and in our land of little rainfall, there were few trees to block the view. It was as though you were standing on a mile-high platform that stretched on and on, its only boundary Casper Mountain, a 3,000-foot ridge to the south that was as much a part of our lives as the sky or the seasons.

A part of the Laramie Range, Casper Mountain had been created eons before in a violent upheaval of earth. Subsequently buried by lava and volcanic sands, it had emerged again in a geological event grandly named the Exhumation of the Rockies. Geologists argue about exactly what forces lifted the mountains and excavated them from the debris in which they had been buried, but had anyone asked us, we would have told them the wind had something to do with it. In the summer, it picked up dirt and whirled it into dust devils and blew tumbleweeds across the prairie until they caught in barbed-wire fences. In the winter, the wind drove the temperature to far below zero, piled the snow in great drifts, and created white-outs, which kept you from seeing more than a few feet ahead.

People who came to Casper as adults were bothered by the wind, particularly the way it howled in the winter, but as children growing up there, we accepted the wind, laughed as we played Annie, Annie Over and a gust took the ball we were trying to throw over the house and deposited it onto the roof next door. We liked to hold our coats open and let the wind fill them out like sails. We would leap into the air when the wind was blowing especially hard, hoping against hope that it would pick us up and put us on a neighbor's roof.

One of the first pictures my mother took after we moved to Westridge shows me and my father standing in our front yard wearing Western gear: boots, saddle pants, and colored shirts, mine peach, his green, both lavishly embroidered across the yoke with white leaves and flowers. The photo is from 1950, the year city officials decided to promote the four-year-old Central Wyoming Fair and Rodeo by asking everyone in Casper to wear Western clothes. My mother and her sisters, all of whom learned to sew from my grandmother, took this as a mission, stitching, trimming, and embroidering until all husbands and children were fully decked out.

We wore our gear to the fairgrounds southwest of town, where there were wheat sheaves, canned beets, and prize-winning biscuits on display. Kids in 4-H walked their champion lambs around. High school girls modeled the outfits they had sewn for the "Make It Yourself with Wool" contest. We would meander through the exhibits, check out the carnival, riding the Ferris wheel, maybe, or the tilt-a-whirl if we were feeling adventurous, throw hoops over bottles in hopes of winning a Kewpie doll, or pay a dime to pick up a floating rubber duck, hoping, always futilely, that our choice would be the one with "$5" written on its bottom side. Finally, we would make our way into the arena, where we'd take our bleacher seats for the rodeo.

The calf roping and steer wrestling, which came first, were a little boring, but the bronc riding, which featured horses with names like Twister and Widowmaker, was definitely not. As soon as a horse was put in a chute, it would try to kick out the sides, becoming more and more agitated as the cowboy lowered him-

Aunt Norma and Uncle Cork.

My mother.

Me.

We didn't wear Western clothes often, but we knew how to get dressed up for a rodeo.

self gingerly into the saddle—or straight onto the horse's back, in the case of the bareback competition. Then the gate would swing open, and the horse would burst out, bucking wildly. The cowboy, one arm in the air, would spur away, trying his best to hang on for eight seconds.

The bronc riding had a certain authenticity about it. Wild horses did have to be broken, though not necessarily by cowboys waving one arm in the air. But the high point of the rodeo, Brahma bull riding, had about as much connection to ranch life as the fancy duds we were wearing in the bleachers. There was simply no good reason to try to ride a Brahma bull—except that it was the meanest animal around and could be counted on to try to kill you. The daring it took to climb aboard a Brahma and try to stay there for eight seconds, your only handhold a braided rope around the animal's midsection, made bull riders the superstars of rodeo—although the clowns who regularly saved their skin ran a close second. As soon as a cowboy fell or jumped from a bull's back, a figure in whiteface, a red nose, and a funny hat would rush into the arena and waggle his fanny at the bull, trying to distract him from the cowboy he was intent on goring. It usually worked, and the bull would take out after the clown, who would run across the arena in his oversize shoes and leap for the fence.

Sometimes the fair and rodeo was an occasion to remember our roots. Girl Scouts would go to Fort Caspar, from which the town got its name (in a slightly misspelled version), and dust and clean the displays there. There might be a reenactment of events in 1865, when hundreds of Lakota, Cheyenne, and Arapaho, enraged by a massacre of Cheyenne at Sand Creek in Colorado, came together to attack the U.S. Army fort at Platte Bridge Station. A young lieutenant with the 11th Ohio Cavalry, Caspar

BLUE SKIES, NO FENCES

Collins, rode out with a small detachment to escort a wagon train into the fort, but he and his men quickly found themselves surrounded. They tried to make their way back, but the fighting was fierce, and as Collins watched, one of his men was shot and fell from his mount. When Collins tried to rescue him, his horse bolted and carried him into the midst of the enemy, where he was killed, his body pierced by twenty-four arrows.

Several months after Collins's death, the military post along the Platte was named in his honor. Two years later, the fort, having outlived its usefulness, was moved, buildings and all, north to Fort Fetterman. I did not understand growing up that our beloved fort was a replica—indeed, the second one that had been built on the spot. The first had come to a bad end in 1933 during a particularly enthusiastic reenactment, when flaming arrows were used and, in the words of one writer, "did just what they were designed to," burning down the fort.

The fair and rodeo were about heritage but also about progress. The local newspapers would begin to build excitement for weeks in advance by advertising this year's celebrities as bigger than ever, better than ever. Rex Allen! Slim Pickens! A trick rider who could spin lassos with both hands while standing on the back of a galloping horse! There would be record crowds and record excitement at the rodeo, the newspapers predicted every year, and no matter what else was going on, they gave the fair and rodeo top billing. On August 15, the day before the opening in 1950, the *Casper Tribune-Herald* headlined "Fair Grounds Here Are Alive with Activity" above "Reds Launch Drive," an Associated Press story about North Korean troops threatening the perimeter that Allied forces had managed to establish around Pusan. The next day, the headline atop the paper was "Big Central Wyoming Fair Under Way Here," and beneath it, "Bombers

Rout Reds," an Associated Press account of the B-29 bombing campaign that had pushed the North Koreans back behind the Naktong River.

Reading the Korean War stories, I see why juxtaposing them with opening-day reports of the fair and rodeo did not strike us as incongruous. Although by this time in the war, the North Koreans had nearly driven allied forces off the Korean peninsula, the emphasis in the August 15 Associated Press story was not that our side had been unable to resist the enemy advance but that "Allied resistance to the Communists had slowed the Red war timetable." Once the air offensive started, an AP story headlined "First Feather Duster, Then the Sledgehammer" emphasized the military's mercy and might, reporting how "one lone B-29," the feather duster, had dropped leaflets urging surrender. Then came ninety-six B-29s, the "massive sledgehammer," dropping 3,500 quarter-ton bombs on the enemy. Another story that day called the air strike "the mightiest air blow of the Korean War." Another described it as "just short of atomic explosive power in concentrated effect." Red troops were described as "stunned by bomb strike" and "retreating in panic." Even toward the end of 1950, when the First Marine Division was forced to battle its way out of a Chinese trap at Choisin Reservoir, the news we read reported on the positive. An AP story, boxed and in bold type on the *Casper Tribune-Herald's* front page, highlighted a Tenth Corps communiqué that termed the withdrawal "one of the outstanding operations in military annals," which, in fact, it was.

Even when the war wasn't going well, we knew that America was great and good, her fighting men capable and heroic; and so, in high spirits, we launched the fair and rodeo festivities with a mighty parade of flags, bands, and floats, so many that assembling them all was a major logistical feat. Maps in the newspapers showed the exact position on certain blocks where each participant was to line up. From these appointed places, everyone gradually moved onto Center Street, where parade watchers lined the curbs and applauded for the celebrities who usually led things off—the senators, the congressman, the governor. One year, we got to see a recent queen for a day, who had come to Casper fresh from her triumph on Jack Bailey's radio show. Kassis Department Store had fitted her out with Western clothes. Stockmen's Supply had given her boots. Employees from Sandison's Tip Top Market waited for her at parade's end and escorted her to a ribbon cutting for their store's new addition.

After the celebrities came the city band, and then the floats, dozens of them. The main method of float construction involved molding chicken wire into the desired shape on the back of a flatbed truck and stuffing the holes in the wire with Kleenex-size pieces of crepe paper. The result wasn't the Rose Bowl Parade, but we thought it was spectacular: an oil derrick surrounded by bathing beauties in hard hats, a giant Indian headdress, a nautical float that featured mermaids.

To add luster to the fair and rodeo, organizers imported Western celebrities such as Gene Autry and the Sons of the Pioneers, but they also tried to broaden the event's appeal by ordering up amazements that had absolutely nothing to do with the West. One year, there was an ice show in the rodeo arena; another year, an underwater ballet. In 1951, there was a re-creation of the Holland Tulip Festival.

But no entertainment brought to town for the fair and rodeo ever topped Sally Rand, the genial performer who had won lasting fame with her fan dance at the 1933 Chicago World's Fair. Wisecracking once that she hadn't been out of work since the day she took off her pants, Sally encouraged people to think she performed in the nude, and perhaps she did, but she also may have worn a body stocking. So dexterous was she at waving her seven-foot ostrich feathers that no one could ever be sure.

Sally performed in a tent set up on the midway just past the fun house and the magic show. A barker out front did his best to make her act seem lascivious, but Sally herself, fifty-two when she came to Casper, was working on a more wholesome image. She sent a publicity picture to a local paper that showed her with her six-year-old son. She invited city fathers to meet her at the airport, which they most willingly did. And on the day before her first performance in Casper, Sally showed up at the Rotary Club, where, wearing a light blue dress with a high collar, she entertained all assembled with the story of how she had been inspired to a career in dance by famed ballerina Anna Pavlova.

The fair and rodeo gave us stories to tell all year long. High school boys would tell lies in the locker room about how they had crawled under the tent and seen Sally Rand's bare backside. The ladies at coffee klatsch would talk about how the women of Beta Sigma Phi, an organization that dominated the float competition, had finally outdone themselves, constructing a Mexican sombrero so large that their float couldn't get under the telephone wires running across Center Street. A story that I never tired of, possibly because I witnessed the event, starred the famed Gene Autry and his ride in the Grand Entry, an event that began every rodeo and involved dozens of people galloping on horses and carrying flags. Riders would charge in from opposite sides of the arena, circle around, and abruptly rein in their horses until everyone was lined up, flags waving in front of the grandstand. Autry, one of the first to gallop in, charged around the circle, pulled up in front of the grandstand—and promptly fell off his horse. Years later, the comedy TV program *Laugh-In* featured an adult character who would furiously ride a tricycle, then suddenly stop and tip over. I never saw the routine without remembering Gene Autry's grand entry.

WHENEVER I LOOK through the family album, the picture of me in Western clothes catches my attention, partly because it was taken with color film, which my family didn't use much until later in the 1950s, and partly because it shows me wearing pants, something I hardly ever did. In winter pictures, I sometimes see snow pants, heavy wool garments with suspenders, but even then I am wearing a dress tucked down inside. In warmer weather, it's almost always dresses—and they were more than inconvenient. Every girl I knew liked to play on the bars under the slide, where certain maneuvers executed in a skirt were positively life-threatening. If you hung by your knees, elemental modesty demanded that you hold up your skirt to keep your underwear from showing, which meant your hands were unavailable for protecting your head should you crash to the gravel below.

Despite the disadvantages of being bare-legged, the society in which we were growing up generally preferred it for us—and we came to prefer it for ourselves. Camp Sacajawea, the Girl Scout camp on Casper Mountain that my friends and I began attending in fifth grade, offered countless opportunities to wear jeans, but in the interest of keeping our legs bare, we liked to wear shorts. We hiked down mountain trails wearing shorts, went to the craft tent and pounded designs into leather bracelets wearing shorts, lounged around our tents and wrote letters home wearing shorts. Unless it was very cold, as it could be at early-morning flag raising, or unless we were going horseback riding, my jeans were folded up alongside my flashlight and collapsible metal cup in one of the orange crates we used for storage.

Long pants would have saved us from many a scratch and

splinter and even protected us from Rocky Mountain spotted fever, a tick-borne disease that was sometimes fatal. Tick fever was enough of a threat around Casper that anyone attending Camp Sacajawea had to have a tick shot, a painful inoculation that offered some protection, but the surest preventive was covering up so the ticks couldn't burrow into you. Still, we wore shorts, usually with saddle shoes, since sneakers for girls hadn't yet made it to Casper.

Part of our prejudice against jeans was that we thought they made us look "country." It was one thing to wear them to the fair and rodeo, where they were a Western costume, like saddle pants, and it was another to show up for a movie at the Rex Theater looking as though you were ready to pitch hay. At the same time as we were learning to love the Rocky Mountain West, we were trying very hard to avoid being typecast. We wanted the world to know that we were cool in the same way that kids in other places were cool. TV hadn't come to Casper yet, so we relied for our images of cool on what we read, with Archie comics being particularly influential. In the early 1950s, neither Betty nor Veronica was in the habit of wearing jeans, and we didn't want to be, either.

For several summers, I spent time at Flagg Ranch, a dude ranch outside the south gate of Yellowstone Park. It was among Oscar Whitlock's real estate acquisitions, and I went there to keep my friend Karen Whitlock company, staying with her and her aunt in a trailer near the main lodge. Even though we were supposed to be contributing to Western atmosphere, we seldom wore jeans. We'd get up in the trailer, put on shorts, though the thermometer was seldom above forty in the mornings, and wander over to the lodge, a big log building where guests checked in as they arrived and were encouraged to buy souvenirs as they left:

beaded moccasins, cedar boxes, copper bracelets, Indian dolls, all arranged on tables near the cash register. At the soda fountain, we would fix ourselves outrageous breakfasts, usually involving ice cream, then look for an adult to accompany us on an excursion, maybe a trip to a nearby hot spring, where we could splash around in inner tubes.

In the afternoons, we had a job: showing tourists to the small log cabins where they stayed. One might expect that since we were at a dude ranch, we guided them on horses, but somewhere Karen's father had acquired a Crosley, a tiny car just the right size for a fifth-grader to drive, and with Karen behind the wheel, we led tourists over dirt roads to cabins designated modern and unmodern, depending on whether or not they had plumbing.

Tourists would ask to take our picture, and that was OK with us. I liked to imagine them pulling out the snapshots at home and saying, "Hey, look at this. These two kids were driving a car." Having them think we were precocious was certainly better than having them assume we were quaint—which they all too often did. Although we dressed as we imagined cool kids anywhere would, particularly favoring midriff-baring blouses with our shorts, some tourist was always asking, "Do you live in a log cabin?" We would wince at such questions, though we'd grown to expect them. The only images of the Rocky Mountain West most tourists had in their heads were the cowboy-and-Indian ones that movies, rodeos—and Flagg Ranch—encouraged.

On our side of things, we also had the tourists pegged. Unless they had Southern accents, we thought of them as Easterners. They might be from Indiana or Missouri or New Jersey, but to us, they were all the same, probably used to going to the seashore, we figured, the way people did in the Bobbsey Twins. Maybe they even played tennis, which teenagers were known to do in Nancy Drew mysteries. There was a tennis court in Casper right next to the high school, but nobody we knew used it for its intended purpose. Our friends all regarded it as a great place for roller skating. We'd tighten our metal roller skates onto our shoes with our skate keys and roar around, delighting in the surface that was so much smoother than any sidewalk.

As much fun as Camp Sacajawea and Flagg Ranch were, they failed to turn me into an outdoorswoman. Pale-skinned, I would burn and blister if I spent more than a half-hour floating in an inner tube. Blue-eyed, I would squint in the outdoor glare. My eyes watered so much that when I was small, my parents often stood me in the shade to take photographs, which made many of their snapshots too dark to see. As I grew older, I tried to tough it out in the sun, which resulted in photograph after photograph of me looking pained—or at the ground.

But you didn't have to be a hardy daughter of the out-of-doors to learn to love Wyoming's clear blue skies and snow-topped mountains. On the hikes we took at Camp Sacajawea, we sometimes sang "Home on the Range," but "Flow Gently, Sweet Afton" and "Kookaburra" were also favorites. Neither of the last two, I know now, has anything to do with the Rocky Mountain West, but to this day, when I hear these songs, one about a Scottish river, the other about an Australian bird, I smell the pine trees on Casper Mountain and long for the pure, dry air of a Wyoming afternoon.

Even someone who held onto the saddle horn for dear life, as I did during moonlight rides at Flagg Ranch, realized that the night sky was an amazement, with stars so thick in places that the darkness paled with them. Looking up from the back of a patient brown horse, I understood that I was not just in Wyoming, not just on earth, but in the universe, and that behind and above and beyond everything human beings could ever know or hope to do was the unimaginable vastness of infinity. It was a realization at once diminishing and exhilarating: I was a small part of such wonder—but I was part of it. And I had been born in a place where the sky and the stars and the distances shocked you into thinking about such things. Resist the stereotyping though I might, I was a Westerner.

FAMILY TRIPS were explorations of our part of the world. Every year or so, we would load up the car—my mother, father, brother, and I—and head for Yuma, Arizona, where my grandmother and grandfather Vincent and brother Leon had moved. We would head southwest on Highway 220, passing Alcova Lake, Pathfinder Lake, and, just before crossing the Sweetwater River, Independence Rock, which rose more than a hundred feet above the prairie and marked the place pioneers had tried to reach by July 4 so they wouldn't get caught in autumn snows as they traveled farther west.

At Rawlins, we'd turn onto Highway 30 and head across the arid expanses of southwestern Wyoming. You could count on one hand the other cars you'd see, and my brother and I got most of our entertainment from the sky, from clouds shaped like elephants or ships, from far-off storms, dark in the distance except for flashes of lightning. Sometimes my mother and I would try to teach Mark the words to songs we liked. I see our car now, a green Buick Special, rolling down the empty highway as we sang:

Oh give me land, lots of land under starry skies above,
Don't fence me in.
Let me ride through the wide open country that I love,
Don't fence me in.

Let me be by myself in the evening breeze,
Listen to the murmur of the cottonwood trees,
Send me off forever but I ask you please,
Don't fence me in.

Occasionally, as we drove along under perfectly sunny skies, rain would fall, a phenomenon I do not understand to this day but that my mother claimed meant the devil was beating his wife.

We'd pass through Rock Springs, a town where eastern Europeans who had come to mine coal had built exotically named fraternal lodges. A half-hour or so farther, we'd stop at a gas station and restaurant called Little America, and while my father took care of the car, Mark and I would admire the stuffed Emperor penguin displayed near the restrooms, no doubt as a tribute to the Little America in Antarctica. After that came Evanston, a pretty town close to the Uinta Mountains that was known to kids in Wyoming as the location of the state mental hospital. In the backseat of our car, I'd whisper to my brother that this was the place we were dropping him off.

From Evanston, we entered the basin of the Great Salt Lake, and from there it was sometimes due south, crossing Utah and entering Arizona so that we could see the Painted Desert, pinks and blues and purples stretching on for miles, and then we were at the Petrified Forest, where fallen trees had somehow turned to stone. But more often, when we left Salt Lake we headed for Las Vegas, where the casinos had more electric lights than the whole state of Wyoming. We'd find a motel, as we did every place we stopped. There were no motel chains, no standardization, so the only way to be sure of what you were getting was to take a look at the room being offered, a job that inevitably fell to my mother, who, since she couldn't stand to hurt anyone's feelings, motel

Me, with my brother Mark, about 1950.

With my brother Leon, on one of the family trips to Yuma, Arizona.

managers' included, went through the motions of looking around but accepted whatever was offered. Details she was willing to overlook—whether the window air conditioner worked, whether the bathroom was clean—usually mattered to my father, but not in Las Vegas, because as soon as we were checked in, he was off to play the slots.

Early the next evening, trying to miss the heat of the day, we'd start across the Mojave Desert, usually with a swamp cooler secured in the passenger window of our Buick. Filled with ice water, the swamp cooler was supposed to blow cold air, but after about fifteen minutes, all it was good for was raising the humidity. My brother and I, both covered with sweat, would collapse in the backseat and moan, while in the front seat, my father eased his misery by drinking bourbon and Coke. He would pour half the Coke out of the bottle, fill it up with bourbon, and take swigs as he drove through Needles, then Blythe, and then we came to Yuma, where Navajo women sold beaded bracelets by the roadside and people plucked lemons and limes off trees in their backyards. And it was so hot that every week or so, somebody would crack an egg on the sidewalk, where, sure enough, it would fry. Sometimes I thought I might smother in Yuma's heat, but my brother Leon considered this the dumbest thing he'd ever heard. Retired today, after twenty-five years as a telephone lineman in Yuma, he still insists that most other places are just too doggone cold.

CHAPTER SEVEN

O UR MOVE TO Westridge meant that I transferred to McKinley, a grand brick pile of a school on the west side of town.
Everything about it was imposing: the eight-foot doors that took
you into the school, the two-story entrance hall inside, and the
woman who stood to the right of the entrance hall offering
a gravelly voiced greeting every morning: Principal Eleanor
McLaughlin.

When I started at McKinley in 1950, Miss McLaughlin,
gray-haired and vigorous, had already been at the school for two
decades. An Irish Catholic from Minnesota, she had originally
been brought to McKinley, so I later learned, to deal with a
gang of bullies, "unmanageable boys," one father called them,
who "were defying the teachers hourly and performing filthy actions before the little girls." With her no-nonsense air—and her
paddle—she quickly brought the boys and the school under control. Although she was nearing sixty when I first saw her, she had
lost none of her power. Wearing glasses, always dressed in a sensible gabardine skirt and lace-up shoes, she made the very idea of
acting up seem impossible.

Strict as she was, Miss McLaughlin inspired affection. Her
toughness didn't come from animosity toward us, we knew, but
from dedication to us and McKinley. We were the center of her
existence, and we loved her for thinking we were important.

Anne Marie Spencer, a sixth-grade teacher at the school, also won our hearts. Married to the manager of Bustard's Funeral Home, Mrs. Spencer, a gorgeous brunette with a beautiful singing voice, was an undeniable celebrity in our small town. She was a soloist at the First Presbyterian Church, had a fifteen-minute talk show on radio station KVOC, and was the person city fathers would pick to escort visiting celebrities, such as the *Queen for a Day* winners who came to Casper for the fair and rodeo. When the canasta craze hit Casper in the 1950s, Mrs. Spencer and her husband, Jim, gained fame together as the best players in town.

Children who became mute in Miss McLaughlin's presence opened up in Mrs. Spencer's, most famously in the case of the Halloween night murder of Pearl Lewis, a fifty-eight-year-old woman from Mills, Wyoming, whose body was discovered near Garfield School, not far from McKinley. When it was reported that Lewis had been raped as well as murdered, kids all over town wanted to know what that meant. They had enough of an idea to figure out that there weren't many adults who would be willing to explain, but one of Mrs. Spencer's students decided he could ask her. And so he raised his hand in class, and when she answered him, calmly and clinically, she became an instant legend.

Eleanor McLaughlin and Anne Marie Spencer, different though they were, knew how to operate in tandem. McKinley School, like Park School, was mostly middle-class, but there were fewer rich kids at McKinley and some whose parents clearly had trouble affording necessities. One family lived in a dugout—a cave with a framed-in entrance—in an area outside Casper known as Mountain View. Conspiring together, Miss McLaughlin and Mrs. Spencer managed to get the Mountain View kids into a bathtub once or twice a week and to see to it that they had clean clothes to put on when they got out.

*Anne Marie Spencer,
a beautiful and
much-loved teacher at
McKinley School.*

*Mrs. Spencer serving at a teachers' coffee. Miss McLaughlin,
McKinley's strong-minded principal, is on her right.*

McKinley School, like many schools in the '40s and '50s, was run entirely by women, but that did not mean it was run for girls. If there was a single thing that defined McKinley, it was sports, and sports were mostly for boys. It was the boys Miss McLaughlin had run lap after lap around the block where the school stood. In every kind of weather, she would be out there, whistle around her neck, yardstick in hand, encouraging them on. It was the boys Miss McLaughlin taught to call plays as they scrimmaged on an empty lot next to the school, the boys she showed how to throw free throws, the boys she showed how to bunt. And with all this attention, the boys became very good athletes. McKinley's teams were feared throughout the town.

She did not entirely ignore girls. At the high school every year, a city track meet was held that had a few running events for girls. You had to qualify to compete, and Miss McLaughlin was there cheering us on as we ran as fast as we could in a street next to McKinley, trying for one of the ribbons that would allow us to advance to the citywide event. I remember winning a red ribbon one year and getting to run on the high school track, but for me and my friends, the track meet was mostly a social event, an opportunity to chase one another around the bleachers in the high school stadium, assess kids from other schools, and get wildly sunburned. Meanwhile, Miss McLaughlin was out on the field, where the boys were doing long jumps, high jumps, and pole vaults, things no one imagined girls could or should do.

All in all, for Miss McLaughlin and so many educators, boys were a better psychic investment than girls. If you put your hopes in boys, you might bring glory to the school, as McKinley's winning teams surely did. I also suspect that Miss McLaughlin thought that girls didn't need attention in the same way that boys did. It had, after all, been a gang of boys that she'd had to confront during her first years at McKinley. I think she discovered early on that organized competition was a good outlet for male energy that might otherwise be misdirected.

My friends and I channeled our competitive impulses into academic contests such as spelling bees. We practiced in our spare time and took special delight in long and difficult words such as *antidisestablishmentarianism* and *Czechoslovakia*. I often came in first or second in the spelling contests, though I never advertised the seconds at home. Anything but first would cause my father to ask, "You didn't win?"

Recess was also a time for contests. Although I was small, I got pretty good at Red Rover, a game usually played in the winter that involved hurling yourself against the clasped hands of members of the opposing team and breaking through their line. The secret, I discovered, was jumping at the last minute so that you brought downward as well as forward momentum onto the clasped hands of your opponents.

As the weather grew a little warmer, my friends and I would jump rope from the minute we got outside until the recess bell called us back, and when the snow had all melted and the spring sun warmed up the sidewalks, we became obsessive—and excellent—jacks players. We would run outside, jacks bags in hand, to claim a prized spot on the sidewalk. The smoother the square of cement, the more desirable, because jacks involves sweeping up metal pieces with your hand and a rough square of cement almost immediately resulted in bleeding knuckles. So we raced for the smooth squares and, as spring advanced, for the shady ones.

The game as we played it was highly ritualized. There was a correct way to sit: left leg bent inward at the knee, right leg out.

There was a correct ball to use: a golf ball. The only time we used the rubber balls that came with a set of jacks was when we got stuck playing indoors. There, on wood or linoleum floors, they gave a pretty good bounce, and golf balls didn't.

Although they were our ball of choice, golf balls were hard to come by. Most of us had just one, but if we happened to get a second, we would set about peeling off the white cover and unwinding the miles of rubber band inside until we reached the hard rubber ball at the center. Inside that center was a yellowish liquid that we firmly believed to be a deadly poison, but that did not deter us. The rubber balls that we excavated bounced like crazy, whether you were indoors or out. Their bounce wasn't as true as a golf ball in its original form, so they weren't the first pick for outside, but inside, they were much preferable to the rubber balls that you got at the dime store.

As for jacks, we mostly made do with what you could buy at Woolworth's, but occasionally, an older sister or a friend who was visiting from out of town would give us jacks that were thicker, heavier, and not so pointed on the ends. We called these jacks stubbies, and when you rolled them around in your hand, they made a wonderful sound, sort of like small pebbles tumbling together. I don't recall that I ever owned six stubbies—which is how many jacks were required to play a game—but I did have one or two and was always hoping more would come my way.

There were no rule books for jacks. Older girls taught younger ones, letting us start by flipping the jacks with two hands, from palms to backs of hands and back to palms again. Whoever dropped the least number of jacks got to go first. By third or fourth grade, pride demanded a one-handed flip, and when the order of precedence had been established, the game would start: babies, baskets, up casts, down casts, up double-quicks, down double-quicks, halves, and wholes. It went from the simple to the more complex, although down double-quicks, which involved passing jacks from one hand to another while bouncing the ball downward and clapping the ground, always seemed harder to me than wholes, which involved picking up jacks and transferring them to the other hand without letting the ball bounce at all.

As people moved from one Casper school to another, they took the culture of jacks with them. All across town, girls were spending hours at the game, sometimes at school and sometimes at home. Our mothers, observing our skinned knuckles and our fingernails worn to the quick, would urge us to take a break, but for the most part, adults ignored us. We were on our own as we sat on the sidewalk, trying as hard as we knew how to beat one another.

We were playing jacks in a world that was becoming an increasingly worrisome place. The Soviets were building a stockpile of atomic weapons, and the resulting anxiety, at least according to some sociologists, was having an impact on the American psyche, making us more anxious to conform, to fit in with the group. Cultural critics seized on a phrase from David Riesman's book *The Lonely Crowd* and labeled the 1950s personality "other-directed," interested in the approval of peers, as opposed to earlier generations of "inner-directed" people, who operated according to their own internal gyroscopes.

But my friends and I, for the moment at least, had not made the shift. We felt no need to be constantly obliging and cooperative as other-directed people were. Perhaps because of some group dynamic, we were not totally caught up in wanting to be liked by our peers; we also understood the pleasure of beating their brains out. Our competitive spirit was every bit as sharp as anything displayed by Frank Merriwell, the superachieving hero of dime novels, who, according to Riesman, provided a model of fierce inner-directedness for generations of boys.

This spirit would serve us well in our later lives. Although many of our teachers and parents encouraged us to go to college and think of careers, the larger society in which we were growing up pressed domesticity upon us. My friends who became professors, psychologists, businesswomen, and software developers were no doubt helped along the way by a certain indifference to the expectations of others.

Competitive spirit, once activated, is a persistent engine, and so in Girl Scouts, when we were supposed to be learning about first aid, photography, and community life, some of us were thinking almost exclusively about earning badges. I decided which ones to work on by flipping through the *Girl Scout Handbook* and figuring out how long each would take. I would survey the starred activities, the things you absolutely had to do, and reject such badges as "Home Health and Safety" because it required making a protective container for household tools, and that sounded like a long-term project. I deemed other badges ("Clothing," "Hostess," "Housekeeper") unsatisfactory because they required discussions at a troop meeting, which our troop leader, Mrs. Finkbiner, might not schedule for weeks. But, particularly in the arts, there were a number of badges that could be whipped out in record time, even if your artistic abilities were as severely limited as mine. I finished "Drawing and Painting" and "Interior Decoration" in a few days, and in a single evening, sitting on my bedroom floor with a compass, a protractor, colored pencils, and paper, I polished off all the requirements for "Design."

My father had joined the Casper Lodge of the Masons, which

meant that I, like a lot of my friends, was eligible for membership in Job's Daughters, an organization for girls from fifth grade through high school. I was very impressed with the idea of becoming Honored Queen, the highest position in Job's Daughters and an office that involved a crown, a long velvet cape, and getting to run the meetings. But after attending a few times, I realized that it was going to take years to work my way to the top, years in which I would have to be a junior custodian or a fifth messenger, or a marshal, a guide, or a princess. That was too much delayed gratification, and I dropped out.

I made new friends at McKinley School, including Linda Ladd, a brown-haired, self-possessed girl, who lived very near the house my Uncle Bub had transplanted from Teapot Dome. Linda's flat-roofed house, built from cinder blocks, had a generous backyard with a dilapidated shed near the alley, and she and I decided to use it to raise pigeons. She had a lead on a couple we could buy, and our idea was that the birds would lay eggs and produce babies we could sell. Meanwhile, we would have the companionship of these adorable birds and maybe even be able to train them to carry messages from her house on Cottonwood Street to mine on Westridge Way. We cleaned out the shed and went into business—for about a week. The birds had bugs, defecated all the time, showed no inclination to be our friends, and certainly weren't about to deliver messages. We gave them back to the high school boy we bought them from.

Linda and I were fond of scaring ourselves to death by going to movies like *The Day the Earth Stood Still*. We'd catch the bus to one of the three theaters downtown, let a uniformed usher, armed with flashlight, show us to our seats, and then scream our way through a summer afternoon. Once, though, a movie at the Rex Theater got so scary that Linda left. I made it through the rest of

When Worlds Collide by myself, although the idea of the world ending was pretty terrifying. It meshed all too neatly with what we knew about the atomic bomb and the fact that the Russians now had one. Our teachers and parents tried not to frighten us. They didn't have us practice "duck and cover," the exercise so familiar to kids in the eastern part of the United States. But we were still well aware that some very bad people were now capable of destroying the world, and this knowledge could inspire immense feelings of dread. Standing outside McKinley School one day, I made myself feel sick imagining a nuclear blast blowing the red brick building to kingdom come.

Given Wyoming's place on the targeting totem pole in those days before Minuteman Missiles were installed in the state, the probability of an atomic weapon getting dropped on Casper was pretty remote. A more realistic threat was polio, which in Casper, as across the nation, claimed victims every summer. The local newspapers would report the numbers, particularly as August approached and the disease started to peak. Wyoming's numbers weren't much compared to national figures, sixteen cases of "infantile paralysis," as it was sometimes called, as of August 1, 1949, compared with 8,000 nationwide, but there weren't many people in the state. Everyone in Casper knew when the fifteen-year-old football player died or the forty-seven-day-old baby was put into an iron lung. In 1951, the year I was turning ten, a nine-year-old whose father worked with mine at the Bureau of Reclamation was stricken and died, which must have thoroughly terrified my parents.

The city fathers tried everything. They spent a fortune spraying alleys with DDT; they had the high school pool drained and disinfected; they shut down the outdoor pool in Washington Park. Most parents had lists of forbidden activities, everything from running through the hose sprinkler to going to the movies, and all lived in dread, until 1955 when the Salk vaccine was released. I have no memory of being vaccinated, but a friend remembers that we lined up in the high school gym for our shots, and she is quite sure that several of the boys fainted.

CHAPTER EIGHT

EVERY WEEK, my father dropped me off at the Sunday school
that met in the basement of the First Presbyterian Church,
but he never went to church himself, nor did my mother, not
even on Easter, when she expended amazing energy getting me
dressed up. One year, I arrived at the red brick church at 8th and
Wolcott wearing a pink corduroy coat my mother had made—a
"duster," she called it—and a straw picture hat trimmed with
pink flowers. I had white gloves and new white patent-leather
shoes, which I was careful not to scuff as I made my way down
the stairs to the basement, where, behind one of the temporary
partitions used to separate Sunday school classes, I listened to the
story of the empty tomb and did my best to absorb the mystery
of the Resurrection. Then, when most of the Sunday school kids
headed upstairs to meet their parents for church, I skipped out to
the curb, where my father was waiting in the car.

One of his objections to church was that it was boring, and
after I tried going a few times by myself, I saw his point. Sermons
did last a very long time. The hymns were great—"Rock of
Ages," "Church in the Wildwood." It was a puzzle to me that we
didn't spend more time singing, since that was the part of church
everyone seemed most to enjoy.

My father was also irritated that Presbyterians (like every

other denomination I've known) encouraged people to pledge a certain amount over the year. They handed out envelopes in which you were supposed to put a portion of your pledge every week, whether you actually attended church or not, and in my father's opinion, this represented grasping after money that hadn't been earned. "I'll pay if I go," he would say. And he didn't go.

My father's real animus, however, was directed not against Presbyterians but against Mormons, into whose religion he had been born. A "Jack Mormon," he called himself, signifying that he was no longer part of the church, but the Latter-day Saints do not give up a sheep easily, and at least twice a year, a pair of clean-cut young men in dark suits would ring our doorbell. My father would chase them from the porch.

He never talked about how his family got to be part of the Mormon church, and I doubt he knew the stories of his forebears' arrival in Utah in any detail. He was so profoundly irritated by the church's refusal to let him go his own way that he wasn't about to spend time thinking about the ancestors who had got him into this fix, but his brother Dale, a more patient man, collected stories about Vincent ancestors, and long after my father died, using Dale's information as a starting point, I learned what hardy souls they were and, in particular, how strong were the women from whom he was descended.

One of my father's great-grandmothers, Katurah Vaughn, was a servant girl in South Wales when she encountered a Mormon missionary in 1848 at a meeting near her home. It had been only a year since Brigham Young had led the first company of Mormons to the valley of the Great Salt Lake, but missionaries were already abroad, and the effort in Wales, led by the charismatic Dan Jones, was an astonishing success. Katurah and a young man named William, whom she met at the meeting and married shortly thereafter, were among thousands baptized in the new faith. They were also part of the first group to emigrate to what Mormons called New Zion, and although it is unlikely that either had ever been more than ten or twenty miles from home, the two of them traveled first to Swansea, then from there by steamer to Liverpool, where they boarded a sailing ship, the *Buena Vista*, to cross the Atlantic. As they waited to depart, local ministers came onboard and tried to persuade passengers not to leave on their voyage, describing every manner of horror awaiting them if they did, including a life in slavery. A rumor common at the time had it that Dan Jones, sailing aboard the *Buena Vista* with his charges, intended to sell them in Cuba.

None of the 249 aboard chose to leave the ship, and when it finally departed from Waterloo Dock, the passengers, accompanied by a harp, joined in "The Saints' Farewell," singing goodbye to "British land,/Our home for a long time," and affirming for themselves and those seeing them off that a better life awaited, "a paradise beyond the great open sea."

The voyage took fifty-one days, not an unusual length of time for sailing ships but miserable weeks for people unused to sea travel. When the *Buena Vista* arrived in New Orleans in April 1849, Katurah, four months pregnant, was probably among the weariest of those disembarking and boarding a steamer, the *Constitution*, for the trip up the Mississippi. At St. Louis, another steamship, the *Highland Mary*, pulled alongside, and the Mormons transferred their belongings for the journey up the Missouri to Council Bluffs, a gathering place for those heading to Utah.

In New Orleans, there had been reports of cholera, and on the rivers, the converts from Wales heard tales of many deaths. They comforted themselves that their faith would protect them, but they had not been aboard the *Highland Mary* long before dozens of passengers were struck down, many of them dying within hours of falling ill. One family lost three children in two days, another three in three days. A new mother died, along with her nine-day-old son. On May 15, 1849, Katurah's husband, William, died and was buried on the east bank of the Missouri.

The captain of the ship tried to force the Mormons off at St. Joseph, Missouri, but authorities there refused to receive them. Nor were they welcomed at Council Bluffs by their Mormon brethren. The living, offloaded with the dead, lay on the river bank until a church apostle intervened. "Brother Smith sent word to the people," one of the passengers wrote in his journal, "that if they would not take us in and give us shelter, the Lord would turn a scourge upon them. It was not long before teams and wagons came down and all were cared for."

In Council Bluffs, on September 16, 1849, four months after the death of her husband, Katurah gave birth to a son, whom she named William after his father. The boy lived only thirteen months. A member of the Mormon church who interviewed Katurah many years later caught some of the desolation she must have felt. "Two of her dear ones," the interviewer wrote, "have been laid in unknown graves."

Without money to travel farther west, Katurah stayed in Council Bluffs until the summer of 1852, when the LDS church had raised a sufficient sum from contributions to take her and others who hadn't been able to pay their own way to the Salt Lake Valley. The train of fifty wagons that Katurah was part of started out on June 28 and traveled along the north side of the Platte, a flat and shining river unlike anything Katurah would have seen before. It was a yellowish color—golden to the more romantic-minded—the result of bits of sand and mica suspended in the water. Its banks, timbered today, were mostly treeless then, adding to the strangeness of the landscape. Under a sky that seemed stupefyingly huge, mirages were common: a lake, a ghostly train of wagons. Strange animals appeared—antelope, elk, and, most notably, buffalo. As the wagons rolled west, women walked alongside and collected dried buffalo dung, fuel for fires in the treeless land.

As the days grew drier and dustier, travelers saw rattlesnakes and eagles and then, rising out of the dry land, rock formations that they had heard about, structures that seemed to belong to another world. Chimney Rock was first, a needle into the sky, then Scotts Bluff, looming like a medieval fortress. After that, Laramie Peak came into view, and then the Mormon train crossed to the south side of the Platte to Fort Laramie, an adobe structure when Katurah saw it. She noted that there were a great number of Indians around the fort, "but all were peaceful."

The country grew rougher, broken hills with gulleys and ravines, before the travelers passed over the Platte once more, ferrying over at Last Crossing, where Casper, Wyoming, is today. The next stretch was probably the worst part of the journey— rough, barren land, littered with the carcasses of cattle poisoned by alkali water that gathered in foul-smelling pools. The wagons probably stopped at Independence Rock, and the Mormons, like pioneers before them, scrambled over the monolith and scratched their names into its granite. Then they moved on to Devil's Gate, a dramatic cut made through the Rattlesnake Range by the Sweetwater, a river aptly named, whose waters grew colder as the trail climbed higher. Katurah crossed the continental divide at South Pass, forded the Green River, and, as the travelers drew near the mountains that create the Valley of the Great Salt Lake, she and the others encountered a familiar figure, their beloved leader, Dan Jones, who was setting out on another mission to Wales. After a joyful reunion with him, there followed another with Welsh Mormons who had been aboard the *Buena Vista* and had traveled straight to Utah rather than staying in Council Bluffs. They rode out from Salt Lake with wagons of watermelons, potatoes, grapes, mushmelons, all the bounty of the valley that the new arrivals would now call home.

Katurah was twenty-five when the wagon train of which she was part traveled through the canyons that penetrate the Wasatch Range and entered New Zion. She married within a year, and with her new husband, Charles Vincent, a widower who had arrived in Utah in 1851, she moved to Provo, where Charles, a farmer, became a landowner, something he could never have hoped to do in his native Wales. The Vincent family, skilled at farming, began to produce large crops of wheat, "so that from [their] bins," a church biography of Katurah reported, "many were fed and seed wheat was supplied to many of the settlers in those early days."

In 1852, the year Katurah arrived in Utah, one of the apostles of the church publicly declared plural marriage to be a tenet of Mormon faith, but there were no such marriages in Katurah's family, nor were there among most Mormons. Estimates vary from 5 percent to 20 percent of the population having been involved in polygamy, but whatever the number, people in other parts of the nation were outraged. The *New York Times* called polygamy "the enslavement of women." A Washington, D.C., newspaper referred to Salt Lake City as "that sink of iniquity." There was also conflict between Mormons and officials sent from Washington to oversee their affairs, with Mormon resentment of outside interference sometimes boiling over into violence toward federal agents. All of this led to a conviction in the nation's capital that the Latter-day Saints had established a theocracy that encouraged immorality and was intent on thwarting U.S. authority. The result was that in 1857, President James Buchanan decided to replace Brigham Young as territorial governor with a non-Mormon and sent a force of 2,500—nearly a third of the U.S. Army—to enforce his order.

The Mormons learned of the army headed their way as they were celebrating their tenth anniversary in Utah, and the news recalled for them earlier persecutions that had led them to seek sanctuary in the far West. Mormons had been killed in Missouri and driven from that state. In Nauvoo, Illinois, their leader, Joseph Smith, had been jailed and murdered. Concerned that the federal force headed toward Utah meant to invade and spill more Mormon blood, Brigham Young sent mounted militiamen to harass the advancing army and ordered hundreds of men, including Katurah's husband, Charles Vincent, to leave their homes and fortify Echo Canyon, the eastern entrance to the Salt Lake Valley. The Mormons piled up boulders to cascade onto invaders, built dams that they could open to send a flood of water onto troops moving into the canyon; and their efforts, combined with freezing weather, persuaded the U.S. Army to encamp for the winter in southern Wyoming rather than advance into Utah.

Sure that the army would come into the valley in the spring, Young ordered those living in the northern part of the territory, some 30,000 people, to prepare their houses for burning and to move south. Some 10,000 set up camp west of Provo, where Katurah and Charles, who was back from duty in Echo Canyon, lived. On land called Provo Bottoms, families found what shelter they could, some even burrowing into the ground. All were aware that everything they had left behind, as part of a scorched-earth policy decided upon by Brigham Young, would be set to the torch if the Army entering the valley proved hostile. But the U.S. forces entered peacefully, and an accommodation was finally reached, with the Mormons agreeing to the new governor, who was sympathetic to them, as well as to the presence of federal troops, and Brigham Young reluctantly accepting a pardon that President Buchanan offered to the citizens of Utah. The thousands who had been living on Provo Bottoms went back to their homes, life in Provo settled back into its seasonal routines, and Charles and Katurah, parents of two boys, had their first daughter.

Some three decades later, Mormon church president Wilford Woodruff announced that plural marriage was *not* a tenet of faith, clearing the way for Utah, which had long sought statehood, to become part of the Union in 1896. By this time, Charles and Katurah's sixth and youngest child, David Jehu, was grown—and they worried about him. Although alcohol is forbidden for members of the Church of Jesus Christ of Latter-day Saints, David made his living from saloons, starting out in the early 1890s as a bartender in Provo's Palace Saloon and later acquiring his own establishment, the Eureka, described in a business directory as a "first-class gentleman's resort." According to the directory: "The bar and the interior are handsomely furnished in cherry and decorated with large French double plate mirrors. The goods handled are the choicest imported and domestic wines, liquors and cigars, and the standard brands of whiskeys, making a specialty of the celebrated Old Crow and Sherwood rye brands." Although a saloon in the heart of Mormondom would not seem a good investment, this one may well have been successful. I suspect it is what an anonymous family historian was referring to when he observed that David ran "one of the most successful dry goods operations in Provo." Perhaps this historian was being ironic, since "wet goods" would be more appropriate, or, more likely, he simply wanted to acknowledge David's business achievement without acknowledging what business he was in.

However successful, the saloon would not have stood David in good stead with the Mormon church, nor was his domestic life tidy. He had married Nellie Elliott, a young woman who, like himself, was a high school graduate from a good Mormon family. Her mother, Fannie Peck, had crossed to Utah the same summer as Katurah Vaughn, though Fannie had been a child at the time—and a very determined one. Just six years old, she walked much of the way barefoot in order to save her one pair of shoes for Sundays when Mormons stopped to worship. Fannie had married Edwin Elliott, an Englishman who converted to the Mormon religion in Australia, and the two had nine daughters. An Elliott family picture shows Nellie, the third daughter, with a tilt of the head and a glint in the eye that makes her look a bit of a rebel, which she, indeed, turned out to be. After five children and many years of marriage, she fell in love with another man, left David, and the two divorced. David married again, this time to a kindhearted woman named Essie, but Nellie's love affair must have ended, for she remained single—and lived to be nearly a hundred. I met her when I was two or three and she well into her seventies, and I remember her hair curling around her face in white ringlets. As an old picture shows, she still had a glint in her eye.

Many of Nellie's and David's descendents became stalwarts of the Mormon church, but their oldest son, my grandfather, was not among them. Leon Edwin, or Lyn, as everyone called him, dropped out of school after eighth or ninth grade and went to Telluride, Colorado, where he worked, according to the 1910 census, "corking flumes," waterproofing the seams of the great

My great-great-grandparents Fannie Peck Elliott and Edwin Elliott,
who traveled the Mormon Trail, shown here with seven of their nine daughters.
My great-grandmother Nellie is in the center.

My father, with his
younger brother,
Dale, during their
Utah boyhood.

conduits that brought water to the silver mines. He then headed to California, where, as a self-taught pianist, he got a job playing on cruise ships traveling between San Francisco and Alaska. Despite his adventuresome spirit, he was a reserved young man, which made his next accomplishment all the more noteworthy. He won the heart of the beautiful, thoroughly extroverted Anna Madsen. She was the daughter of Swedish and Danish immigrants deeply committed to the Mormon church, and they may have tried to increase Lyn's commitment, but if so, they merely irritated him. He usually began his description of my grandmother's relatives by declaring them to be "too religious."

After his marriage to Anna, Lyn went to work for American Express, a company then known for parcel delivery and travelers' checks, and by 1925, he was earning ninety dollars a month, enough to rent a two-bedroom house in Provo for his family, which now included two sons, my father, Wayne, and his brother Dale. The boys fished, swam, hiked along the Provo River, and climbed Provo Mountain. They earned money during harvest season picking string beans for a penny a pound and spent their hard-earned wealth on silent movies starring Tom Mix and Buck Jones. In 1927, they heard their first radio broadcast, sitting on the lawn of a neighbor who put his radio in the window with the volume turned up so that kids outside could hear the Dempsey-Tunney fight.

Anna, like her husband, had only a grade-school education, but she wore clothes well, had an air of authority, and became a successful saleswoman and buyer for Butler's, a women's ready-to-wear store. She attracted people with the joy she took in life, but the spontaneity with which she would exclaim over a sunset or burst into song ("Springtime in the Rockies" was a favorite) did not mean she was casual in her opinions. If she decided that zinnias were the best flowers for her garden, then zinnias it would be, no matter that the seed envelope said they needed more sun. And her flower gardens bloomed, as though they dared not do otherwise.

As determined in her housekeeping as she was in her views, Anna believed in keeping drawers tidy, making beds first thing in the morning, and ironing underwear. To her way of thinking, letting dishes dry by themselves in a dish rack was a sign of laziness, as was clutter. While she might have allowed a piece of trash, such as wrapping paper, to stay inside overnight, anything she designated as garbage, such as potato peelings, had to be wrapped and disposed of in an outside receptacle as soon as it was produced.

Lyn's job took the family from Utah to Wyoming, Colorado, and Arizona, and as they moved, he, who had always loved his gin, began to drink more. When Anna complained, he hid a bottle in the car and another in a drawer, once precipitating a major family crisis when he tucked a bottle into the corner cupboard and, upon trying to retrieve it, destroyed most of the family china. But it wasn't until he slipped and fell after a bout of drinking, breaking his arm in three places, that he decided to quit. He resolved never to touch another drop, a vow he kept for the rest of his life. But perhaps sobriety wasn't easy, or perhaps age did to him what it does to many and made him more the way he already was—in his case, an essentially private person. He spent the hours when he wasn't working sitting in his chair reading, a radio nearby turned up just loud enough so he could hear it. He left the socializing up to my outgoing grandmother.

One connection he did keep was with his Masonic lodge. Faithful about attending meetings, he was extremely proud when he became a 32nd-degree Mason, an attainment that would only have deepened his estrangement from the church. Its hierarchy was irritated by Masonic claims that Mormons had purloined some of their rituals and suspicious that the Masons were trying to be a church themselves. Whether these disputes meant anything to my grandfather isn't clear, but he did cast his lot with the Masons and quit going to church entirely. Anna became an enthusiastic member of Eastern Star, the Masonic women's organization, but she didn't let that stand in the way of her religion. She simply ignored whatever arguments the Masons and Mormons were having and kept going to church on Sunday.

Mormons were the main religious irritant in my father's life, but he also continued to resent the Catholic church, blaming it as he did for the death of his first wife, Tracy. In the early 1950s, a movie casting the Catholic church in a bad light came to the America Theater in downtown Casper, and although we didn't typically make family trips to the downtown movies, going instead to whatever was playing at the Skyline Drive-In west of town, for *Martin Luther* my father made an exception. He wanted me to see the church taking advantage of people, he said, with Tetzel, the fat monk selling indulgences to the poor, being a case in point.

Tetzel was repulsive, but Martin Luther, as portrayed in the movie, was to my eyes an odd hero. I could not get over his head, mostly shaved but with a ring of hair left to grow around the edge. Today I know this hairdo, called a tonsure, was historically accurate, but in Wyoming in the 1950s, it served mainly as a distraction. Anti-Catholic feeling would have been hard for me to whip up in any case, because I knew so many Catholic kids. Toward the end of the nineteenth century, O'Mahoneys, Sullivans, and Tobins had come into central Wyoming, bringing sheepherding skills and Catholicism with them. "A weird, lonely place," one of the O'Mahoneys called it, but he also observed that it had "fine, fresh air and plenty room to kick and feel free." Early arrivals encouraged others still back in Ireland to join them, and by the time I was growing up, Casper had a substantial Catholic community. Although most Catholic kids went to St. Anthony's, a parochial grade school founded in 1927, the town was small enough that we all knew each other anyway, and I couldn't connect these kids with what went on in Martin Luther's time. In fact, I quite admired the exotic things they got to do, such as eating fish on Friday, electing May queens, and going to some exclusively Catholic event called Sodality, which I imagined to be an ice-cream social.

Driven to the Presbyterian church every Sunday by my father, I earned a white zippered Bible with my name stamped on the front in gold for my faithful attendance. I spent hours reading every word of it, including the begats, prompted in large part by the fact that my friends were doing the same thing. I read through my Bible twice for good measure, emerging from the experience not only with bragging rights but with the wonderful cadences of the King James Version lodged in my mind. Occasionally, I will hear a Bible verse from the Revised Standard or New International Version that seems just right, but more often than not, I find myself turning to King James, the one I first read.

I have no idea why my parents chose to send me to the Presbyterian church. None of my relatives went there, and the fact that my parents didn't go either left me without much denominational loyalty. In fact, with the exception of my Mormon grandmother, no one in my family had much of that, which was in some ways no doubt a loss, but it also led to a kind of genial tolerance. When a grade-school friend persuaded me to attend after-school revival meetings ("Good News" meetings, they were called) in temporary housing from the air base that had been relocated next to Westridge, my mother seemed totally unconcerned. I think she was of the general opinion that whatever religion was being advanced, it was probably good for me. Even my father mellowed some over the years, becoming marginally more polite to the Mormon missionaries who appeared on our front porch and being no gruffer with the Catholic boys I dated than with other male teenagers who showed up at our house. Many years later, when I joined the Methodist church, everyone was fine with that. And when my brother Mark fell in love with a Jewish woman and decided to convert, it caused hardly a stir.

There was, however, one dear relative, Maxine and Bub's grandson Mike Lockwood, whose approach to religion definitely raised eyebrows. I had left home by the time he began to preach on street corners but received reports, particularly when he built a large wooden cross, attached a wheel to the bottom, and began pulling it up and down CY Avenue. Hearing of this, I rolled my eyes along with everyone else, certain he had gone 'round the bend.

Years later, I found myself wishing I had tried harder to understand what he was doing: testing his faith, perhaps, strengthening himself in it, knowing as he must have how people would respond? When I called him much later and asked about the cross with the wheel, he had a very practical explanation. "It was a way to get attention," he said with good humor. "People would stop and say, 'Christ didn't have a wheel, why do you?' And I'd say, 'Well, it would be a real drag without one.' Then I'd have a chance to talk to them about why Jesus died, how he died for them." Mike is no longer walking the streets with his cross but continues his ministry by volunteering at a local rescue mission.

CHAPTER NINE

In 1952, MY MOTHER appeared in "Mrs. Casper's Cooking Class," a feature that appeared irregularly in the *Casper Morning Star*. She was photographed standing behind our kitchen table, cracking an egg into a bowl in which dough for something called Chinese Chews was being churned around by a Mixmaster. My brother, about to turn three, is sitting on a kitchen chair beside the table, looking directly into the camera, an expression of total skepticism on his face.

But three is too young for skepticism, so I'm no doubt reading into what I see and finding disbelief on my brother's face, because I know that my mother's prowess didn't lie in cooking. She basically hated to cook, except for a few dishes that she had grown up with. Hominy was one, and when she fried it up with bacon, it was delicious. Her version of grits, which was basically cream of wheat with butter, salt, and pepper on it, was a little puzzling. Cream of wheat deserved sugar and milk. But the menu item that caused most resistance was head scrapple, the basic ingredient of which was meat scraps from a pig's head, with some tongue and brains thrown in. She would slice the scrapple and fry it in lard, with my father proclaiming all the while that it might be her dinner, but it wasn't going to be his—a sentiment I wholeheartedly shared.

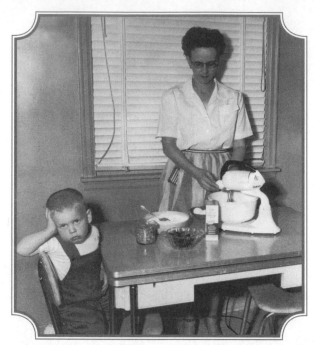

My mother, appearing in a newspaper feature, "Mrs. Casper's Cooking Class." My brother Mark seems skeptical of the enterprise.

Casper's police force in the 1950s. My mother is the only woman.

For supper on Sundays, she always made chicken and noodles, a recipe served over mashed potatoes that left everyone pleasantly stupefied for hours after we ate. She would mix up flour and eggs, roll the dough out, let it dry a couple of hours, then roll it up and slice it. Meanwhile, she cooked a chicken in a pressure cooker, a device much in favor in the 1940s and '50s that saved cooking time, but you had to cook on low, something my mother, always in a hurry to get out of the kitchen, didn't like to do. And so, periodically, the pressure cooker would explode, coating the kitchen in broth and leaving bits of chicken hanging from the ceiling.

My mother also hated doing laundry, and no wonder, I think to myself, when I realize that until I was in junior high, she got the excess water out manually, running just-washed clothes through a wringer attached to the washing machine. When I was in high school, she got a tumble dryer, but in all the years before then, she hung the laundry out on a clothesline to dry, not such a terrible task in warm months, but in the winter, it meant aching fingers and clothes that froze on the line. She'd bring my father's shirts in and put them on the couch, where they'd lie all puffed out as though someone were inside them.

She liked to have the house look nice, but to her way of thinking, the way to achieve that was not by scrubbing but by redecorating. If she found herself with a few extra hours on a weekend, she did not spend it making beds, but instead would buy wallpaper for the front room. She would lay long strips out on the kitchen table, brush them with paste, and put them up right over the old paper. I have been told many times since that this is a method doomed to fail, sure to result in everything coming loose from the wall, but my mother did it repeatedly, and it worked, though my brother and I often joked that she had put so many layers of paper on the walls that the front room of our Westridge house had grown several square feet smaller as a result.

She once decided that she would get rid of any reason ever to wax the kitchen floor by having liquid plastic poured on it. A team of men who must have been of strong constitution, since as far as I know, they, like we, survived the fumes, spread the gooey mixture around our kitchen floor, throwing red and gray flakes in it for decorative effect. Called Torgenol, the plastic coating lasted all the days my parents lived in the house and I am sure has resisted every effort to remove it since.

My mother looks so pretty in the picture where she's mixing dough. She seems the very picture of health—and I know that isn't right. She was ill for years after my brother was born—pale, tired, weepy. Someone decided that maybe her teeth were the problem, and so she went to Midwest, the town in the Salt Creek oil field where she had grown up, to see Marvin Shidler, a dentist who offered good prices and would take all your teeth out at once. He had a theory that it was very important to force the dentures in as soon as the teeth were pulled, and I remember seeing my mother right after this had been done. She was wearing pedal pushers, sitting on the front lawn, trying hard to smile with her new teeth, but her gums were bleeding. She was not yet thirty-five.

Having her teeth pulled, it turned out, wasn't the answer. She was still sad and tired from the moment she got up in the morning. Finally, one doctor suggested that she wasn't really sick, that it was her nerves, a diagnosis that she decided was maybe right. She needed to be busier, to quit thinking about herself so much, and so she got a job. She went to work as a clerk in the local police department and felt better almost from the day she started—not because the job calmed her nerves but because, I think, it gave her a life outside the home and people to relate to besides my father. She loved him, and he loved her, but theirs was a difficult marriage. His needling—"You got an A minus?" he would say to me, no matter that all the rest of the grades were straight A's—was probably productive in my case, a spur to perfect report cards. But when he, having been raised in one of the cleanest houses on the planet, fulminated about my mother's housekeeping, it was devastating for her. She suspected that there were niceties she hadn't learned growing up in the oil fields, and his criticism would convince her that she was right. She'd stand at the sink, taking dishes from the soapy water and putting them in the dish rack to dry, and he'd see they were still dripping soap suds. "You're going to make us sick," he'd yell. "Were you born in a barn?" It was a popular expression of the time, but because she actually had been born in a roadside barn, she would run from the room in tears.

Her work at the country courthouse was perfect for her in many ways. She had always loved reading about crime. Every Sunday, at her request, my father and I would stop at Westridge Drugstore on the way home from Sunday school and buy her a New York tabloid she liked that almost always featured a gruesome murder on the front page. She and my Grandmother Vincent shared a love for crime magazines such as *True Detective*, which could be found in abundance around our house. Now, working in an office decorated with knives and guns that had been seized from evildoers, she was part of the action. The policemen she worked with liked to talk to her about their jobs, the reporters who covered the courthouse liked to talk about everything, and she suddenly was in possession of a lot of interesting information. When a prominent businessman was caught in the

Van Rooms, a house of ill repute down in the Sandbar, my mother knew all about it. When a local man's wife was found buried in concrete in the basement of their home at Fifteenth and Melrose, she knew all the details before they appeared in local papers: the faithful St. Bernard that led police to the grave by scratching at the cement; the former wife who had moved back in when the current wife had disappeared.

She loved to help people, and when she was promoted to being in charge of collecting traffic tickets, she had real power to do so. The dean of girls at the local high school came in to pay a parking ticket, and while she was in the courthouse, she got another one, which my mother, seeing the injustice of it all, tore up. Myrtle Lybyer, married to my grandfather's brother Leonard, swore the red light she was charged with running had something wrong with it. My mother, seeing the injustice of that, too, took care of Myrtle's ticket.

After a decade of collecting parking tickets, my mother became secretary to the police chief, controlling who saw him and who didn't, which made her someone to be reckoned with. "She was strong," says Jennie Brown, who worked with her then, "and she had to be. She was between the chief and everybody else." But when Brown contacted me a few years ago, her main point was my mother's kindness. "I couldn't have been poorer," Brown says, describing her situation as a young mother with a second husband who spent everything she earned. "Your mother would say, 'I have some clothes out in the car, and maybe you know someone who could use them.' And I'd take them and wear them, and she'd never mention it again." Brown, who would start college when she was thirty, eventually became a college teacher and writer.

My mother eventually became a deputy sheriff, performing

duties that were mostly clerical—typing, filing, and, in her beautiful handwriting, keeping the department's payroll records. She enjoyed her work, did it well, and was very proud of her uniform and badge. In later years, after I had moved far from home, she would come visit me, and when I picked her up at the airport, she would inevitably introduce me to three or four fellow passengers whom she had awed with her gold sheriff's star. It had the Wyoming state seal at its center and around the top part of the seal, her jurisdiction, Natrona County. Around the bottom was her name, Edna L. Vincent.

My brother and I, self-centered as children are, focused on the ways her working deprived us. Mark didn't like the babysitter my mother found for him and wanted to stay home rather than go to her house after school. I was old enough not to have a babysitter, so that wasn't a problem for me, but I did envy the more orderly lives of children whose mothers were at home full-time. The Bishops, across the street from us, were a case in point. Every night at 5:00, Mrs. Bishop would call her two daughters, Marybeth and Susan, in to have a bath. By the time Mr. Bishop arrived home, the girls would be scrubbed and shiny in clean dresses, and the family would sit down at a dining table to a carefully prepared meal. I had no desire to trade places with the Bishop girls, and when I grew up, I would fall miles—millions of miles—short of providing my own children with the soothing rituals that were part of their daily life. But as an eleven-year-old, I admired the way the Bishops organized their lives, perhaps because I was attuned to what the culture of the '50s was saying about the way families were supposed to be. I'm more inclined to think, however, that I was seeing a way of living that was, in fact, very pleasant—but that could be sustained only if women found gratification in creating it.

CHAPTER TEN

IN THE SUMMER, my mother looked for ways to keep me busy while she was at work. Swimming lessons were out, since my eyes would turn bright red after about twenty seconds in the heavily chlorinated high school pool, and my mother, remembering the near-drowning her mother and sister had witnessed in Midwest, wasn't all that eager to have me in the water in any case. And so she signed me up for baton twirling. By the time I walked the mile or so to the high school, took a class, and walked home again, half the day was gone, and I would spend the rest of it practicing the loops and twirls I'd learned. When the six weeks of the twirling class were over, the instructor, a thoroughly glamorous high school junior named Delores Bissacca, wanted me to enter the state twirling championships being held at the Central Wyoming Fair and Rodeo. My mother made me a costume from a pattern in the Simplicity pattern book, a red and white satin creation with a flared skirt and epaulettes, and bought me a pair of majorette boots and a tiara. I performed on a wooden platform erected in the rodeo arena and, much to my surprise, came in second.

I immediately began to imagine myself the winner the next year, and so did my mother, who arranged private lessons with Delores Bissacca. I'd go to her house on South Grant, where her

My mother made my first baton-twirling costume from a Simplicity pattern book.

She also arranged for the police department to sponsor me in a national contest. While Chief C. J. Carter hands me a police department emblem, reporter Lou Musser, who covered the police beat, turns over $56 to help pay my way.

mother, Mary, who specialized in Rayette perms, had a beauty salon in the rear, and Delores would show me rolls and slides to add to my twirling routine. We'd practice on the sidewalk out front, creating something of an obstacle course for Mary's clients, and later I'd perfect what Delores had shown me in our front yard in Westridge. Thanks to the shadow cast by the house, it was shady out there in the afternoons, and I'd plug in a radio and listen to baseball games—preferably the Yankees—as I wore a circle in the lawn lunging and spinning around. When fall came and then winter, I practiced inside, in the front room, and usually kept going until 7:00, when *The Lone Ranger* was over. The ceiling and the furniture suffered, and my parents must have as well, since the room was maybe twelve feet by fifteen, and there was no place else for them to sit after work. So accustomed was I to twirling in the front room that once, when my mother sent me to bring in the milk left by the milk man on the front porch, I twirled the glass bottles on my way to the kitchen. As I executed a particularly challenging maneuver, they slammed together and broke, splashing a white coat of milk over couch, chair, radio, rug, and ceiling. My mother cried as we cleaned up the mess, and who could blame her?

Although more intense than most, I was by no means alone in my passion for baton twirling. All over Wyoming, girls were practicing, doing their wrist twirls and flat spins in Cheyenne and Rawlins and Lander. Lusk, a town of a couple thousand in the eastern part of the state, was a baton-twirling center, because Joan Lund Berry, who had won the Miss Wyoming contest with twirling as her talent, lived there. In a small town, you took advantage of what expertise you could find, and so Lana Templeton, Bonnie McKelvey, Donna Osborne, and Leila Lewis took lessons from Joan and became forces to be reckoned with at the state championships. The Lusk girls came to the 1953 state contest in gorgeous costumes: white satin with red fringe, sky-blue satin with gold glitter, pale green satin with gold fringe, lavender corduroy with white appliquéd flowers. My mother and I had advanced beyond the Simplicity pattern book, but I was not in the Lusk league.

The city fathers of Casper imported a genuine twirling celebrity for the state contest that year: Bob Roberts from California, who led off the Central Wyoming Fair and Rodeo parade flinging two batons high into the air, higher even than the Henning Hotel, while zooming around on roller skates. Roberts confirmed our worst fears when he declared that we were living in a twirling backwater. He told a local paper that "Casper twirlers are several years behind other sections because they are isolated from the districts where twirling is far advanced." Undaunted, wearing the creations sewn by our mothers and grandmothers and aunts, we smiled and twirled for the judges, and when the day was over, I was the junior state champion. In the rodeo arena where the cowboys rode horses and bulls at night, I was presented with a trophy and $150 toward a trip to the national competition.

The next January, on the first plane trip for both of us, my mother and I flew to St. Paul, Minnesota, where the National Baton Twirling Association's national contest was a part of the St. Paul Winter Carnival. All dressed up, as was everyone who traveled by air in the 1950s, we boarded a Western Airlines DC-6, which, after stops in Bismarck, North Dakota, and Pierre and Sioux Falls, South Dakota, finally touched down in the twin cities of Minneapolis and St. Paul, which were, by far, the coldest places I had ever been and, to my mind, the most exotic. I was in that mysterious place called the East, I kept telling myself, although, of course, I was actually in the Midwest. But it was the East to me, and a big city, I thought, as we made our way through the crowds and bustle of the airport. My uncle, Wilbur Lybyer, a mechanic for Braniff Airlines who lived in Minneapolis, picked us up and took us to the Lowry Hotel, where I met my first genuine TV celebrity in the elevator. I asked Robert Q. Lewis, whom I knew from the quiz program *What's My Line?* for an autograph, which he gave me, though not too graciously, as I remember. We stayed at the Lowry for three nights for the grand sum of $31.66, including phone charges, which were, in part, I am sure, the result of my mother calling her newspaper friends in Casper.

One newspaper story explained the competition. Each contestant started with one hundred points and, during the course of her two-and-a-half-minute routine, received deductions for failures to be perfect—as in dropping the baton, for example, which was about the worst thing you could do, though not smiling was nearly as bad. The story headlined the fact that we had a "great time," a nice way of saying I didn't win anything, but we had learned a lot—about costumes, for one thing. No more buying sequins by the yard for my twirling outfits. From that time forward, we spent hours applying sequins one at a time, bead in the middle, creating flashing swirls and flowers of great intricacy—just like the ones we had seen in St. Paul.

We also learned that what Bob Roberts said was, sadly, true: Wyoming was indeed a twirling backwater. The finalists were mostly girls from places like Zionsville, Indiana; Cudahy, Wisconsin; and Dundee, Illinois. I took a lesson from Sonie Rogers, a lovely brown-eyed girl from Watervliet, Michigan, who had won the national championship the year before, and my mother began to worry about what to do when we got home. She put her ear to the ground and came up with the name of Mary Joe Budd, a statuesque blonde who was the star twirler with the University of Wyoming band. Mary Joe didn't exactly live next door. Her home was in Sinclair, Wyoming, a tiny refinery town about 120 miles from Casper, but her family was willing to have me come stay with them and take lessons when she was home for the summer. My mother put me, my suitcase, and a baton on a Trailways bus for Rawlins, the nearest town of any size to Sinclair. The Budds picked me up at the bus station, and I spent a week with them, most of it in their backyard learning slides and rolls and leaps from Mary Joe.

I won the junior state championship again, and my mother, making plans for us to go to the nationals the following January, decided to be sure I was fully appreciated. She began by arranging for the Casper Police Department to sponsor me, which was all the hook she needed to get her pals at the local newspapers to give us plenty of coverage. In one of several pictures she arranged, I am accepting a police department emblem from Police Chief C. J. Carter and an envelope from Lou Musser, a columnist for the *Casper Morning Star*, containing, the newspaper explained, $56 "collected from people who wish to remain anonymous to help aid in the expenses of the trip." The *Casper Morning Star* also noted that the police department had contributed about $90, much of which I suspect was from my mother.

In St. Paul, she arranged for the police department there to roll out the red carpet, which was fodder for more stories in the hometown papers—and a picture of me performing for my assigned escorts—policewoman Dorothy Thimmell and Detective Richard Ferber—in the *St. Paul Pioneer Press*. My mother accomplished all this publicity from her position as a police department clerk. I've often wondered what would have happened had she been, say, a lieutenant. Would I have been on the cover of *Life*?

I smile as I write this, but there's truth in it. My mother and her siblings were part of a breakthrough generation for the Lybyer family, the first to grow up with a high school education as an expectation, the first to have white-collar jobs, the first to spend adulthood in the middle class. She and her sisters came from a long line of women who were no doubt capable of many things but whose days had been consumed by the hard work of farm life. Freed from that, my mother's generation had opportunity to demonstrate other abilities—limited opportunity, to be sure, compared with what women would later know, but enough to indicate talents waiting to be tapped. My mother was a force I can easily imagine being multiplied many times over had her connections reached higher and farther.

I suspect, though, that whatever her circumstances, her focus would have been the same: her children. As my brother grew, she took him to the photo studio as she had once taken me, encouraged his interest in baseball, and marveled over his accomplishments. He became a steady, sturdy boy, who gave my baton-twirling achievements about as much respect as he should have. He had a total lack of awe for the trophies displayed in our front room, using them as battlefield obstacles for his toy soldiers. He occasionally helped me out by running the record player I put on the porch so I could practice to march music, but he insisted on a nickel a start—probably not too much, given that the record player delivered an electrical shock about every third time you touched it. When I think of what a well-balanced little boy he was, I am not surprised that he turned into a fine man. Husband, father, and now grandfather, he still lives in Casper, where he manages a law firm.

Whenever a twirling contest was coming up, I would imagine myself winning it, see myself standing at the microphone graciously accepting the first-place trophy—and then it would happen. Deciding that this technique deserved to be applied to other fields of endeavor, I began to imagine myself receiving the Outstanding Girl of the Year award, a prize given to an eighth-grader every year by the American Legion. I pictured myself standing up on the stage in a blue dress holding my certificate, and lest these thoughts not be enough, I began to write "OGY, OGY" (for Outstanding Girl of the Year) in patterns on my notebook, around the edges of school papers, even on the soles of my shoes.

A few years ago, in a book about female ambition, I read about a reporter who once did something similar, only she wrote "IWBF, IWBF," letters that stood for "I will be famous." The author of the book didn't identify the reporter but did thank Lesley Stahl in her book's preface, leading me to wonder if Stahl might have been the ambitious girl. She did get to be famous, and I got to be Outstanding Girl of the Year—though whether my imaginings had anything to do with it is doubtful. Eight years later, my brother Mark managed to become Outstanding Boy of the Year without defacing his possessions.

The picture that ran in the newspapaer in 1955 shows me standing alongside Zirn Hayden, Outstanding Boy of the Year and a fellow eighth-grader. At six feet tall, he is as oversized as I am undersized and could be one of the adults in the picture. Genial as well as smart, he regularly let himself be taken advantage of by my father, who watched to see when Zirn was visiting his buddy Bill Chrisman in the house next door. Spying Zirn, my father would send me out to mow the grass, a chore I was too small to perform very effectively. Before I'd push the lawn mower more than a couple lengths of the lawn, Bill and Zirn would be over the fence putting all their thirteen-year-old energy against the task, and my father, quite satisfied with his cleverness, would have his weekly mowing done.

Looking at the picture of me receiving the Outstanding Girl

of the Year award, I see that I did not think that the photograph, which shows me in a puffed-sleeve dress, made me look shapely enough, so I shadowed in my waist with a pencil. But the most important thing I see is not in the picture but in the story below, where all the eighth-graders, some four hundred of us, are listed. I don't know him yet, but there is his name in section four, right after Walter Chase and before Viola Mae Clark. There he is: Dick Cheney.

PART TWO

CHAPTER ELEVEN

THE FIRST THING he remembers is riding on a bus with his mother and his younger brother Bob. The bus is full, mostly with servicemen, and one of them offers his mother a cigarette. She takes it and smokes it. The boy, three and a half, has never seen such a thing, and he never forgets it.

It is fall, 1944. The boy's father, Richard, has been in the Navy since spring, stationed first at Great Lakes Naval Training Station in Illinois, then sent to San Diego, where he expected to be shipped out but instead was assigned to the Shakedown Group of the Pacific Fleet, which trains sailors heading to sea. The boy's mother, Marge, wants to go to California and be with Richard, but there are no guarantees of how long he'll be there, and even if she could get to San Diego, she'd probably have trouble finding a decent place to stay. In August, Richard sent her a story from the *San Diego Daily Journal* describing the "pitiful squalor" in which wives were living. A marine's wife told the *Journal*, "We've had to sleep on the beaches, on park benches. We've had to walk the streets because there was no place to go." A picture accompanying the article showed one woman living with her young daughter behind a refrigerator in a six-by-nine breakfast nook.

So instead of going to San Diego, Marge and her sons, Dick and Bob, are taking the bus from Lincoln, Nebraska, where

Dick Cheney, Lincoln, Nebraska, 1944.

they've been living, to Sumner, Nebraska, population 296. There they will live with Richard's parents, Thomas and Margaret Cheney, in a pretty single-story house that Thomas built just east of Sumner School in 1906. It has two bedrooms, the smaller of which the Cheneys often rent out to schoolteachers, but now they give it to Marge, and they turn a storage area off her bedroom into a place where the boys can sleep.

Thomas, the slender, white-haired man who greets them on the front porch, comes from a family that has been in the country more than three hundred years. First arriving in America before 1640, the Cheneys were part of the great immigration of Puritans escaping persecution in England and hoping to establish a community that could be a "city on a hill," a model for the world. Thomas's first ancestor in America, William Cheney, farmed a 24½-acre homestead in Roxbury, Massachusetts, where he was apparently respected by the town's other residents, who elected him to the village's board of assessors as well as to the board of the Roxbury Latin School. But for many years, William was not a "freeman," a full citizen of the colony, because he was not a church member, status that could be achieved only by proving that you were among those chosen by God for salvation. An aspiring church member had to stand before the congregation and undergo a cross-examination by church elders, an experience that could be painfully intrusive, particularly for those who were reticent. Puritan theology was also tricky, involving as it did a careful balancing of the notion that God gives his grace freely with the idea that what a person does in this life matters, and there was a powerful example of what failing to achieve the proper doctrinal stance could cost. In 1638, Anne Hutchinson was held under house arrest in Roxbury before being expelled from the Massachusetts Bay Colony for putting too much store in the idea of God's freely given grace.

But in the end, it is impossible to say why William did not join the church until 1666, the year before he died, or to know why his wife joined much sooner. Church records show her becoming a member before 1644, although apparently the Reverend John Eliot, who kept the records, could not remember her given name and drew a blank where it should have been, listing her as "———— Cheney, the wife of William." In her later years, Margaret was well known to Reverend Eliot, though not for reasons that she or her family would have wished. According to church records, Margaret became "bound by Satan under a melancholick distemper . . . which made her wholly neglect her calling and live mopishly," a description that seems to tell of a woman suffering from depression who did not keep her home as Puritan women were expected to do. It wasn't until 1673, six years after William's death, that Margaret's decade-long crisis ended and she "gave thanks to God for loosing her chain, . . . confessing and bewailing her sinful yielding to temptation."

For several generations, the Cheneys lived in Massachusetts, with a few venturing to nearby Connecticut to farm. In the 1750s, William's great-great-grandson, also named William, served in the French and Indian War in Nova Scotia and decided to live there, eventually settling on the island of Grand Menan. He farmed, fished, raised thirteen children with his wife, Elizabeth, and, when the Revolutionary War broke out, failed to see the virtue of the patriot cause. A family genealogical chart lists him as U.E.L, or United Empire Loyalist—a Tory.

Many Cheneys fought the British. One was at Lexington, another was killed at Bunker Hill, another is on the muster rolls at Valley Forge. William's refusal to join their ranks must have caused dismay and even outrage. When Joseph Cheney, William's wealthy uncle, drowned in 1776, William did not share in his estate, although his siblings did.

William's oldest son, Ebenezer, returned to Massachusetts, but life as the son of a United Empire Loyalist may not have been easy there, and he soon moved to New Hampshire, where, like his forebears, he worked the land. Ebenezer's grandson Samuel Fletcher Cheney, born in 1829, returned to Massachusetts to marry, but shortly after his first child was born, he moved with his family some 800 miles west to Defiance, Ohio. There his wife, Harriet, died, leaving Samuel, who was working as a mechanic, to raise their daughter, a responsibility that his sister, Frances Strong, who had also moved to Defiance, probably helped him with. When Fort Sumter was fired upon in April 1861, Samuel responded to President Lincoln's call for 75,000 state militiamen to put down the rebellion, joining the 21st Ohio Volunteer Infantry for a ninety-day term. He returned home at the end of his duty long enough to reenlist for three years and to marry again, this time to Ella Phillips, the twenty-year-old daughter of a shoemaker.

Described by his mustering officer as five feet seven and one-half inches tall, with hazel eyes and auburn hair, Samuel, a first lieutenant now, fought steadfastly at Stones River in Tennessee, earning high praise from his brigade commander, Colonel John F. Miller, who listed him among those deserving "highest credit for the ability displayed in the discharge of their duties, and for their distinguished gallantry and cool courage on the field." A fellow soldier from Defiance, George T. Squire, also paid him tribute, writing to his mother and father in January 1863 that "Cheney is clear grit." One imagines the Squires passing their son's words along to Ella Cheney, who in April 1863, bore Samuel's second daughter, Belle.

In September, Samuel was in Georgia at the battle of Chickamauga, in which both Union and Confederacy suffered terrible casualties: 16,000 for the North and 18,000 for the South. De-

*Samuel Fletcher Cheney, who moved from New England,
home of his Puritan forebears, served in an Ohio regiment
in the Civil War, and homesteaded in Nebraska.*

spite greater losses, Confederate forces won the battle—but not decisively enough. Although they broke through the Union line, sending thousands of federal troops fleeing in panic, they did not accomplish the total rout that would have broken the Army of the Cumberland, and the reason they did not was General George Thomas, the commander of the corps in which the 21st Ohio, Samuel's regiment, served. When the Confederates broke through, Thomas, who, though a Virginian, was fighting for the Union, inspired his men to hold fast. They withstood repeated assaults until nightfall, when they made an orderly retreat, thus saving the Army of the Cumberland to fight another day.

Thomas's performance at Chickamauga led General Ulysses S. Grant to promote him to lead the Army of the Cumberland. It also won him a nickname, "The Rock of Chickamauga," and the undying affection of the men whom he had commanded. At an inspection near Chattanooga, Thomas noted that the 21st Ohio, which had lost its colors and more than half its members at Chickamauga, seemed but a fragment of a regiment, and he dismounted from his horse to talk to the men who, like Samuel Cheney, had made it through. He told them he knew how saddened they were at their losses but that they had fought bravely and should be proud of what they had done. "It was not a speech," one member of the regiment remembered. "It was more a fatherly talk, and when he moved away, there was not a dry eye in the line."

By the time of the victorious Atlanta campaign, the 21st Ohio, its numbers replenished, was once again a force to be reckoned with. After the fall of the city, the regiment joined in the pursuit of Confederate General John Bell Hood and his army, trying to prevent them from disrupting Union supply lines.

General William Tecumseh Sherman, commander of all forces in the West and the leader of this effort, decided while pursuing Hood that it was time for a different strategy. Instead of trying to protect his supply lines, he would cut his army loose from them and march across Georgia, demoralizing the Confederacy by destroying factories and railroads along the way and letting his men live off the land.

On November 13, 1864, as the 21st Ohio moved back toward Atlanta to begin the march to the sea, the men paused in the late afternoon near Acworth, Georgia. Samuel Cheney, a captain now, was with his men near a railroad track when Lieutenant Colonel Arnold McMahan approached and demanded to know why Company B had not yet pulled up the tracks. "My men have not had their supper, and I will be damned if they work until they get their supper!" Samuel snapped, prompting McMahan to place him under arrest for "conduct prejudicial to good order and military discipline." Samuel remained in detention for almost two months, marching across Georgia to the sea at the rear of his brigade rather than leading it, a position he surely would rather not have been in but one that, given the nature of his offense, his fellow Ohio volunteers likely regarded as a place of honor. In Savannah, he was court-martialed, found guilty, and sentenced to a public reprimand, a light punishment that was probably the result of testimony that McMahan's orders about the railroad had been confusing, leading many to think that the men were supposed to eat before they started pulling up tracks. Asked in court about the orders he had received, Lieutenant J. R. Porter, in command of Company G, testified, "Build fires, get supper, and destroy railroad."

As the 21st Ohio left Savannah to march through the Carolinas, Captain Cheney, now in command of both Companies A and B, seemed to have suffered little damage to his military career. After the Battle of Bentonville, where the South made a last futile effort to stop Sherman's progress, Lieutenant Colonel McMahan was chosen to lead the 3rd Brigade, and Samuel assumed command of the 21st Ohio. His regiment was in camp in Martha's Vineyard, North Carolina, when news came that Lee had surrendered. "Such rejoicing! Such noise!" wrote one of Samuel Cheney's fellow officers. But that was followed shortly by word that Lincoln, the commander in chief who had never wavered in the cause for which they fought, was dead. "It was easily discernible among the private soldiers," wrote the officer, "that they felt that they had lost their best friend."

The 21st Ohio marched toward Washington, D.C., and encamped about three miles from Alexandria. The men began brushing their uniforms in preparation for a grand review of Union troops in the nation's capital. On May 24, 1865, the Army of the Cumberland crossed long bridges over the Potomac and paraded through a flag-bedecked city, passing a reviewing stand where President Andrew Johnson, in office just more than a month, presided. Seated with the president were his cabinet and General Grant, who had commanded the Union Army. Standing for six and a half hours as his men passed by was General William Tecumseh Sherman.

Samuel mustered out of the army, returned home to his wife and daughters, and began to farm land he purchased north of town. As his family grew to include three sons, Samuel also began to work in a sash and door factory co-owned by his brother-in-law, Charles Strong. On February 10, 1872, after coming safely through a war in which 600,000 had died, Samuel suffered a grievous accident. While using a circular saw to split siding on clapboards, he realized that the frame holding the saw needed adjusting and knelt to turn a nut on the lower outside of the frame. As he rose, he later testified, he "slipped and partly fell bringing his left hand in contact with the saw while in motion causing the loss of all the fingers on his left hand."

Samuel sold his farm, which would have been difficult for him to work, and bought out his brother-in-law's partner in the factory, which for a decade thereafter was known as Strong and Cheney. Samuel and his brother-in-law tried to keep up with the times, buying machinery that allowed them to work in metal as well as wood, but these were not good years to own a small business. What some economists call the Long Depression began in 1873 and lasted more than two decades. Characterized by falling prices, it was particularly hard on those trying to pay off debt, as Samuel and his brother-in-law were. They had to attract more and more customers to keep up with mortgage payments, but those who used their services were in trouble themselves. In 1883, Strong and Cheney, like thousands of other small enterprises, was assigned to a trustee and sold to pay off creditors.

Samuel, now in his fifties, made a second 800-mile move, this time to Buffalo County, Nebraska, where he established a homestead claim. He cut bricks of sod from the grass-covered prairie, stacked them to create a four-room dwelling, then returned to Ohio to get his family, which by now included four sons, three of an age to be able to help farm. By Christmas 1883, the Cheneys had moved into the sod house.

Using credit for time served in the Army, he proved up his homestead claim of 160 acres in 1885, and by planting trees— oak, cottonwood, and box elder—on an adjacent timber claim, he acquired another 160 acres. Through the decade of the 1880s, the rains came regularly, and the Cheneys thrived, but in 1890, drought struck, killing the trees and devastating the crops, leaving only enough grain to feed the family. Samuel managed for a time, helped by an 1890 law that made it possible for any disabled veteran of the Civil War, whether or not his disability was the result of his service, to qualify for a pension. With his mangled hand, he was paid twelve dollars a month.

But in order to plant a crop, Samuel needed more than that, and, as he testified in an affidavit, "The banks will not loan to anyone at present." The economic circumstances that had driven him under in 1883 were worse now. Money was in extremely short supply, a situation that was soon to catapult a congressman from Lincoln, Nebraska, William Jennings Bryan, to national prominence and the Democratic presidential nomination. When Bryan brought the crowd at the 1896 Chicago convention to its feet by declaring, "You shall not crucify mankind upon a cross of gold," he had in mind farmers like Samuel, who, with the money supply restricted by the gold standard, found it difficult to borrow in the first place and to redeem debts once accumulated.

Samuel sold his timber claim to a son and finally managed to get a thousand-dollar mortgage on his homestead from an insurance company, probably by agreeing to a high rate of interest. When the loan came due in 1896, the year Bryan made his famous speech, Samuel could not come up with the money to pay it off. The court ordered the Buffalo County sheriff, Silas Fund, to hold a public sale of Samuel's farm on the front steps of the county courthouse in Kearney, which Sheriff Fund duly did. But perhaps sympathizing with Samuel's plight, which was a common one, Fund did not execute the deed to the purchaser. Not until 1902, after Fund had left office, was the property conveyed to Phoenix Mutual Life Insurance.

Samuel had once again lost everything, but he remained a man of determination, and after he and Ella had lived in Omaha for five years, he filed for a second homestead, as permitted by a 1904 law meant to encourage settlement of the Nebraska Sand

Hills, a vast area of grass-covered dunes. In his seventy-ninth year, he moved to the claim with Ella, and although she died less than two years later, he managed to prove up the homestead. A government inspector who visited him the year he turned eighty-one described him as "an intelligent old gentleman," but age finally caught up with him, forcing him to move in with his second son, who lived on an adjacent Sand Hills homestead. In 1911, in the home of Sherman Cheney, who'd been named after the supreme commander of the armies in the West, Samuel died.

It was his third son, Thomas Cheney, named after George Thomas, "The Rock of Chickamauga," who welcomed Marge and her boys to Sumner. Born four years after the end of the Civil War, Thomas had reached manhood as his family struggled on their Buffalo County homestead. No doubt hoping to avoid a life spent at the mercy of Nebraska's weather, he chose not to farm, instead teaching school for a few years, then moving to Sumner, Nebraska, where he worked for a bank. He married Lillian Byers, and they had a daughter, Mildred, in 1894. After Lillian died of tuberculosis, Thomas married Margaret Tyler, and on June 26, 1915, they had a son whom they christened Richard.

In the nine generations of Thomas's forebears in America, this name had never before been chosen. Margaret, a serious student of genealogy, probably decided on it as a way of memorializing the Prichard family of Maryland, who were among her earliest ancestors in America. A 1915 genealogy that she owned notes that the name Prichard likely derives from an elision of the phrase *ap Richard*, meaning "son of Richard." It's also possible that she knew the surprising fact that her son was descended from Cheneys not only on her husband's side but on hers as well. His Cheneys, Puritans arriving in Massachusetts before 1640, had fled persecution under King Charles I; hers, coming to Maryland before 1660, were possibly royalists who found themselves out of favor once Charles was beheaded and the Puritan Oliver Cromwell in power. His Cheneys may not have been partial to the name Richard, but hers were, since that was the name of the first of them to arrive in Lord Baltimore's province. Richard Cheney would become a substantial landowner, leaving his name on various places in Maryland: Cheney's Hill, Cheney's Resolution, Cheney's Purchase.

It could be, of course, that the echo back to the first Richard is simply happenstance. Stranger coincidences have certainly happened. I had no Cheney family reason for naming my daughters Elizabeth and Mary or for thinking—and telling my family rather often—that if I had a third daughter, I would name her Ann. And so I was struck—and moved—when I came across a page in a genealogical journal listing the daughters of the Richard Cheney who came to Maryland so long ago: Elizabeth, Mary, and Ann. It occurred to me that scripts are written for our lives that we act out unknowingly, except for now and then when we catch a glimpse of them, but I pushed the thought away, telling myself the names were a coincidence—as was the fact that a few years before we were aware of the Cheneys who came to live on Chesapeake waters in the seventeenth century, my husband, a Westerner like myself, decided he wanted to live—part of the time, anyway—on a creek flowing into the Chesapeake Bay.

Thomas, forty-six when Richard was born, delighted in his son as the little boy did in him. One of the sweetest baby pictures I have come across is of Richard, maybe four months old, with his father in the Nebraska sunshine, an expression of pure bliss on his baby face.

Margaret, thirty-eight when she became a mother, had come

*Dick's grandfather Thomas, seated,
working at Farmers and Merchants Bank.*

Dick's grandmother Margaret, center, at her high school graduation.

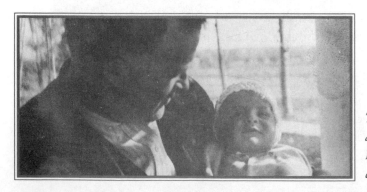

*Thomas, holding his
and Margaret's son
Richard on a fall
day in 1915.*

to Sumner to teach and had been made principal of the town's only school not long after her arrival. She gave up that job to marry Thomas, and when their son Richard was born, she lavished her attention on him, bundling him up to take his photograph in a wicker stroller and buying him toys: a miniature table and chairs, a rocking horse that attached to a small wagon. She made the bright little boy her star pupil, teaching him to read before he went to school. She told him her family history, how a group of her ancestors had traveled from Pennsylvania to Brown County, Indiana, in a wagon train led by Daniel Boone's brother; how her father bought land from the Union Pacific Railroad along Plum Creek in Nebraska and then moved the family, their belongings, and their livestock in a boxcar to their new home.

Richard completed his first five grades in just three years, making him thirteen when he started Sumner High in 1928. Two years later, when he had turned fifteen and was eligible to drive, the family took a summer road trip. Richard's half-sister Mildred and her husband, Elmer Ericson, went along, so there were five of them in a 1928 Chevy. They strapped a luggage carrier on the back, headed to Iowa, then Indiana, staying with relatives most of the time. In West Virginia, with Richard behind the wheel, they drove to the town of Welch, where a relative arranged for them to go down into a coal mine. In Defiance, Ohio, they found the swimming hole that Thomas had cannonballed into as a child. In Chicago, they toured the Field Museum and got caught in a traffic jam right after a gang slaying. Newsboys walked up and down the line of stalled cars hawking extras about the big murder.

It was a great adventure, all 3,000 miles and thirty days of it, a carefree month on the road that in memory would seem a sharp contrast to the time of crisis they were about to enter. Drought bore down hard on Nebraska in the early 1930s, making it increasingly hard for farmers to repay their loans. Thomas drove from farm to farm trying to collect on notes and mortgages for Farmers and Merchants Bank, where he had worked for twenty-five years, but it was futile. The capital reserves of the bank plummeted from more than 30 percent in June 1931 to 7 percent in December, well below state requirements.

Knowing what the bank examiner would find when he came to Sumner, Thomas summoned the board of directors, sending his assistant to a nearby town to make the telephone calls so that word of the emergency meeting wouldn't spread over Sumner's party lines. As the board gathered in the Cheney living room, sixteen-year-old Richard, who happened to be downtown, was spotted by the bank examiner, who was waiting for someone to open the bank. Did Richard know what was going on, the examiner demanded? Did he know where everyone was? People were getting suspicious since the bank wasn't open, the examiner said, and somebody had better do something fast. Richard ran home to report the encounter and found a heated discussion going on in the Cheney living room. Some board members were urging that the bank borrow to stave off the crisis, but others, led by Thomas, were firm that they should close the bank's doors. Thomas carried the day, but the decision was so painful and final that the men in the living room could barely bring themselves to announce it. Finally, with heavy hearts, they made their way to the bank and declared it closed. In the weeks ahead, Farmers and Merchants, one of 2,294 banks to fail in 1931, paid out its remaining assets. Depositors collected somewhere between thirty and forty cents on the dollar.

Thomas and Margaret had long been active in the community, he as a school board member, church treasurer, and Democratic county committeeman and she as state chairman of the Baptist women's organization and a trustee of Grand Island Baptist College. After the bank's closure, they remained respected figures, and townspeople continued to seek out Thomas for services he had provided while at the bank: advice on taxes, help with wills and warranty deeds, an insurance policy now and then. But the fact that people who had trusted him lost their savings weighed on Thomas the rest of his life. He had made the right recommendation to the board. Banks that borrowed when they got into trouble—and there were many—ended up paying their depositors only pennies on the dollar. But that was cold comfort. When Thomas died fifteen years after the bank's failure, among the items found in his strongbox was a letter in spidery handwriting dated January 11, 1932, from a widow, Mrs. Ella Frew, urging him not to feel guilty. "I thought when I deposited that check in October that something was worrying you," she wrote. "Of course I am sorry this happened but it has and we must make the best of it. Please don't take the blame on yourself for we know better."

Also in the strongbox were stock certificates from Farmers and Merchants Bank that had been issued to Thomas over the course of more than a decade. Handsomely engraved, affixed with a gold seal, they were worthless once the bank closed its doors. What Thomas and Margaret had thought of as their nest egg was gone.

Witness to his parents' trauma, Richard found a way to pay for college himself. A crack typist, he landed a job in the mimeograph department at Kearney State Teacher's College, some thirty miles down the road. He produced typewriter-cut stencils, attached them to the mimeograph's inked cylinder, and cranked out copies of course lists, assignments sheets, and tests, earning forty dollars a month for his work, enough for his room, board, and the few fees the college charged. There wasn't much left over, but he didn't spend much, not then and not for the rest of his life. Perhaps he was naturally frugal, but his parents' experience in the Great Depression no doubt made him more so. He believed in wearing out his clothes, buying secondhand cars, and saving. In his eighties, he would set aside for a rainy day about a third of the government pension he drew.

At Kearney State in the 1930s, he was hardly alone in being short on funds. Most students had to scrimp, and, judging by old yearbooks, they had a pretty good time anyway. Richard's yearbooks were signed by male pals who waited tables, worked in the library, and liked to kid him about his sarcastic sense of humor. The girls wrote about times they'd gone roller skating, to the movies, or to a lake nearby. In 1935, a young woman named Doris wrote that "I have had the best time of my life these last few months, thanks to you."

Majoring in commerce, Richard got good grades, but after four years, he was still at least a year away from his degree. Because of his job, he carried a partial course load, nine or ten hours a quarter instead of sixteen, and in the spring of 1936, contemplating the time ahead of him at Kearney State, he sat for a Civil Service exam. When he was offered a $120-a-month position as a senior typist with the Veterans Administration in Lincoln, he took it, even though it was only temporary and meant he'd have to leave school. His friends, aware of how hard any job was to come by, congratulated him. "I sure wish I would fall into your luck," wrote one in his yearbook.

At the Veterans Administration, Richard processed applications for World War I bonuses. Since the beginning of the Depression, veterans had been agitating to have money due them in

1945 paid out immediately, a demand that President Herbert Hoover had resisted. When violence broke out between police and Bonus Marchers who came to Washington to insist on the payment, Hoover had ordered federal troops to clear them out of their camps. President Franklin D. Roosevelt, worried as Hoover had been about the cost of paying out the bonuses early, vetoed a bonus bill, but when Congress overrode him in 1936, veterans began receiving their checks.

Richard spent three months going through records and determining eligibility, and when that job ended, another offer came his way, this one from the Soil Conservation Service, a federal agency born of the dust storms of the 1930s. Working with the Civilian Conservation Corps, one of President Roosevelt's efforts to combat the joblessness of the Great Depression, the Soil Conservation Service had begun demonstrating techniques such as crop rotation and contour plowing that could prevent farm soil from being lifted into the sky when winds blew across the Great Plains, and Richard, assigned to one of these projects, moved to Syracuse, Nebraska, a town of about a thousand in the southeastern part of the state.

A bachelor living in rented quarters, he was soon eating most of his meals at Dickey's Café, a small place with a soda fountain on one side, a few oil-cloth-covered tables on the other, and stick-to-your-ribs items on the menu. The café also had a pretty and friendly waitress, Marge Dickey, daughter of the owner, who in addition to helping out her dad, worked for C. R. Williams, the new doctor in town. She was also an outstanding athlete, feted in Syracuse as a member of the Bluebirds, the local women's softball team that had against all odds won the Nebraska state championship and come close to conquering the nation.

CHAPTER TWELVE

WITH PEOPLE LOOKING for ways to forget their troubles during the Great Depression, softball, both men's and women's, came into its own, not only in Nebraska but across the country. Equipment was cheap, meaning people could afford to play, particularly if, as in the case of the Syracuse Bluebirds, players made their own uniforms. Marge and her teammates sewed up sleeveless, ankle-length culottes, elasticized at the waist. They splurged on blue store-bought hats but not on getting them personalized. Instead, they painted their names and nicknames—Dotty, Andy, Daffy, Dizzy—on the bottoms of the bills that they turned up when photographers were around.

For a girl like Marge, who'd grown up with three brothers, getting out on the diamond was just plain fun, but the Bluebirds were tough competitors, particularly their pitcher, Nina Korgan. With Nina hurling and Marge and Betty and the other girls smacking the ball out into the cornfields, the Bluebirds became the softball queens of Nebraska, defeating even the big-name teams from Omaha, and that wasn't the end of it. Twice the Bluebirds went to national championships in Chicago, and twice they made it all the way to the semifinals only to be defeated by the Cleveland Bloomer Girls, who went on to become national champs. The Bluebirds didn't end up with "the glory and honor

Dick's mother, Marge Dickey, on the right, was a champion softball player. She and her friend are standing in front of the Dickey family café.

of ruling an entire nation," as the local newspaper had hoped they would, but Syracuse loved them anyway. In Marge's scrapbook, a newspaper clipping from 1935 describes them arriving home "amid plenty of welcoming noise. The band played, folks cheered, car horns blared, and there were plenty of handshakes and congratulations tendered the vanquished in tourney play but winners in spirit." Declared the newspaper, "Syracuse and the state of Nebraska have a right to be proud."

Photographs of Marge from these years show a lighthearted, outgoing young woman who smiles big and sometimes strikes silly poses for the camera. Richard appears to be quieter, a little studious, even, especially when he is wearing his wire-rimmed glasses, but the two hit it off. He got along particularly well with her father, although it is hard to imagine a person more different from Richard's staid Baptist parents than café owner David Dickey. A small, engaging man, who loved to drink whiskey, play cards, and enjoy life, Dickey was two decades younger than Richard's father and a decade younger than his mother. As old photographs make apparent, there was also a wide cultural chasm between the two families. A studio portrait of Margaret Cheney, taken for her graduation from high school, shows her coolly composed in a white lace-trimmed dress. Immaculately groomed, she sits with her ankles gracefully crossed, her hands folded in her lap. One of the few photographs of young David Dickey, who didn't make it past sixth grade, shows him on a wintry plain, wearing a jaunty hat, carrying a shotgun over his shoulder. He holds a newly killed rabbit in one hand and has a half-dozen or so recently shot ducks dangling from his waist.

While both Thomas and Margaret Cheney came from English stock, David Dickey's male forebears were Scots Irish, Presbyterians who emigrated from Scotland to northern Ireland in the first half of the seventeenth century. The British government had encouraged Protestants to settle in Ulster as a way of curbing Catholic influence, but when Charles I came to the throne in 1625, he viewed the Scots Irish as dissenters and demanded that they conform to the Church of England. His royal successor, Charles II, also hounded the Scots Irish to abandon their faith, and they found themselves under assault as well by Irish Catholics, who regarded them as interlopers. In these struggles, Protestants living in Ireland were well served by a system of clanship they had brought with them from Scotland. It bound many families with the same surname together, often through intermarriage, to face whatever danger might threaten.

In the early eighteenth century, in addition to their other troubles, the Scots Irish faced crushing rent increases from their English landlords and saw the linen industry they had built up destroyed by an English embargo. When crops failed as well, they began to emigrate to American by the tens of thousands. Not only families but clans picked up and sailed across the Atlantic Ocean, many of them landing in Philadelphia. Encouraged by the Quakers, who found them entirely too boisterous, they quickly moved south and west, following the Appalachian Mountains. Hardy and proud, they pushed the American frontier inland.

David Dickey's great-grandfather James, part of the Scots Irish push westward, moved from North Carolina, where he was born in 1788, to Tennessee, where most of his children were born, to Ray County, Missouri. Although James's forebears had been in America for several generations, the ways of the clan seem to have persisted. Two of his ten children married Dickeys, and two married McGaughs, members of a Scots Irish family that

Dick's beloved grandfather David Dickey, whose family was Scots Irish, hunting in Nebraska as a young man.

David and Clarice Dickey, at the door of the Union Pacific Railroad car in which they lived. He cooked for repair crews.

moved from Tennessee to Missouri about the same time as the Dickeys and seems to have been part of an extended Dickey-McGaugh clan. There were also two instances in James's family of women marrying into the Dickey-McGaugh group, becoming widowed, and then marrying their husbands' nephews. An anthropologist might explain these marriage patterns as clan-strengthening, pointing out in the latter instance that keeping widows in the clan by having them remarry their husbands' relatives was a way of ensuring that children born into the clan were raised by its members.

But lives are usually about more than theories. Consider Laura Nora Dillman, who married her husband's nephew. She came from a long line of Dunkers, or so outsiders called them, because the group believed that a proper baptism consisted of three immersions. Persecuted in Germany, the Dunkers emigrated to America, bringing with them a tradition of pacifism but producing many who fought in America's wars. Laura Nora's ancestors served in the Revolutionary War and the War of 1812. Her father, David, was in the Union Army for a year before being discharged on account of ill health.

By 1870, Laura Nora's family was living in Nebraska, and there she met one of the McGaughs, Edward, a bearded tenant farmer who had come to Nebraska Territory during the Civil War, as had many young Missourians with Southern sympathies when service in the Union Army became compulsory in that state. In 1872, Laura Nora, age fifteen, married Edward, age twenty-nine, and between 1873 and 1883, they had seven children, one of whom died when she was a little more than a year old. In September 1884, Edward died, leaving Laura Nora, now twenty-seven, in charge of the farm and six children, five girls and a boy, ranging in age from ten years to one.

Laura Nora hired twenty-seven-year-old Alonzo Dickey, Edward's nephew who had been helping on the farm, to work for her for fourteen dollars a month and wrote down their agreement in the ledger book that Edward had used to record home remedies. In 1888, after Alonzo had been working for her for three and a half years, she began to use the old ledger for a diary, recording some entries that were about things she had known most of her life: the hard work of the farm, the men in the fields, the women washing, sewing, cooking, scrubbing, ironing, and helping plant as well. She wrote about the wind that swept over the Nebraska prairies. "Wind in the north, very cold," begins a January entry, and in February, "Wind in north, cold as Greenland." But there are also lovely days, she notes, particularly in the spring, and there is Alonzo, whom she nurses when he is sick and worries about when he is gone longer than she thinks he should be hauling a load of cattle to Wyoming. She visits neighbors with him, they go to dances and church socials, and at the end of May, she buys fabric and begins work on a dress for herself, a project that takes her weeks, and then she begins sewing for her girls and Alonzo as well.

The diary breaks off at the end of June without explaining the new clothes, but a wedding picture from July 19, 1888, tells the story. In it, Laura Nora, slender with deep-set eyes and long hair, is wearing a dark frock with a bow at the neck that ties sharply in the way that new fabric does. Alonzo, dark and handsome, is wearing a jacket and vest with a collar so white it is likely new. The photograph probably helps explain the diary as well: Laura Nora wanted to record, if only in an elliptical way, the happiness of being in love.

Five and a half months after Laura Nora and Alonzo were wed, future café owner David Dickey was born. In 1900, after bearing four more children, Laura Nora died at age forty-one. The younger children were sent to live with half-sisters from their mother's first marriage, but eleven-year-old David, a small, slender boy, was deemed old enough to help in the fields and stayed on the farm with his father. He grew into a cheerful, outgoing young man, fell in love with Clarice Miller, a quiet farmer's daughter who loved to play the violin, and they were married in May 1911. Eight months later, their first child, Ward, was born, followed by two more sons, Vancel and Gerry, in whom David also delighted. He worked at all kinds of jobs—in a drugstore, running a meat market—and though he always seemed happy, he had one regret. No matter how hard he worked, he couldn't get enough money together to buy a home, something he had yearned to do since he was a boy working as a tenant farmer with his father. Twice he traveled to Saskatchewan, thinking that the Canadian government's relaxed homestead policies might provide a way for him to own something, but both times he returned to the United States.

In 1918, while David was working at the grain elevator in Burr, Nebraska, he and Clarice, on whom he doted, had their fourth child and only daughter, Marge. Burr's population wasn't much—500 or so—but on weekends, there might be as many as 1,000 people, farmers and their families shopping, visiting with friends, and enjoying Burr's special attraction, moving pictures projected onto the side of a downtown building, free for anyone who wanted to pull up a hay bale and watch. David decided a restaurant might make money, opened a lunch counter, and quickly began to draw people in with his cooking and congeniality. He served up jokes along with lunch, one of his favorites being a recipe for carp, a bony and aromatic fish. "First thing you do," David would say, "is nail the carp to a board. Then you put it in the sun for ten days. Then you throw away the carp and eat the board."

In December 1925, a fire broke out in the back of Burr's general store, and most of the town's small business district burned down. David's restaurant survived, but with the general store and the drugstore gone and the moving-picture machine destroyed, farmers began bypassing Burr on the weekends to shop in Sterling and other towns in southeastern Nebraska. David shut down the restaurant and began driving an oil truck to make a living. He also hauled cows, two or three at a time, to the stockyards in Omaha.

He was running a creamery in 1929, when his fifteen-year-old son, Vancel, died of a ruptured appendix. David, Clarice, and their three remaining children wept for Vancel at his funeral at Hopewell Methodist Church, then buried "the promising boy who was just entering manhood," in the words of the Burr newspaper. Someone took a photograph of Vancel's flower-covered grave, and the family put it in their picture album along with photographs of happier days: Ward and Vancel driving a goat cart; Ward, Vancel, and Marge striking silly poses in front of somebody's Model T.

No one ever recovers from the death of a child, but by the time David opened Dickey's Café in Syracuse, Nebraska, a few years later, he was laughing again, enjoying his family, his card games, and life. He opened the restaurant early and cooked until 2:00, turning out solid meat-and-potatoes meals as well as some specialties, such as a scrambled eggs and brains sandwich and a chili flavored with suet. After lunch, he would go over to the pool hall and play pinochle until it was time to go back to the café and cook supper. He usually kept the place open until the town movie got out at 11:00 or so.

Clarice, who worked the cash register, loved the movies, and twice a week, when the feature changed, she left David on his own. One night after she departed, snow started falling, and because there weren't many customers, David had a few drinks. Then somebody came into the café with a pair of wooden skis and the idea of hitching a tow rope onto the back of a car and skiing the roads around Burr, which was a million laughs, whooping and swerving along snow-covered byways, until David careened into a ditch and broke his arm. One of his friends rushed into the movie theater to get Clarice, who was frantic until the whole story emerged, and then, for the first time anyone could remember, she lost her temper with David. He was chagrined, but only slightly, and continued to play cards, enjoy his highballs, and seek out his beloved Clarice and kiss her every time he came into a room and she was there.

David managed to move his family out of the rooms they'd been living in over the restaurant and into a rented house, which was good but not quite what he'd been hoping for. He was a great cook and a boon companion but never enough of a businessman to accumulate the funds to buy a place. A nephew, Bill Parkinson, who worked in the café, remembers that anybody who needed an extra buck or two took it out of the till, which was just fine with David but not conducive to home ownership. Still, David remained a man of unfailing good cheer, the kind of person who lit up any gathering.

David's daughter Marge married Richard Cheney, the young man who'd come to Syracuse with the Soil Conservation Service, on June 1, 1940, and on January 30, 1941, in Lincoln, Nebraska, where Richard had been transferred, they had their first child. Named after his father and known most of his life as Dick, the baby arrived at Bryan Memorial Hospital, where the bill for his birth, carefully saved, shows that the cost of his delivery was $37.50. David Dickey wrote to his daughter and son-in-law that he was "disappointed it was not twins." He also urged the new parents to let President Franklin D. Roosevelt, who had a January 30 birthday, know of the arrival of the "little stranger." Richard wrote to his parents in Sumner, inviting them to Lincoln to see the baby and saying he'd send bus tickets, but there's no record that they came. Thomas may have been too proud to have his son pay his way. Margaret, who left the clear impression that she thought her son had married beneath him, may not have been quite ready to bestow her blessings on the seven-pound, eight-month baby the marriage had produced. A photograph of her with the little boy when he is an irresistible six or seven months old shows her reserve melting—a little.

Fourteen months after Dick's birth, Marge and Richard had a second son, Bob, and two years after that, Richard received his notice to report for a preinduction physical. Marge tried living by herself with the boys in an apartment in Lincoln, but after an attack of appendicitis sent her to the hospital, she decided to move in with Richard's folks. They'd be backup for her, and she could save money, paying them rent, of course, but not as much as she was paying for the apartment in Lincoln.

As she unpacked in Sumner, Marge must have thought how much she would have preferred to live with her mother and father. They'd understand if she had a cigarette once in a while, and with her dad around, there would be jokes, card playing, some fun, which she wasn't likely to find in Margaret Cheney's strict Baptist household. But David Dickey had taken a job on the Union Pacific Railroad—or, to be precise about it, Clarice had taken a job that David was doing. He had heard from a relative about an opening as a cook, a good deal like all railroad jobs because it came with benefits and retirement. Figuring that the problems he was having with his hearing would keep him from being hired, he had Clarice apply, and when she got the job, he began cooking for crews repairing line in Nebraska and southern Wyoming. So they could follow the crews, he and Clarice moved into a railroad car, which was a great place to visit but no place for Marge and the boys to live.

In the well-regulated house in Sumner, Marge tried hard to turn the boys into orderly children. One day, after joyously splashing in a puddle, they appeared covered with mud, leading Marge, usually relaxed about such matters, to grab a yardstick and begin spanking Bob. She let Dick know he was next, but then the yardstick broke—and so, too, did her determination to punish her sons. Dick, older and usually the ringleader when it came to trouble, got off free, which became the point of the story when family members told it later, but it's easy to imagine that it meant something different to Marge. Perhaps in that moment, it was clear to her that she couldn't raise her children to satisfy someone else's expectations.

Sunday was the best day of the week, because Richard's half-sister, Mildred, and her husband, Elmer Ericson, a cheerful, hard-working Swede, came after church to pick up Marge and the boys and take them out to their farm. After many years of living in Sumner, where Elmer worked at the grain elevator, the Ericsons had traded their house for eighty acres west of town, on which they grew crops and raised livestock to meet most of their needs. There was also a small cash crop of corn every year, which Elmer harvested with the aid of two large plow horses. When the corn was ready, he would attach a large wagon to the horses and send them down the rows of corn while he walked alongside, tearing off ears and throwing them into the wagon. He allowed

Dick's dad, home on leave, with Marge, Dick, and Bob.

Dick and Bob spent time on their uncle Elmer Ericson's farm during World War II.

small boys, much to their delight, to ride along on the wagon seat.

Elmer's farm was unmechanized, but he did own a car, a Ford coupe that he used to drive back and forth to town. When he picked up Marge and the boys on Sundays, he'd jam everyone possible into the front seat, since there was only a front seat, and tuck any leftover child onto the ledge behind. When they'd pull into the farm, Elmer's two white collies would run barking to greet them. Large and gentle, the dogs not only tolerated small children but followed them, tails wagging, all around the farm. There were chickens in the yard, and Mildred would catch one every Sunday, using a coat hanger bent into a loop to capture the bird and a small ax to chop off its head. When the chicken had quit its headless run, she'd clean it, pluck it, and fry it for Sunday dinner.

After Marge and the boys had been in Sumner a couple of months, Richard sent notice that he was coming home on leave, prompting Marge to write, "Oh, happy day," in her diary. He walked into the house on January 30, 1945, just in time for his older son's fourth birthday. Why had he been gone? the little boy wanted to know. Richard pointed to the arm patch on his uniform, on which a white eagle was embroidered, explaining that he was now a yeoman. The boy, still young enough to think magically, was only slightly dismayed that his father was spending much of his time as some kind of bird.

Marge bought a scrapbook in which she neatly arranged all the documents of Richard's service: his induction notice, his leave papers, and news clippings he sent her about the officers he was serving under. When President Roosevelt died on April 12, 1945, she cut out all the articles about his death from the Omaha *Morning World-Herald* and made a folder for the clippings in the scrapbook. When Germany surrendered, she did the same, neatly cutting and folding the scenes of celebration and tucking them inside envelopes in the scrapbook. It looked as though America and her allies would win this war, but how long was it going to take?

Marge decided to go to San Diego. She bought herself a coach ticket for $68.83, carefully recording the amount on her ticket envelope and saving it; took the boys to Mildred and Elmer's; and on June 19, 1945, boarded a train in Kearney. It was so crowded that she had to spend one night sitting up in the ladies' lounge, but she didn't mind. Many of the passengers were women who were also going to see their men, and Marge loved the camaraderie. She also loved seeing the country, and every time the train stopped, she got off to look around. When she arrived in San Diego on the 21st, she checked into a hotel that cost five dollars a night, a lot of money, but Richard and Marge figured they could afford it for the couple of weeks she'd be there.

They had so much to tell each other, Marge filled with news about how the boys were growing and Richard with the people he'd met and the sights he was seeing. Perhaps he talked about the ships he'd readied for war. In the papers she saved is a list that includes the battleships *West Virginia*, *Colorado*, and *Iowa*; the cruisers *Flint*, *Tucson*, and *Chester*; the escort carrier *Block Island*; the destroyer *Strong*—perhaps some of the ships that he'd been aboard as part of the shakedown crew.

Marge and Richard got to know a couple from Kentucky, Earl Combs, a yeoman who'd been part of Richard's draft, and his wife, who had followed Earl to San Diego and managed to land a job at Lockheed Aircraft that provided housing. The Combses had two little girls, Mrs. Combs was about to deliver a third child, and they needed someone to live in with them and help out. Marge eagerly volunteered, no doubt telling herself that the boys would be just fine at Mildred and Elmer's farm— and that she, going back to live in the small house with her mother-in-law, would not be.

Making the job even better was that the Combses had a car and an unusually large number of gasoline coupons that they willingly shared with the Cheneys, which meant that when Richard wasn't on duty, they could sightsee or drive to the San Diego Padres baseball park, where Marge kept track of the action in the official programs that you could buy for a dime. Using a code familiar to serious fans, she drew an entire diamond if a player made it all the way around the bases but only half a diamond if he made it just to second. By specifying a number for each player in the field, she also indicated how the players at bat were put out: "5-3," for example, meant that the third baseman (number 5) had thrown to first (number 3) for the out. She indicated when someone struck out with "K." A wild pitch was "WP." If all else failed, she wrote out the information: "Ump threw Aleno out for arguing."

On Mildred and Elmer's farm, meanwhile, the boys were having their own adventures. One day, the Holsteins that Elmer kept for milk tried to cross a swinging bridge and managed to fall into the creek below. Elmer called a neighbor, who hooked the cows to his tractor and pulled them from the mud with a most satisfying *pop*. Another day, the boys, pretending they had their own navy, floated pieces of wood in the horse tank. It was a great game, which they decided would be better if they had a better view of the tank, so they stacked up logs lying around and climbed up on them, which did improve the game—until Bob reached out too far and fell in. Figuring that it was not good for his brother to be floating in circles facedown in the water, Dick ran to get Elmer from the tool shed nearby. Elmer grabbed Bob's collar with one hand, his belt with the other, and lifted him out of the horse tank as though he were a toy.

Eventually, the boys began to worry that Marge, whose two weeks in California had stretched to two months, might not come back on her own, and they decided they had better go get her. Ages three and four, they made it all the way from the farmhouse to the main road, where they had planned to hitchhike to California, before Mildred intercepted them.

Marge started home on August 13, 1945, and while changing trains in Ogden, Utah, heard the news that the Japanese had surrendered. Back in Summer, she began to clip details out of the newspaper: American prisoners of war being released, the planes of Bull Halsey's Third Fleet off Tokyo, MacArthur landing at Atsugi Airfield. Surely, Richard would be home soon.

But demobilization was no quick and easy matter. Men were discharged according to a point system that took seniority into account, and since Richard had been in the Navy less than two years, he had a long wait in line. Finally, on April 4, 1946, nearly eight months after the end of the war, the telegram came: "Finished today, will arrive Kearney on number eight Saturday at five pm love." In a photo album, a snapshot taken in front of the Cheney house in Sumner shows a happy Richard in civilian clothes with a happy Marge standing beside him.

Richard had to get back to the job that the Soil Conservation Service had held for him in Lincoln, but with everyone coming home from the war, it was impossible to find a house or apartment. He rented a room at Mrs. Fern Burns's, a place he had lived before he was married, and continued to look for a house, no doubt with plenty of encouragement from Marge, who had to stay in Sumner with the boys until he found something. Finally, some friends living in Lincoln, the Volkmans, came to the rescue, offering their unfinished basement. Four Cheneys would have to share the upstairs bathroom with four Volkmans, and Marge would have to cook on a hot plate, but none of that mattered. Marge packed the suitcases, and she and the boys boarded the bus for Lincoln.

CHAPTER THIRTEEN

A FEW MONTHS AFTER the Cheneys moved into Inez and Dwayne Volkman's basement in Lincoln, they found a house under construction in College View, a small town fast becoming a Lincoln suburb as developers converted cornfields into housing tracts. Richard financed the house—purchase price $8,350—with a VA loan, and the family drove out to watch it go up in a '37 Buick they had inherited from an uncle back in Sumner. A "salesman's coupe," the car was called, because there was room behind the front seat for sample cases, space that Richard and Marge used for the boys, putting a couple of wooden boxes back there for them to sit on. On weekends, the boys on their boxes, the family would head for College View to check on the progress of 2915 South 44th Street, all five rooms of it: living room, kitchen, two bedrooms, and a bath.

Dick started school at Randolph Elementary, where his first teacher, Margaret Van Neste, noted on his November 1946 report card that he "seems a little self-conscious when speaking before the group." By February 1947, the family had moved to College View, and Sylvia Harney, Dick's kindergarten teacher at College View Elementary, noted that he was "speaking more confidently" and asking "worthwhile questions." "Richard is observant and is often alert to certain elements in a situation not readily perceived by everyone in the group," she wrote, adding that he also had admirable health habits: "He always tries to sit and stand correctly, and to use his handkerchief in the right way."

Marge saved his report cards, so a half-century later, it would be possible to know that his second-grade teacher, Helen Annan, found his work "highly commendable" and that his third-grade teacher, Katharine Duffield, one of his favorites, thought he had "the qualifications for a good leader." Miss Duffield did worry, though, at the trouble he was having in imitating musical tones, a difficulty that Marge, who loved the piano, the violin, and group singing, took seriously and tried to help him with at home. But four years later, he still couldn't sing. "How can I help Richard improve?" Marge would write to his seventh-grade music teacher.

The Cheneys settled into the suburbs, a postwar phenomenon that urban social observers loved to hate. "Conceived in error, nurtured by greed, corroding everything they touch," according to social critic John Keats, suburbs were denounced as a triumph of mediocrity, the ultimate expression of conformity. They were, apparently, terrible places—unless you happened to be living in one. After the dislocations of war and the housing shortages that followed, the suburbs seemed a piece of the postwar dream to many middle-class families and paradise to their kids.

And there were lots of kids in College View: Eddie and Vic Larsen, two houses down from the Cheneys, and next to them, on the corner, the Frazier girls, Patty and Betty. Across the street was Denny Carsten and, down the block, the Turner kids and Kenny Tenhulzen. Pets abounded, including Butch, the Cheneys' dog, tossed into their living room one day by Granddad Dickey, who'd found the scrappy little mutt scrounging for food around the railroad tracks. Butch could sit up like nobody's business. He could perch on a bicycle seat, even sit up on the palm of your hand as you lifted him into the air. Well behaved when human beings were watching, Butch, always sporting a wound or injury of some sort, apparently had a violent secret life. Some of it may have involved a large tomcat named Boots that the Cheneys had taken off a neighbor's hands. The terror of the neighborhood, Boots was known to disappear for days at a time.

The boys in the neighborhood loved to play in 44th Street's tree-filled dead end. Neighborhood storm sewers dumped into a ditch back there, and if you had some lunch meat, a piece of string, and a little patience, you could usually catch crawdads. The trees were great for tree houses, and it didn't take long for the kids to discover you could travel quite a distance without touching the ground by climbing out onto the end of a branch of one tree, grabbing hold of a branch on the next one, and transferring yourself. Bob was particularly good at making his way across the treetops, and one day, he and Dick invited their grandmother Clarice Dickey, who was babysitting, to come admire his skill. She was impressed, particularly when a limb that had been climbed on a few too many times broke, sending Bob falling ten or fifteen feet to the ground. He landed flat on his back at his grandmother's feet, the wind completely knocked out of him.

When she heard about it, Marge shrugged off the accident, but she wasn't so complacent a few years later, when Bob had a mishap involving his chemistry set and a garbage can. The idea was to set off an explosive mix inside the metal can, which would create a really great noise, but when the fuse didn't work, he sprinkled a trail of gunpowder to the can and lit it, figuring he'd have plenty of time to get out of there before it went off. But the trail ignited in seconds, and the can blew with Bob standing right beside it. Fortunately, all he lost were his eyebrows.

The neighborhood had a hill perfect for wintertime sledding, a two-block-long shot down the street running between the Fraziers and the Carstens, which was pretty safe if you set out watchers to warn of cars coming on the cross streets. At one holiday party, the adults in the neighborhood decided that the sledding looked like too much fun to leave to the kids, so they rounded up all the American Flyers they could find and went down the hill themselves, wrecking a sled or two at the bottom because they didn't quite get the part where you had to turn sideways to stop.

Kids in the neighborhood rode their bikes everywhere. Dick liked to take his to school so he could ride home for lunch. Even after Marge got a job as a secretary with the State Health Department in the Capitol Building in downtown Lincoln and was gone all day, he still rode home at noon, cooked himself a hamburger or warmed up leftovers, then rode the nine or ten blocks back to school.

Buses expanded the universe further. Dick and Bob would take one to the stadium and for fifty cents sit in the knothole section in the end zone and watch the University of Nebraska football team play. On days when school was out, they sometimes took the bus downtown to the Capitol, where their mother worked, going once at her special invitation for a ceremony in the Rotunda honoring Master Sergeant Ernest Kouma, a Congressional Medal of Honor recipient from Dwight, Nebraska. Under assault for more than eight hours near Angok, Korea, Kouma, a tank commander, had held his ground and killed more than 250 Red Chinese.

On Saturdays, the boys would catch a bus to the movies in Lincoln, or sometimes the whole family would load up in their '47 Frazier, the car they traded up to after the '37 Buick, and go to the movie theater over in Havelock, where for a dollar, all four of them could watch a double feature. Lincoln had an AA farm team, the Athletics, and going to those games was a Cheney family pleasure, as were Soil Conservation Service softball games. Richard coached the SCS team, and Dick and Bob were batboys.

Dick and his brother played Little League baseball in the spring and summer, and in the fall, Dick signed up for Pop Warner football, a kids' league named after legendary football coach Glenn Scobie "Pop" Warner. The boys liked to fish, and sometimes their dad would take them to Oak Lake, where they might catch a carp, or to one of the slow-moving streams around Lincoln, where they might get a bullhead. Granddad Dickey liked to go after catfish, which could be found in the rivers along the Union Pacific rail line where he was working. The secret, he told the boys, showing them pictures of his catches, was the combination of blood and chicken guts that he used for bait. It worked best if you kept it for a couple of days until it took on a fearsome smell that catfish loved—though people weren't so fond of it, as the family discovered when Granddad left his car parked in their driveway for two weeks, forgetting that some of his special catfish bait was locked in the trunk.

Dick and Bob were in Cub Scouts, Pack 54, Den No. 2, sponsored by the Sheridan Boulevard Baptist Church. Marge was their den mother, presiding over meetings in the Cheneys' unfinished basement. When they became Boy Scouts, Jim Murphy, a senior scout, acted as the troop's mentor. Much admired by the parents of the boys in the troop, and even more by the boys themselves, Murphy had a part-time job in a drugstore, which meant he had access to cigarettes. He didn't steal them, which would have been a violation of the Boy Scout code, but instead carefully left money in the till for a pack he would bring to Monday night meetings at the Baptist church. After the meeting, the Scouts would all sneak out for a smoke.

Dick, far right, and his brother Bob, second from left, with neighborhood pals and fellow Little Leaguers Vic and Eddie Larsen.

Marge Cheney supervises Pack 54, Den 2, while the Cubs produce a radio drama.
Dick is at the typewriter.

Marge stands outside the house the Cheneys purchased in Casper
when they moved there in 1954.

Richard bought a Craftsman mower at Sears and Roebuck, and Dick used it to earn money mowing neighborhood lawns. He also had a paper route that got him up early most mornings. He'd ride his bike over to the drugstore on Calvert Street, where bundles of the *Lincoln Star* had been dropped off, roll and rubber-band his papers, and jam them into cloth bags tied to his bike's handlebars. Then it was just a matter of riding the streets from 40th to 48th between Van Dorn and Calvert and throwing the papers onto the right porches. On really cold days, he'd use a small chrome hand warmer that he'd bought at an army surplus store, filling it with lighter fluid, putting a match to the wick, covering the device, and sticking it in his pocket, where he could warm his hands on it. Once a month or so, he'd collect, but he tended to lose motivation for getting people to pay their bills once he had enough for his papers and a little extra left over. His parents nagged at him until he'd knocked on all the doors, and he was making about thirty dollars a month when the *Lincoln Star* featured him in the paper as "Star Carrier Dick Cheney." He'd bought a clarinet with his newspaper earnings, he told the *Star*, and he was saving for his college education, which he figured he'd need since he planned to become an architectural engineer.

For the Cheneys, as for many Americans across the country in the years after World War II, car trips were a favored form of recreation. Sometimes they'd take the weekend and drive to wherever David and Clarice Dickey were, some spot on the UP line in Kansas or Nebraska. After their first trip to visit the Dickeys, when they had observed rats hanging around the dining car, Dick and Bob started taking their BB guns along. They'd pick off rats during the day, and then at night, when the grown-ups had lit the kerosene lamps and were playing Pitch, a card game they loved, the boys would go out and shoot at night hawks. When the card game was over, the adults would call them in and bed them down on the oil-cloth-covered tables where the crew ate during the day.

One summer, the Cheney family drove to Colorado to visit Melba Kreifels, a cousin of Marge's, and her husband, Pete, who had leased a dairy farm outside Denver. The boys watched for the mountains, which they had never seen, watched as the blue line on the horizon grew thicker, then peaks appeared, and then the boys were in the mountains, riding horses, milking cows, and taking hikes, once finding refuge in a cave when a hailstorm started pounding them.

In the summer of 1950, the family drove to California to visit Grandmother Cheney. After Thomas had died in Sumner in 1947 at age seventy-eight, Margaret had "had her sale," as people spoke of it in rural Nebraska. She had called in the auctioneer and sold most of her possessions, including her home, which Mildred and Elmer purchased. Then she had moved to Whittier, California, to be near a sister.

Richard, Marge, and the boys started out from Lincoln in the '47 Frazer with an ice chest filled with food, and when they'd stop for the night, they'd get a motel with a kitchenette so that Marge could cook. They carried a Coleman stove with them, too, and sometimes she'd cook lunch by the side of the road, or maybe they'd have cold cuts. Taking a route that passed through Yellowstone Park, they saw Old Faithful, the mud pots, and their first bear. They went fishing in Idaho, sightseeing in Hollywood, shopping for souvenirs in Tijuana. They stopped in San Diego to see where Yeoman Cheney had served and watched as the aircraft carrier USS *Philippine Sea* pulled away from the dock, sailing for Korea.

And they did see Grandmother Cheney, which was, after all, their main purpose, though you wouldn't know it from the diary Marge kept. Her way of dealing with a difficult mother-in-law was simply not to mention her. She did record daily expenses for what turned out to be a 5,500-mile journey by the time they went through Nevada, Arizona, New Mexico, Oklahoma, and Kansas on the return home. On June 20, 1950, for example, they spent $3.13 for gas, $7.00 for overnight lodging in Winnemucca, Nevada, and $4.20 for meals for four. Marge also noted in her diary that they saw fifty-four different license plates on the trip.

In 1952, there was another trip to California, this time with David Dickey riding along. Clarice, his wife, had suffered a stroke and died, and since she had been the official Union Pacific employee, even though he had done the cooking for the road crews, her death put him out of a job—and out of his home in the railroad car. He was spending a couple of months with one of his children, a couple of months with another, and they were always glad to see him. Three grown-ups and two boys in a car headed to California didn't seem crowded at all when Granddad Dickey was the third adult.

But David liked his Seven and Seven, a highball of Seagram's Seven and Seven-Up, and Margaret Tyler Cheney, whom they visited in Whittier, was a teetotaler. He smoked, too, but not in her house, Margaret made clear. David and Richard and Marge also played cards whenever they had the chance, but that wasn't going to happen in Margaret Cheney's house, either, so the visitors spent a lot of time out of the house. They went to Knott's Berry Farm, where they hissed at the villain and cheered the hero in an old-fashioned melodrama at the theater. "Quite a hilarious show," Marge wrote in the diary she kept. They went to Hollywood, where they saw Art Linkletter's and Curt Massey's radio shows during the day and Bob Moon's talent show at night. "Enjoyed a nice little visit with him after the show," Marge wrote of Moon. They drove to Huntington Beach and swam in the ocean, and to Newport Beach, where they took pictures of a 1,000-pound manta ray. "Some fellows in a motor boat had fought it for eight hours before it finally gave up," Marge noted. "Quite a sea mammal."

But after every day's adventures, they had to return to Whittier, and there was relief when it was time to start home. As they left, David Dickey instigated a stop at a liquor store, where he and Richard picked up a couple of Cokes and a bottle of bourbon. They passed the Cokes to the backseat, where the boys drank them down a little, then David and Richard topped them off with the bourbon and celebrated their departure from Whittier.

WHILE THEY WERE on the road, as when they were home, the boys read a lot. A fourth-grade summer list shows Dick completing Arthur Draper's *Wonders of the Heavens* and Jerome Meyer's *Picture Book of Astronomy*, as well as books about the childhoods of famous Americans: Miles Standish, John Quincy Adams, Kit Carson, and Lou Gehrig. He read *Tom Sawyer*, *Huckleberry Finn*, and *A Treasury of Heroes' Stories*, a book ahead of its time. Authors Joanna Strong and Tom B. Leonard held up not only Daniel Boone and George Washington for admiration but also Molly Pitcher, Harriet Tubman, and Booker T. Washington.

The entire family listened to the radio. On summer evenings when there was no relief upstairs from the heat, Marge would set up a card table in the basement, and the four of them would go down there to eat supper and listen to *The Lone Ranger*.

About 1949, the year that television station WOW in Omaha started up, TV sets began to appear in College View. The

Turners had one of the first, and on Friday nights, when *The Gillette Cavalcade of Sports* was on, the neighbors would gather at their house. Everyone would crowd into the living room, waiting for the bell in Madison Square Garden to clang and announcer Jimmy Powers to declare, "Friday night fights are on the air!"

By 1952, when the national political conventions were televised, the Cheneys had a set, and Aunt Delores, who happened to be visiting during the Democratic convention, caused quite a stir when she took up a seat in the middle of the living room and began shouting at Adlai Stevenson and the other Democratic politicians appearing on the screen. A half-sister of David Dickey's, Delores had twice married well and twice been widowed. Out of her hearing, Richard, a lifelong Democrat, who knew there were Republicans in the world but had never seen a show like Delores was putting on, said that he thought her money had gone to her head.

Eisenhower won that year, and although Richard and Marge had voted for Stevenson, Ike was going to be president, and that was something they thought kids ought to know about. They invited Dick's sixth-grade class to come to their house to watch the inauguration on January 20, 1953. As the kids crowded into the living room, none of the family had any idea that the historic event they were watching was going to affect them personally, but it would, in fact, cause them to pull up stakes and move west, as their ancestors had been doing for generations. Once in office, Dwight Eisenhower would reorganize the Department of Agriculture, and that would mean moving Soil Conservation Service offices around. In 1954, SCS employee Richard Cheney, a GS-11 administrative officer in the Lincoln office, would be given a choice of transfers: Great Falls, Montana, or Casper, Wyoming.

He chose Casper, and he and Marge presented the move to the boys as a great adventure, one that would take them to the mountains and to some of the best fishing in the world. They sold the house in College View for $9,750 and bought one at 505 Texas Place in Casper for $15,000. The new house had three bedrooms instead of two, but the best thing about it was that you walked out the front door to nothing but prairie for as far as the eye could see.

Not knowing anyone in Casper, Dick spent many days that first summer at the Carnegie Library downtown, which had a pretty good collection of military history. He'd catch the bus down to the brick, white-domed building at Second and Durbin and check out books such as Ross Carter's 82nd Airborne memoir, *Those Devils in Baggy Pants*, correspondent Rich Tregaskis's *Guadalcanal Diary*, and Slavomir Rawicz's *The Long Walk*, an account of the trek to freedom that Rawicz, a Polish officer who escaped from a Soviet labor camp in 1941, made out of Siberia and across China, the Gobi Desert, and the Himalayas to British India.

Dick signed up for Pony League baseball, practiced his pitching in the front yard with his mom catching, and at the end of a good season was named to the all-star team that would travel to Richland, Washington, to play in a three-state competition. Treated like celebrities by the hometown papers, the all-stars appeared in group photographs, were shown getting on their bus, and were followed closely on the sports pages as they succumbed to the Richland team, triumphed over the Idaho state champs from Blackfoot, and ended up with a third-place finish. A sports writer from the *Casper Morning Star* who accompanied them cast their trip in the best possible light, pointing out that it was a fine experience for the boys, who, after all, were part of a first-year club, going up against kids from towns where Pony League had been around for years.

On the trip to Richland and back, Dick met Tom Fake, a round-faced Catholic-school kid with whom he would spend a lot of time once they were both students at Casper's public high school. A good athlete who would become excellent once his height caught up to his weight, Tom ate memorably on the trip, sometimes ordering as many as three breakfasts, until finally, Father Taylor, the Catholic priest who coached the team, put his foot down, establishing a one-breakfast rule.

When school began, Dick started hanging out with John Mayer, a loose-limbed, perpetually smiling kid who'd just moved to Casper from Waterloo, Iowa, and had a motor scooter that took them all over town. They managed to get into a lot of mischief together, mostly harmless, such as the time they were going a little too fast, hit a pothole on a road east of town, and bounced Dick off the scooter and into a cactus patch. But there was also the time they decided to toss snowballs at passing cars and, not realizing that one driver had her window down, smacked her in the head. That earned them a trip to the police station.

In Lincoln, Dick had been on the honor roll, was even chosen at a seventh-grade honor roll ceremony commemorating great men such as Washington, Webster, and Lincoln to represent youth and speak about the future. But eighth grade in Casper was a different story. His math teacher, Mrs. Treglown, gave him 1's and 2's (A's and B's) and wrote that he "can do better than this." His history teacher, Charlotte Evans, who gave him 1's, 2's, and even a couple of 3's, wrote that he "whispers too much. Conduct poor." His arts and crafts teacher, N. Duggins, gave him a 4, commenting that he was "capable of doing much better. Too much time wasted foolishly." And, he added, "he needs to get over his very smarty attitude." According to John Mayer, Dick's parents decided that Dick and John were not bringing out the best in each other. "Mr. and Mrs. Cheney told Mr. and Mrs. Mayer that their sons ought to spend less time together," he says now, laughing.

There were happy family times in Wyoming, many involving fishing. On a 1954 trip to Dubois to fish the Wind River, Granddad Dickey came along, making the trip all the more fun. His health was a worry. He'd had a couple of heart attacks and just couldn't give up his beloved cigarettes entirely, though he was down to four Pall Malls a day. Still, when he was around, everybody had more fun. They stayed in a motel and fished the Wind River right in the middle of town, which was the kind of thing only greenhorns would do, but what did they care? They fished and laughed and couldn't have had a better time.

David Dickey visited again in the spring of 1955, and while he was at the house at 505 Texas Place, he had a heart attack. Dick went out in front of the house and flagged down the ambulance, then held open the screen door for the emergency workers as they took his granddad out of the house on a stretcher. His folks got into the car and raced to the hospital after the ambulance but returned a few hours later with sad news. David Dickey had died.

The Cheneys couldn't go to the funeral in Lincoln because Marge was nine months pregnant, and a week after David's death, his granddaughter Susan was born. The new soul was much welcomed, her birth an occasion for joy. But David had been deeply loved, and with his passing, some of the light went out of the world.

PART THREE

CHAPTER FOURTEEN

WHEN TELEVISION CAME to Casper in 1954, we Vincents figured out pretty quickly that the house we were living in had not been built with TV watching in mind. At one end of our front room was a dining table where we seldom ate, preferring the kitchen, but since that space was the designated dining nook, it didn't seem right to put the TV there. The couch took up a second wall and the picture window a third, leaving only a wall directly to the right as you came in the front door. Since there was a hallway entrance at the far end of this wall, the only blank space it offered was very near the front door, so that's where the television went. It was a vexing location, since anyone coming in from outside had to duck around the TV and the cabinet it sat on, and in the winter, anyone who pulled up a chair to watch TV was subject to arctic blasts every time someone entered.

It wasn't long before my parents found a house on the next street to which a den, paneled in knotty pine, had been added. Attached to the kitchen, it was the perfect place to watch television, and so we sold the house on Westridge Way and moved to 1735 Westridge Drive, propelled by one of the most powerful forces of the age, moving images in a box.

Neither we nor anyone else in Casper would have had TV if it hadn't been for Bill Daniels, who had come to town in 1952 to sell insurance to the oil industry. A Golden Gloves champion in his youth, Daniels loved watching the *Friday Night Fights* and was dismayed when he arrived in Casper to find there was little prospect for the town getting television. We were too far from a major city to pick up a signal from a television station and too far from being a major city to have a television station of our own.

Daniels frequently traveled to Denver just so he could go to Murphy's Bar on South Broadway, order a corned-beef sandwich, and watch the fights live from Madison Square Garden. He knew a little about technology, having been a decorated fighter pilot, but was no engineer. He'd never been to college. But he exemplified a belief that expertise was simply knowledge you hadn't yet acquired, and as he sat in Murphy's and watched the fights, he kept telling himself that if it was possible to get a TV signal from New York to Denver, he could figure out how to get one up to Casper.

When he heard that there was a fellow named Martin Malarkey in Pottsville, Pennsylvania, who was importing TV signals from Philadelphia by means of cable, Daniels hopped on the plane to go see him—and forked over the $500 that Malarkey declared to be the price of a meeting. After picking the brains of other entrepreneurs in other places who were using coaxial cable to transmit television signals, Daniels began to raise money from Casper oilmen for a cable venture of his own. He hired two honors graduates from the University of Texas College of Engineering, Richard and Gene Schneider, ex-GIs like himself, and the three came up with a system whereby signals from Denver would be transmitted over mountainous terrain to Casper by a microwave relay system, then distributed to homes by means of cable.

Daniels persuaded Mountain States Telephone and Telegraph to build the relay system, which required six towers between

Denver and Casper, and in January 1954, with the last structure in place, Community Television, as the Daniels enterprise became known, put on a three-day show at Casper's National Guard armory to demonstrate how the microwave and cable scheme worked. Half of Casper wandered through roomlike settings in which local dealers displayed television sets and offered advice on proper placement. And the armory visitors watched TV, programs such as *Ted Mack's Amateur Hour* and Walter Cronkite's *You Are There*. Some of the programs they saw that weekend—Saturday night wrestling and *Dragnet* on Sunday—carried special salutes from Denver stations welcoming Casper's citizens to the wonderful world of television.

Following all this in the newspaper, my parents decided that even though Community Television's $150 hookup charge and $7.50 monthly fee were steep, we had to have television, and they and thousands of other Casperites made Daniels's venture an immediate success. Knowing a good thing when he saw one, Daniels opened a Denver office to expand his business and was on his way to a legendary career in cable television in which he would accumulate fabulous wealth and gain a colorful reputation. "The best is good enough for me" became his motto as he traveled the country in a Learjet and accumulated wives and girlfriends. In a biography authorized by his estate, Matt Tinley, Jr., a great-nephew and an admirer, describes Daniels as "the kind of guy who always had the free cash, the girlfriends, the Cadillacs, the T-Birds, the fancy clothes, and he threw the best parties." Daniels had, Tinley said, "a lot of Hugh Hefner in him." He also had a generous spirit, and when he died in 2000, he left more than a billion dollars to charity.

Westridge, where we lived, was wired early in 1954, and not long after came our first TV. For me, slightly neurotic as most twelve-year-olds are, it was a source of concern as well as entertainment. What if it should be discovered in twenty years that too much TV watching blinded you? I tried shutting my eyes for five minutes every half-hour or so, not imagining that I'd be the last sighted person in the country but figuring it was possible I would be one of the last.

In the beginning, we had no choice about what we watched. Community TV provided a single channel, and although the company sent out a poll every three months asking which programs broadcast by the Denver network affiliates its customers would like to see on that channel, Gene Schneider admitted several years after the fact that he, his brother, and Bill Daniels actually made the decision according to their own viewing pleasures. "Which, of course," he said, "were all the sports, all the fights."

And that may account for the fact that I have absolutely no memory of the McCarthy hearings. When I read about the 1950s, the hearings always loom large, but I know them only in a historical way, perhaps because from May 5, 1954, onward, Casper television did not carry them in full but instead provided a nightly recap, which in the Mountain Standard Time Zone ran at 11:15 P.M. No doubt, there were citizens of Casper who watched the late-night summaries and saw McCarthy at his thuggish worst, but as a twelve-year-old, I didn't stay up that late, nor do I recall any of the adults around me talking about the hearings. In these days before news saturated all our lives, the McCarthy hearings also may have been an example of events that took on gale-force strength in other parts of the country while barely ruffling the cottonwoods in Wyoming.

I do remember *The Mickey Mouse Club*, which was on for an hour every day right around dinnertime. I generally thought of it as a program for my little brother, but it had some pretty snazzy dancing by the Mouseketeers that I, fourteen when the show started, found appealing. Several of the Mouseketeers were teenagers, and they got my attention, particularly Annette Funicello, who wasn't gorgeous but got prettier as the show progressed. During one *Mickey Mouse Club* season, there was a serial within the program that starred Annette, and in it she did a complete ugly-duckling-to-swan transformation, great viewing when you are a teenager yourself, hopeful that a new short hairdo will change your life.

American Bandstand was another program I dropped in and out of, watching when they were playing songs I liked and ignoring it when they had singing groups I'd never heard of, which was often. I didn't find the dancers nearly as interesting as did some of my friends, who hurried home after school so they wouldn't miss a thing. That was too much dedication for me, and I missed many an afternoon, putting me at a decided disadvantage when it came to identifying Kenny and Justine or doing the Stroll.

Every program that aired in the evenings was OK for kids, so we watched TV together, my dad in his flowered lounge chair, my mother in a smaller one like it, and Mark and I on the couch or the braided rug that covered most of our den's red and white vinyl-tiled floor. We watched *I Led Three Lives*, the story of Herbert Philbrick, citizen, Communist, and counterspy. The plots involved Communists distributing literature on how to blow up viaducts or coercing Americans who had relatives behind the Iron Curtain into becoming Party tools. The show was never played for laughs, and we didn't find it funny, though all these years later, some of the episodes cause me to wonder that we took them seriously. In one, Communist agents try to launder counterfeit money by giving each of a thousand teenagers a phony ten-dollar bill and instructing the teens to spend less than a dollar, collect the change, and turn it over to the agents. Presumably, none of the writers on the show had ever tried to organize ten teenagers, let alone a thousand. Watching these fifty-year-old shows today, I'm also struck by how low-tech the spying is. In one episode, the FBI puts paint on a tire so they can follow a car. But, of course, we were all low-tech in the '50s, and when I learned from *I Led Three Lives* about how to use lemon juice to do secret writing, I thought I had come into possession of some pretty important knowledge.

Sunday nights were great because a half-hour after *Lassie*, a three-handkerchief event in our family, came *The Ed Sullivan Show*, with its quirky host and amazing range of guests, from singer Mario Lanza to puppeteers to Elvis Presley. That was followed not long after by what I thought was the best of the night, *What's My Line?* which introduced me to something I'd never seen before: men wearing tuxedos. The women on the panel dressed formally, too, and actress Arlene Francis's entrances in her long gowns made you sit up and take notice, as did columnist Dorothy Kilgallen's questions, artfully phrased to avoid the no answer that ended a panelist's turn. "Would it be safe to assume that you're not an acrobat?" she might say. Random House publisher Bennett Cerf was a charmer, making fun of himself and others with terrible puns and offbeat words, such as *tabescent* and *eupeptic*. The result was a show both sophisticated and silly, as the erudite group tried to guess offbeat occupations such as "feeds a whale underwater" or "manufactures revolving doors."

I especially loved moderator John Charles Daley's long and carefully parsed answers to questions from panelists that didn't have a clear-cut yes or no answer. "Is it a machine?" actor Tony Randall, a guest panelist, asked one evening, to which Daley responded, "I assume you mean an entity that has a motivating force and through the use of the motivating force and other implements attached thereto does something to something else in terms of turning or shaping or slicing." "No," Randall replied, going for the laugh, "that's not what I meant." Daley and the panelists chatted about Broadway shows and vacations in exotic places like Caneel Bay the way we talked about going to the Skyline Drive-In or a picnic on Casper Mountain. It was a glimpse inside a world that I hadn't known existed, an elegant party, with very pleasant and clever guests.

Watching old reruns of *What's My Line?* as I write this book, I also realize that, like many programs in the 1950s, it brought us the unexpected surprises of live television. One night, Bennett Cerf's microphone started smoking, prompting John Charles Daley to walk across the stage and pour a glass of water on it. I don't remember this episode from when it first aired, but if we saw it, I'm certain we all slapped our foreheads and exclaimed, "Water on an electrical fire!" Maybe these Easterners didn't know everything after all.

On Tuesdays, we watched *The $64,000 Question*, a quiz show that took a familiar expression ("the $64 question"), added three zeroes, and went to the top of the TV ratings. It gave seemingly ordinary people the opportunity to use deep knowledge of some subject—opera or history or cooking—to gain what seemed fabulous wealth. In order to succeed, they also had to take double-or-nothing gambles, which added suspense to the show's appeal. The most memorable contestant was Dr. Joyce Brothers, a risk-taking psychologist who knew everything there was to know about boxing and won the big prize. Years later, when she had gone on to a successful career offering advice on TV and in the newspapers, we would learn that she had overcome more than the usual odds to win. The show's sponsors, deeming her insufficiently telegenic, had tried to get rid of her by giving her especially hard questions.

But the quiz show of all quiz shows, as far as I was concerned, was *Twenty-one*. The prizes were even bigger than those on *The $64,000 Question*—contestants could win more than $100,000—and the show had a star, Charles Van Doren. I had never heard of the distinguished Van Doren family, but Charles seemed to share the mysterious and urbane world that the panelists on *What's My Line?* were part of, though he was younger, more self-effacing, and even smarter—or so we thought. We would later find out that he had been given the answers, that all his angst inside the isolation booth was acting, and that all the adoration that America had bestowed on him was undeserved. I remember my shock that someone who had seemed so decent had let himself become a con man and my mystification about why a person of such promise would do something that brought his downfall.

The quiz-show scandal became public at the end of the '50s, giving it a symbolic weight that, in a way, it deserves. News that shows had been rigged demonstrated that deserving a reward and receiving one could be very different things, a revelation that ran counter to the confident belief of the postwar era that the world was a meritocracy. But we also saw in the disgrace of Charles Van Doren that cheating is high-risk and that when a society in which honesty is valued uncovers it, there is a substantial price to pay.

The 1950s are sometimes portrayed as an era in which Americans were unaware of social problems, but I think it is more accurate to describe it as a time when we were becoming aware of them and had confidence they could be solved. In 1957, television brought us deeply disturbing images as nine black students attempted to integrate Central High School in Little Rock, Arkansas. Governor Orval Faubus called out the Arkansas National Guard to prevent them from entering the school, but the pictures that lodged in memory were mobs of angry white people, faces contorted with hatred, screaming at high school kids, earnest students the same age as we were. We knew nothing of race relations in the South, but you didn't have to in order to know what was right in this situation and what was wrong. In Wyoming, as in most of the country, we saw Eisenhower's decision to send in federal troops as exactly right, a proper way to resolve the matter. We had no idea that getting the students in the door was just the beginning or that there were so many other battles yet to be fought. We failed to realize either the depth of racism or the many forms it could take, and in that we were naïve. But as I look back over the forty years since those images from Little Rock played on our television set in Casper, I think our confidence in America was warranted. Although work remains, our country has undergone fundamental change on matters of race—and we are all better off for it.

Television connected us to current events in a very compact way, with just fifteen minutes of network news a night on weeknights and none at all on weekends. Most of our television hours were spent watching entertainment, and I remember Saturday night, particularly in the years when we first got TV, as the best night of the week. *Your Hit Parade*, a beguiling cross between a contest for most popular song of the week and a musical review, came on then. It was sponsored by Lucky Strike cigarettes, and after Dorothy Collins or one of the other *Hit Parade* singers invited us to "light up a Lucky," the top songs, as determined by a national survey (or so the show claimed), were presented by a troop of singers and dancers. Giselle MacKenzie might sing

"Autumn Leaves" in a bistro, or a group dressed as coal miners
would render "Sixteen Tons." Sitting in our den, we'd try to
guess what the number one song would be, but suspense over the
winner was less a reason to keep watching than were the songs
themselves, which often struck an emotional chord—nostalgia
with "Moments to Remember" or religious inspiration with
"He," a song about God's power, love, and forgiveness. "Love Is a
Many-Splendored Thing" was wonderfully romantic, so much so
that one critic suggests that in our more jaded times, "it may
evoke laughter more than passion and tears." But in the '50s, romance was alluring. Early in the decade, my friends and I bought
glossy publications that contained nothing but the words to
popular songs so we could memorize the lyrics to "Stardust,"
"Kiss of Fire," and "Secret Love."

As I was standing in the high school gym one day during my
freshman or sophomore year, a new girl in town asked me if I'd
heard of Elvis Presley. When I admitted I hadn't, she took it as
clear evidence that kids in Casper were hopelessly behind the
times. Her parents had moved her to the middle of nowhere, she
was sure, but soon enough, the news arrived even to the high
plains of the Rockies, and we were listening to "Heartbreak
Hotel" and "All Shook Up" at the Charles E. Wells Music Company on Second Street. Wells's had booths where you could pre-
view records, and after we'd listen to Elvis, we'd buy his 45s or
sometimes even an album. But we were also buying Tab Hunter's
"Young Love," Debbie Reynolds's "Tammy," and the Plat-
ters' "Twilight Time," and about the same time that Elvis burst
onto the scene, so did another young singer, Pat Boone, and we
bought his records, too: "Friendly Persuasion," "Love Letters in
the Sand," and my favorite, "April Love."

Elvis was great—we loved dancing to "Don't Be Cruel"—but

he wasn't *the* greatest, not yet. We also loved dancing to the Everly Brothers' "Bye Bye Love" or the Diamonds' "Little Darlin'." And the Elvis phenomenon—the screaming girls, the gyrations—seemed a kind of weird distraction to me, though some of my classmates seemed to get it. One took iron-on letters and ran "Elvis" down one side of her sweater and "Presley" down the other, leading a few boys to remark cleverly and cruelly that she had named her breasts.

The tunes we chose from the jukebox at the Canteen, a community center where we went to dance, spanned a wide range, wider, it turned out, than the singers on *Your Hit Parade* could manage. Snooky Lanson and the others, great at pop songs with sweet lyrics, simply didn't have it in them to do the shimmying and pounding and wailing that "Hound Dog" or "Rock around the Clock" required, and it was embarrassing to watch them try. As more and more rock 'n' roll numbers made it into the top ten, the show went downhill, ending as the sentimental decade ended, last airing in April 1959.

The family shows of the 1950s—*Leave It to Beaver, Father Knows Best*, and *Ozzie and Harriet*—seemed boring to me then, as they do now. *I Love Lucy*, a family show of a kind, was regarded as well worth watching in our household, but we didn't look forward to Lucy and Ricky Ricardo nearly as much as we did to Alice and Ralph Kramden, who, in the years when we first got television, were the highlight of our week. At first, they were part of *The Jackie Gleason Show*, a program with many things to recommend it, including the June Taylor dancers, whose precision maneuvers opened the show, and Gleason as host, crossing his legs in the shape of a 4 and heading into the skits with "Away we go." But *The Honeymooners* was the best part, and in 1955, when Ralph and Alice got a show all their own, we thought the powers-that-be in TV Land were pretty smart to give us an entire half-hour of what we really wanted. Ralph, of course, was played by Gleason, and his resemblance to my father, who had put on weight over the years, was so uncanny that friends and neighbors remarked on it. The two shared not only substantial girth but curly hair, and both were surprisingly light on their feet. In one of his most memorable shows, Gleason, as Ralph, did a surpassingly good mambo, and my father, too, could execute a fine and fancy step. With my mother as his partner, he twirled and dipped and spun with such grace that the dance crowd at the Riverside Club, a favored place for ballroom dancing, had been known to clear the floor so that everyone could watch Wayne and Edna perform.

Ralph yelled at everyone—at the passengers on the bus he drove, at his neighbor Norton, and especially at his wife, Alice—but for all his bluster, he had a soft heart. In one episode, he refuses to let Alice keep a puppy from the pound and takes it back himself, but when he discovers what happens to puppies that don't get adopted, he emerges from the pound with three small dogs. In another episode, he has a fifteen-dollar bill to pay but refuses to dip into the money he's squirreled away in the sugar bowl for a bowling ball. When a priest seeking help for the needy comes along, however, Ralph hands over his savings.

The Honeymooners reminded us that, like Ralph Kramden, my father was a complicated man. You worried about going to the store with him, because if there was a line and he perceived anyone to be crowding in front of him, a scene would develop in which he would play a very loud part, but in other circumstances, he could be amazingly patient. He taught me to drive, and I was not the most apt of students. One day, when he was letting me practice on a flat area beside the Platte River, I got the brake, clutch, and gas pedals confused and headed straight for the water.

"The brake, Lynnie, the brake!" he kept repeating, voice calm, until finally, only a few feet into the water, I figured it out. He never once shouted, though I do remember my brother, six years old at the time and in the backseat, screaming.

He coached my brother's Little League team for several years and aided and abetted all the schemes my mother came up with for Mark's and my benefit, whether it was a baseball camp in Montrose, Colorado, she thought he ought to attend or a twirling contest in North Platte, Nebraska, in which she thought I ought to compete. My father was so committed to things going well for us that it was hard for him to watch us at crucial moments. Mark might throw the ball too high, or I might drop the baton, and such events were too painful for him even to contemplate. I can remember seeing him peer around the door of the high school gym once when I was twirling. I suppose he thought that if I were having a bad day and he needed to get out of there, he could do it more easily standing in the hallway than if he were seated in the bleachers with the other parents.

But if he had any idea we were in real trouble, his approach changed totally. Early in my driving career, I pestered him one day when he got home from work into letting me take his 1949 Chevy to my grandmother's. Daydreaming as I drove down CY Avenue, I didn't see the car in front of me signal a left turn and stop to wait for oncoming traffic to pass, and I plowed right into it. I wasn't hurt but thought I needed a parent around and asked someone to call my mother, who was still at work, not thinking to call my father because I knew he was without a car. But before much time had passed, I looked up to see him coming toward me, pedaling furiously down CY Avenue on my seven-year-old brother's bike. Heedless of the spectacle he made, he was intent on being sure I was all right.

My father's job paid about $9,000 a year while I was in high school, a good salary in that time and place, but his work was definitely bureaucratic. "I am responsible for the interpretation and application of all policies, procedures and regulations pertaining to the programming, scheduling and budget functions of the North Platte River District," he wrote on one form, as well as "for the preparation, issuance, and operation of the work order system." He didn't hate his job the way Ralph Kramden hated being a bus driver, but neither did he find much satisfaction in it. Early in his career, he had polished his credentials with math courses at Casper College and tried to improve his public-speaking skills by joining Toastmasters. One of the speeches he practiced for delivery was entitled "Water Does Run Uphill," and he went through it so often that both my mother and I could recite large parts of it. He'd been preparing himself to move upward and onward, but by his mid-thirties, he had settled in for the long run, working for bosses who were nice enough but about his age, so he knew there was little chance of advancing. He did his job well, judging from what superiors said about him on personnel forms, but I think, restless as he was, the sameness of it wore at him.

He joined my grandfather, Ben Lybyer, in one of his attempts to strike it rich, exploring terrain north of town with a Geiger counter. He bought bags of coins that people had dropped into the town's parking meters and sorted through them, pulling out the Indian-head pennies and buffalo nickels and hoping he'd come across one of the rarities, like a 1943 copper penny. Once at Christmastime, he was sure he could make a fortune by marketing miniature bales of hay for Santa's reindeer, but that, too, came to naught. He went to work week after week, year after year, to a job he did not love and thereby made our middle-class life possible. This is not, I know, an unusual gift for a parent to give. Still, I wish I had been more aware. I wish I had thanked him.

My father never shouted at my brother or me, but he did raise his voice when he and my mother quarreled, although never so spectacularly as Ralph Kramden, who was always threatening to send Alice to the moon. My dad saved his threats for people outside the family, but his blowups were still memorable—and frequent. I wanted my mother to give right back the way Alice Kramden did, and she got a little better at that over the years, but in the end, she couldn't outshout him. She'd come home from work, put some round steak in a pan, and turn the stove on high, then leave the kitchen to change her shoes. He would tip-toe across the kitchen to turn down the heat, a reasonable idea, but he'd overdo it, and when she got back, she'd discover the burner turned so low that the meat juices were congealing. She'd tell him to leave the stove alone, which would spur a loud outburst from him about her domestic skills, which would lead her to suggest that if he didn't like the way she cooked dinner, he should cook it himself, which would lead to an explosion from him that stopped all rational discourse in its tracks and usually left her in tears.

None of my friends had divorced parents, but I thought if such a thing were ever to happen, this kind of quarreling was likely a road to it. Maybe one day he'd leave and not come back, or she'd get fed up and be the one to walk out. Their fighting filled me with dread. It made us all miserable, including, I think, my father, who was inevitably subdued after one of his blowups but seemed incapable of controlling his temper, particularly after he'd had a couple of highballs, which he usually did before my mother got home from work, and then maybe a couple after that. And so there were unhappy evenings in our house, although not usually on Saturdays, because that was when we watched Ralph Kramden, who was so much like my father. However much he yelled, he had a tender heart, and however much he blustered, he loved his Alice. "You mean everything in the world to me," he told her once when he thought she was dying.

Ralph was never going to change. We knew that. But in moments of clarity, he wished that he could. "I'm pretty stupid, yelling at people and screaming," he confessed to Alice one Saturday night. "I don't know why you stick around." And she, too, spoke words that reassured us: "Because I love you, Ralph."

CHAPTER FIFTEEN

OUR HIGH SCHOOL was the most beautiful building in Casper, if not in all Wyoming. With its turreted tower, triple ogee arch, and clerestory of five arched windows two stories high across the front façade, it rose like a castle from land that within living memory had been empty prairie. As an entering freshman in 1955, I loved its grandeur, as had students for nearly thirty years. In a time and place when most construction was done with today and tomorrow in mind, we had a high school for the generations. In one of my annuals, some astute observer, no doubt a teacher, has placed a quotation from English critic John Ruskin alongside a picture of the school: "When we build, let us think that we build forever."

Architect Arthur Garbutt, who designed the building in 1924, did not think small. His design called for building the new high school around the old high school, then razing the old school to create a huge courtyard. He proposed an exterior adorned with quoins, quatrefoils, and coats of arms, and interior corridors lined with travertine and verde antique marble. When he presented his plans, Casper was in the middle of an oil boom, and the school board gave them quick approval, but hardly had the cornerstone for the building been laid when grumbling about extravagance began. At the next school board election, the grum-

Natrona County High School, the most beautiful building in Casper.

blers went to the polls, and no member of the board who approved the project was reelected.

When the doors opened in 1927, the price had escalated from $600,000 to $1 million, and the oil boom was over, leaving Casper's economy so constrained that architect Garbutt, seeing no future in the local building industry, left town to take up ranching in the Big Horn Basin. Thus, there was more reason for discontent at the building's completion than when construction started, except for one overwhelming fact: the building was gorgeous. It instantly became a source of community pride.

Those of us entering its arched doors in 1955 didn't know this history, nor did we know much about our high school's Gothic style. A few kids with brothers or sisters at colleges like Duke or Bryn Mawr might have been able to say that NCHS looked like college buildings "back East," a concept into which we fit North Carolina, where Duke is located, as well as Pennsylvania, the home of Bryn Mawr, but beyond that, most of us would have been mute. Still, we knew NCHS was grand, and that conveyed a message that education—and our education in particular—was important.

If we got into the building without remembering our high purpose for being there—as we did rather often—teachers reminded us, and the reminder-in-chief was Frances Feris, a gray-haired teacher in her mid-fifties when the class of 1959 entered NCHS. With a piercing gaze and an air of utter determination, she reigned over the debate team, the English department, and, indeed, the entire school. As an entering freshman, unaware of the prevailing hierarchies, I was surprised when Miss Feris, of whom I had just begun to hear, had an upperclassman deliver me a message. "She isn't going to ask you to be in debate," the upperclassman announced, "because you have too many irons in the fire." I knew right away that "irons in the fire" meant baton twirling, but why was Miss Feris sending me word that it was keeping me out of debate? And why would I want to be in debate, anyway?

All these years later, I wonder if she didn't anticipate this reaction. I had no appreciation at the time for the intellectual training that debate under Miss Feris offered, the skill in research it helped develop, the experience it provided in framing issues and rebutting opponents. It would have been pointless to present it to me as an alternative to baton twirling, she might have thought, since I wasn't likely to choose correctly. My friend Karen Brewer, on the other hand, must have seemed a wiser fourteen-year-old, because Miss Feris gave her a choice: continue being a cheerleader or sign up for debate. Karen put away her pom-poms and joined Miss Feris.

But why did she let me know that I wasn't being chosen? To put me in my place? To motivate me to show her what I could do? A classmate, Mary Ann Garman Hoff, who married in her junior year, remembers Miss Feris saying to her, "I don't know why you're going to school. Girls who are married are just wasting their time." And Mary Ann, who would become the first woman in upper management at the Farmers Home Administration in Wyoming, has asked herself the same questions I have: "Was she down on me? Did she tell me that to give me a challenge?"

If you did make it into Miss Feris's debate class and she decided that you were less than fully committed, she could make your life miserable. When one student took a weekend off to go to a meeting of a leadership group, she immediately called due all the papers from which he previously had been excused because of his activities in debate. When a student she had recruited went out for football, she talked openly and often in class about his lack of commitment—both before and after she kicked him out.

Although Miss Feris's irritation extended to boys as well as girls, I am reminded of her when I read how cantankerous Susan B. Anthony could be when women around her wanted to marry or have babies or do anything that she believed distracted from the cause of female equality. Frances Feris had the same sense of mission about keeping students focused on improving their intellectual skills, disdaining anything that interfered with that and, in addition, probably thinking we were soft, growing up as we were in times so much easier than the ones she had known.

She had come to Wyoming as a child in 1907, when her father, a storekeeper in Missouri, was advised to go west for his health. As she described her early life in a brief autobiography, her family lived in a one-room shack in Riverton, then a town of many bars, several churches, and no schoolhouse. Her father farmed a homestead outside town, and every six weeks, in order to prove up an additional 160 acres, Frances and her mother drove a buckboard twenty-five miles and lived for two weeks in an abandoned saloon that her father had moved to the acreage to serve as shelter. As they drove along, Frances's mother sang her songs, told her Bible stories, and recited poetry.

She had other teachers, as well. They taught her reading and writing in a room above the Fazon and Lamar saloon, then presided over classes held in the Baptist church, until finally there was a red brick school building for Riverton-area children. Among the dedicated teachers she remembered in her autobiography was Helen Petersdorf. "We had both respect and fear for her," Miss Feris wrote, "two attributes of a great teacher." She also remembered a Professor Twitchell, a Latin and Greek instructor who had been dismissed from his previous job, she said, "because he was either an atheist or an agnostic. In those years 'agnostic' could have meant anything from drug addict to homosexual," she explained. "Although our community did not keep him long, he gave us much."

Frances Feris earned a B.A. at the University of Wyoming, an M.A. at the University of Iowa, and spent forty-one years at Natrona County High School, where she led debate teams to seventeen national championships. If you became one of her prized debaters, you were the equivalent of a valued athlete, practicing after school and spending weekends on the road, bound for Cheyenne, Wyoming, and Fort Collins, Colorado, and and Spearfish, South Dakota, to compete. The honors won by Miss Feris's forensic champions were trumpeted on the front page of the *Gusher*, our student newspaper. In the top right-hand column, just below the newspaper's oil derrick logo, you'd read "NCHS Debaters Win First at Denver Speech Meet."

Some students had heard that Miss Feris was once engaged but that her fiancé had been killed in World War I. Most of us knew that she lived in a house on Spruce Street and that Miss Hill, an English teacher a few years younger, lived in the basement. In our yearbooks, which Miss Feris and Miss Hill cosponsored, there is a picture nearly every year of the two of them, overseeing the annual, a food drive, or the English department. When Miss Feris died at age seventy-three, she left Miss Hill $5,000 and put the bulk of her estate, $100,000, into two trusts, designating half the trust income as well as use of her house to Miss Hill until her death. But the main purpose of the trusts, as the lawyer who helped Miss Feris draw up her will explained it, was to continue "her life work of helping deserving young people" by providing college scholarships to worthy students.

It's hard to overstate what a strong figure Frances Feris was.

Teaching during days when progressive educators were arguing that schools should emphasize cooperation, not competition, she was unhesitating about encouraging her students to win. Indeed, she was not above intervening in their personal lives if she thought it would advance the cause of victory, once suggesting to a girl dating a star debater that she quit seeing him because she was a distraction.

Progressive educators, whose ideas had become conventional wisdom by the 1950s, were also convinced that students should learn life skills at school rather than concentrate on bookish knowledge, and this idea had some slight impact on Natrona County High School. All freshman girls had to take home economics, and freshman boys took a class called shop, a bargain I believe girls got the better of. Although I remember little of the cooking part of home ec, the sewing part has stayed with me, enabling me still today to put in a pretty good hem. My husband, on the other hand, remembers nothing of shop except learning to drill holes in metal, a skill he has not often been called upon to use.

We had tracks at our school, one in vocational education, another in general education, a third in college prep; and an effort was made to make all seem equally worthy. Our yearbooks show girls in a Family Living class and boys adjusting the head bolts on an engine, as well as math students holding up slide rules ("Learning the use of a slide rule will be pretty important in a world dominated by math and science," reads the caption). But a student who was doing very well in a general education math course would be encouraged to take a more challenging one, and the idea that we should continue on with education after high school was constantly emphasized. "Today a college education is almost a must," an article in the February 14, 1957, *Gusher* begins, and looking through issue after issue, I see that almost every student interviewed is asked about future plans, and almost everyone replies that he or she is college-bound. That's what the strongest teachers at our school wanted for students, and students said it was what they wanted, even, I think, some students who didn't really intend to go on to college.

One of our teachers, a lovely woman named Margaret LaViolette, thought grades were overrated, as progressive educators generally did, and she didn't think we ought to spend time studying war in her world history class. While progressive educators didn't necessarily share this aversion, many did believe that teachers ought to shape the curriculum in ways that would improve society, and perhaps this was behind Mrs. LaViolette's approach. Perhaps she thought the world would be better off if we moved right past wars to peaceful achievements.

Born in Ohio, Mrs. LaViolette had been educated at Wellesley College, and although her way of teaching world history left some big blanks to fill (why were Alexander the Great and Napoleon significant?), she never doubted that the study of the past was important, an idea underscored by a wealth of reference materials ("Acropolis to Zinjanthropus," she labeled them) that she gathered for students to use. I found her gentle ways appealing but also unique among the women I knew best at Natrona County High School. Most had early lives that had been tough and demanding, and they had become forceful adults, no-nonsense, take-charge women utterly unsympathetic to the soft-hearted—they would have said soft-minded—ideas that progressive educators advocated.

Kathleen Hemry, an endlessly enthusiastic redhead from whom I took English as a sophomore, had spent her early years on the prairies west of Casper, where her family grazed sheep, living in a tent and a one-room cabin before they finally built a house. In her early fifties when I first knew her, she had earned two degrees at the University of Wyoming, loved Shakespeare, and required us to memorize passages from the plays, such as Portia's speech from *The Merchant of Venice* and Julius Caesar's "The fault, dear Brutus, is not in our stars but in ourselves that we are underlings." She was also a stickler for grammar, not hesitating to interrupt midsentence if you said "who" when it should have been "whom." And she taught us to diagram sentences, an exercise that appealed to me for the sense it made out of the English language.

Miss Hemry wanted people to know that even though she'd never married, she had led a full life, breaking many a heart in her youth and once even dancing on the roof of the Wonder Bar—though after any such revelation, she would make clear that she'd never drunk so much as a drop of liquor. In her eighties, she noted in an essay that she had spent most of her years in Casper, forty of them, teaching school. "Some might call her life a rat race," she wrote of herself, "[but] she views it as a gallop over the open prairie with her hair streaming out behind her in the wind."

She lived to be a hundred, which gave her many years after retirement to put her organizational skills to work in a variety of causes, from a library book sale to Meals-on-Wheels, which took food to the elderly. She dragooned people into helping her, including my father-in-law, who thought Meals-on-Wheels a fine program but one he deserved a break from now and then—a concept foreign to Miss Hemry. She liked to describe herself as "Irish by name . . . Swiss, German, French by ancestry—and Scotch by nature," and her frugality was famous. When she undertook to raise money for community health screenings, she ordered the cheapest envelopes she could find, which happened to be blue, thereby giving a name to this charitable endeavor that endures today: the Blue Envelope Fund.

Miss Hemry saved so she could give. On her eightieth birthday, she contributed her house to an organization that wanted to establish a group home for girls. In her nineties, she wrote an essay in which she observed: "There's no U-Haul behind the hearse. Don't leave your loot in a will for relatives and lawyers to squabble over. The descendants won't like each other any more and the lawyers will get the money." As she approached her hundredth birthday, she had become an institution. Girl Scouts came to visit her, bearing cards that they often addressed to "Mrs." Hemry, which earned them a lecture, and if they asked if she had children, she told them that in her youth, she had much preferred dancing to diapers. Before she died in 2004, Kathleen Hemry, who had never earned more than $7,000 a year as a teacher, had given $1 million away to good causes in Casper.

The most important teacher for me personally was Margaret Shidler, a small woman with blue-gray hair who taught Latin. Former students almost inevitably describe her as "feisty," probably because she didn't behave as an older woman was expected to, zipping around town in a snazzy little Nash Metropolitan, smoking, though not in public, and cursing mildly. "They're raising hell and putting a chunk under it," she'd say when students drag-raced down CY Avenue or got into an after-school fight.

Part of the same generation as Misses Feris, Hill, and Hemry, Miss Shidler had been born in the farm town of Knob Noster, Missouri, in 1902. Her mother died when she was born, leaving behind six children in addition to new baby Margaret. Two unmarried aunts took her in and cared for her, and she grew up in their household, graduating from high school and then attending a teachers' college in nearby Warrensburg. When her father and three of her brothers, hearing about one of the early Salt Creek oil booms, decided to seek their fortunes in Wyoming, Margaret followed with her aunts, settling in Casper. She got a job as a physical education instructor at Natrona County High School and then, in the early 1930s, began teaching Latin. By the time we entered her classroom in the '50s, she was well practiced in the art of letting students know she wouldn't put up with nonsense. Under her clock hung a sign—"Time will pass. Will you?"—and if you didn't work, she had no mercy. She once flunked her nephew.

She also felt an obligation to motivate those she thought were loafing. One of my classmates, Joe Meyer, who would go on to become a lawyer and Wyoming's secretary of state, as well as its state treasurer, remembers her announcing in class that one of the students in the room who was doing mediocre work actually had a high IQ. As he passed her desk to exit when the bell rang, she said to him, "You know who I'm talking about, don't you?" "It was the first time I thought of myself as smart and figured I could do more," he remembers.

I approached her class as I'd done every other, completing all the assignments and studying for tests, and was thoroughly dismayed when she gave me a 2, our equivalent of a B. Being able to translate Virgil wasn't enough for a 1, she made clear. I needed to be able to explain how the language worked, and so I began to memorize declensions and conjugations and to pause over words to see the signals that placed them in relationship to other words. I still remember with pride the day she called on me to identify a construction in *The Aeneid*, and I was able to say with some certainty that it was the ablative absolute. With Miss Shidler's

English teacher Frances Feris, on the right, dominated Natrona County High School. Gwendolyn Hill helped her run things.

English teacher Kathleen Hemry, whose enthusiasm was as boundless as her generosity.

Margaret Shidler, a Latin teacher, taught me the pleasure of hard intellectual work.

Barbara Scifers, dean of women at Natrona County High School, kept our eyes firmly fixed on the rules.

prodding, I learned the difference between skimming over the surface of a subject and delving into it. She showed me the satisfaction that hard intellectual work can bring, a gift that I have treasured.

After her retirement and the deaths of her aunts, for whom she had cared in their old age, Miss Shidler moved to Vancouver, Washington, to be near some younger friends. When she was dying, she asked them to sell her belongings and establish a scholarship at the First Methodist Church.

So many of our teachers were older single women without children of their own. Iva Smith, Clara Francis Gadbury, Ruby McBride, Ethel Lindsey—the list is long. Had they been born half a century later, they might have gone into other professions. I can easily imagine Frances Feris running a major corporation, Kathleen Hemry in charge of a large nonprofit, or Margaret Shidler as a professor of the classics. Instead, they taught us, and we were lucky for it.

Ione Gibbs, from whom I took geometry my sophomore year, was divorced, a rarity in that time and place, and had a child, Catherine, a year ahead of us. She was a marvelous teacher, conveying the wonderfully ordered world of plane geometry with a clarity that made me love it. If you knew two sides of a right triangle, you could figure out the third: a^2 plus b^2 equaled c^2 every time. And if you knew the first two parts of a syllogism, the third followed: If all men are mortal, and Socrates is a man, then Socrates is mortal. Perhaps because not everyone was as taken with the world of plane geometry as Mrs. Gibbs and I, we formed a bond that lasted beyond the class, and when it was time for me to apply to college, she had some definite ideas. Although she herself had been born in Colorado and received most of her education in Oklahoma, she was determined that I go to an Eastern school, Barnard College in New York, in particular. I'd never heard of the school, nor had I been to New York, but it seemed like a fine idea to me.

We had some very good male teachers, too, usually married, often with children, and sometimes quite young. Bob Lahti, a tall South Dakotan in his twenties, held us to high standards in his chemistry class, for which I am grateful, as I am for his moving me one day in the fall of my junior year from a seat where I was talking too much to Tom Fake, a gregarious quarterback I'd dated as a freshman and sophomore, to another seat, this one next to a halfback named Dick Cheney, who was cute, quiet, and unavailable since he was going steady with a cheerleader.

Don Weishaar, a big guy with a great grin and a crew cut, was in his early thirties when I took a class with him our senior year called Math Analysis. The point of the class was to take students who tested well, teach them advanced algebra and beginning calculus, and along the way deepen their understanding of math, which I suspect happened, though what I really remember is that the class was fun. Dick Cheney was in Math Analysis, as was Joe Meyer, also a football player and, since his encounter with Miss Shidler, a pretty good student. A few kids in the class were brilliant in math. One of them, Curtis Strobeck, famous for doing his homework in ink, went on to earn a Ph.D. in theoretical biology at the University of Chicago. Most of us were simply pretty good, and Mr. Weishaar, fresh from getting his master's degree in mathematics at the University of Colorado, brought immense enthusiasm to his subject. I carried it with me to college, where I was a mathematics major until my junior year, when I realized that equations had become drudgery for me. It was poetry I loved. Reading Gerard Manley Hopkins was like standing on a Wyoming mountain and looking at the stars.

Bob Lahti, Don Weishaar, and Harry Geldien (clockwise from upper left)
were great teachers—and great coaches. Geldien, who taught biology,
led the football team to many winning seasons, with Lahti and Weishaar,
who taught chemistry and math, among his assistants.

Math Analysis was part of a program that had enrolled its first students in September 1957, the month before the Soviets put Sputnik into orbit, alarming Americans and spurring demands for school reform. President Eisenhower had tried to allay the nation's concerns, but how could we not worry about the Reds, as the newspapers called them, putting a satellite into space? We listened to the beeping sound it made replayed on television, went out in the backyard at night to try to see it—unsuccessfully in my family's case, though others saw it overhead.

Just a month after Sputnik's launch, there was another shock, another satellite, this one with a passenger, a space dog that the *Casper Tribune-Herald* insisted on calling Curly, though her name was Laika. We tried to see that one, too, again with no luck. Nearly everyone was examining the skies, and in these anxious times, they saw—or thought they saw—things even more alarming than satellites. There were feverish reports in the *Casper Tribune-Herald* of fireballs streaking across the western sky and glowing objects hovering on the horizon. Two news carriers provided an especially vivid description of an orange cigar-shaped object with a long plume behind it over the east end of Casper Mountain.

Experts spoke out about what had gone wrong. Vanover Bush, who'd help guide U.S. development of the atomic bomb, declared in an article that ran in the *Casper Tribune-Herald* that the nation was doing too little to encourage promising youngsters to study science. Admiral Hyman Rickover, father of the nuclear Navy, laid blame at the feet of progressive education and declared its day over: "Our technological supremacy has been called in question and we know we have to deal with a formidable competitor. Parents are no longer satisfied with life-adjustment schools. Parental objectives no longer coincide with those professed by the progressive educationists." As cries for school reform swept the country, teachers and administrators at NCHS must have taken some satisfaction in the efforts they had under way to encourage students with potential to delve deeper into mathematics. They had already begun what the rest of the nation was being urged to do, and when it came to ridding classrooms of the notions of progressive educators, they were also ahead of the game. Teachers like Frances Feris and Margaret Shidler had long been defending the intellectual ramparts at Natrona County High School, and there was almost nothing of significance to get rid of.

SECOND ONLY TO the high school in terms of its beauty was the library, a red brick structure with a low neoclassical dome at the corner of Second and Durbin. It had been built with the help of Andrew Carnegie, a diminutive immigrant from Scotland who at the turn of the century had begun using some of his vast wealth to build libraries across the country. After the city fathers agreed, as Carnegie required, to fill the library with books and provide for its maintenance, he provided funding for construction, and the building opened in 1910 to a celebration of music and dancing. It had oak-trimmed interiors, and by the time I started going there, some forty winters of hot-water heating had worked to combine the scent of varnished wood with the slightly acidic odor of aging books to create a wonderful smell, one unique in my experience. I've come across hints of it since in the stacks of great libraries and been instantly taken back to the Carnegie Library in Casper, which was a wonderful place to spend an afternoon. I can easily understand why Dick Cheney, a new boy in town in 1954, chose to read his way through the summer there.

I first started going to the library by myself in the fall of that

*Casper's Carnegie Library, pictured here when it was new,
was in the 1950s a haven for kids who loved books.*

year, looking for information to write reports. My parents had purchased *Great Books of the Western World*, a set of fifty-four volumes that a door-to-door salesman had convinced them were encyclopedias but which were nothing of the sort. University of Chicago president Robert Hutchins and Mortimer Adler, a professor determined to bring the classics to the general public, had conceived the project as a way to present the works of great thinkers from Homer to Freud, and years later, when I fell under the spell of the great books, I wished many times that I had the set my parents purchased. But in 1954, I couldn't make heads or tails of it. When I was assigned to write a report on jade, the Wyoming state stone, I could see no way to wrest information on such a topic from the *Great Books of the Western World*. There was an index of sorts, called a Syntopicon, but under "J" there was only "judgment" and "justice," no "jade." I understand now that to pose a question about a gemstone to the Syntopicon was a complete misuse of what was an elegant attempt to span the range of human wisdom on topics such as "the moral theory of the good," but a report on a gemstone was what I was stuck with, and so I went to the library.

Once there, I couldn't resist the rows after rows of books. Sometime in high school, I decided to read my way through the fiction section, not by reading every book, just those by authors I'd heard of. I'd loved *A Tale of Two Cities*, which we'd been assigned in school, so I pulled some Charles Dickens off the shelf, but I found *David Copperfield* heavy going. *Great Expectations*, though, with its tighter plot, caught my fancy. After Dickens, I came to Lloyd C. Douglas, whose book *The Robe*, about a soldier and a slave who left Calvary with Christ's crucifixion garment, had been made into a popular movie. It was a wonderful read, as were the other Douglas books I checked out, *Magnificent Obsession* and *Green Light*. I somewhat guiltily passed over George Eliot, of whom I had heard, but I knew her through *Silas Marner*, a book assigned in school that was so lugubrious it nearly ruined Eliot for me for a lifetime. Fortunately, I later learned to appreciate her work, indeed, to love her masterpiece *Middlemarch*.

In the J's, I found James Joyce, whom I wasn't sure I'd heard of, but one of his books was called *Ulysses*, and that sounded familiar, so I checked it out. When I opened the book on the bus on my way home, I nearly fell off my seat at the graphic descriptions of sex—though with no punctuation, you had to concentrate hard to catch them. Somebody would be thinking about the weather and then suddenly veer into territory that was entirely new to me—and pretty interesting. Did Miss Burke, the librarian, have any idea what she had on her shelves?

I'd never seen anything like *Ulysses* before, and while I didn't think my mother would open it to check what I was reading, just to be on the safe side, I hid the book in the laundry hamper as soon as I walked through the front door. In the middle of the night, it occurred to me that anyone coming across it there would figure out it was hidden, so I got up and put it under the couch, though not too far. If someone found it, it should look as though it had been accidentally kicked there, and besides, I needed to be able to retrieve it without making a scene. For the entire time that I had *Ulysses* checked out, I worried that my parents were going to find out what was in it, which didn't prevent me from keeping it for the full two weeks and skimming through it whenever I could, looking for the good parts.

Even in the '50s, Miss Burke, the librarian, was talking about tearing down the Carnegie building and putting something better in its place. The old building no doubt had its disadvantages, but the urge for new construction was characteristic of Westerners and still is today. Perhaps it has to do with our being descended from people who wanted to leave older parts of the country for someplace new. Maybe we're determined to keep it new, or maybe we just want better, as our ancestors so fervently did. Whatever the cause, many a building with some age on it has gone under the wrecking ball, including, in 1970, the Carnegie Library. A new library with a curving window wall stands in its place.

About three-quarters of a mile away, Arthur Garbutt's high school building remains, though there is talk about its having outlived its usefulness as a school. That may be true if you consider such measures as the square footage of individual classrooms, small by today's standards, but surely there are other matters to keep in mind: the soaring spaces in the auditorium, the crenellated tower reaching to the sky, and the words from the time of our country's beginning engraved by the front door: "Religion, morality, and knowledge, being necessary to good government and the happiness of mankind, schools and the means of education shall forever be encouraged."

CHAPTER SIXTEEN

ALTHOUGH NATRONA COUNTY HIGH SCHOOL was a public school, girls wore uniforms, and Barbara Scifers, dean of women, was in charge of making sure we did not deviate from the requirements: straight, dark skirts (no pleats) and white blouses (always with collars and sleeves). We could wear sweaters, but they had to be in addition to the blouses, not in place of them, and Mrs. Scifers could spot a dickey, a forbidden item of clothing that was basically a blouse collar with no blouse attached, a mile away. She also had a keen eye for skirt lengths, and if she asked you to kneel (the rule was your skirt had to touch the floor when you were on your knees), you generally knew your goose was cooked.

I suppose that on the theory that boys were unlikely to become consumed by clothes, they had no uniforms, except during their sophomore year, when they were required to take ROTC. Girls didn't seem to mind this difference in rules, mostly, I suspect because we didn't mind the uniforms. If they seemed aimed at disguising our shapes rather than revealing them, so did most of the clothes of the '50s. The skirts we wore to dances and on uniform holidays assumed *Gone with the Wind* proportions after we put layers of starched petticoats underneath. Even when we wore that most daring of gowns, a strapless formal, we might as well have been fully armored, since underneath it was a "merry widow," a contraption of corset stays, foam, and snaps that I knew from family experience was incompatible with a full meal. My mother once fainted at the Elks Club after consuming several banquet courses in her merry widow.

Girdles were also part of our lives, insurance that no part of us bounced when we wore the outfits we particularly prized, Jantzen suits, which were sweaters with matching knit skirts that you saved your money and bought for about twenty-five dollars at Kassis Department Store or in the sportswear corner at Kistler Tent and Awning. Girdles for underneath came in many brands—Lastex, Formfit, Youthcraft, Gossard—but most popular was Playtex, which came in a slender tube, the advertising point being that you would be slim if you wore it. Playtex advertised its product as having no seams, stitches, or bones, a feat achieved by constructing it completely of rubber. The garment had "pores," ostensibly to let air through, but when you encase yourself in rubber, little holes are little help. The Playtex girdles were not only sweaty but also noisy. When you sat or bent over, the top rolled down, and when you straightened up, it unrolled with a loud snap.

Uniforms weren't sexy, but little we wore was. And uniforms were easy, limiting the number of fads you had to worry about on any given school day. A necklace of pop-it beads was a possibility, as were furry balls on a velveteen cord, another accessory that we considered the height of fashion. You could wear the beads, the balls, or a scarf as long as you ran them under your collar, but if you were so daring as to wear them above it, you were going to hear from Mrs. Scifers.

And even if your uniform was perfect, you might hear from her. Joining the other adults in our lives who monitored what we were doing, she took it upon herself to try to steer us past trouble.

BLUE SKIES, NO FENCES

She once called in one of my friends, Beverly Bunce, to tell her to stop dating a certain boy because he was just too wild, advice that Bev, no shrinking violet, took to heart.

For the most part, we didn't think about our teachers having a life outside of school, but we were aware of Mrs. Scifers's because with her husband, Leland, an accountant at the Texaco Refinery, she opened an Arthur Murray dance studio in Casper. Later named the Barbara-Lee School of Dance, it displayed a neon sign impossible to miss as you drove down CY Avenue and was the place where thousands of Casperites, including my sixth-grade brother, learned their way around the dance floor. Mark was there under protest, not agreeing at all with my mother's assessment that he needed to polish his dancing skills, but he reports that he behaved himself—being left absolutely no choice by Mrs. Scifers. "I was scared to death of her," he says, and so were we all.

Like so many of our teachers at NCHS, Barbara Scifers had grown up in the West. She'd ridden horseback from her family's Montana homestead to a one-room schoolhouse in Pleasant View and later sold her horses to pay her way to the University of Montana. She moved to Casper to marry Leland, began to work in the schools, and as the years passed and they had no children, she directed her considerable energy not only toward students but to a host of benevolent organizations, from the American Association of University Women to philanthropic and service groups such as Zilah and Zonta. Together with her husband, she also taught a credit course in ballroom dancing at Casper College for fifty-one years, and before he died in 2003, the two of them, savers and investors, gave the college a gift of $1 million. Mrs. Scifers, still formidable in her ninth decade, also endowed five scholarships to benefit the college's students and faculty.

Not long ago, she videotaped a birthday greeting for me.

"Lynne Ann," she said, "you will always be a girl to me," a sentiment that brought tears to my eyes with its reminder of how few remain of the adults we knew in our youth. It also called up long-ago times when the world was innocent, and Mrs. Scifers, striding forcefully down the halls, was bound and determined to keep it that way.

One of her methods was to make sure her girls knew the rules right from the beginning. She organized orientation events for incoming ninth-graders, such as one in 1956 in which she had members of Girls' League Council, a group of elected representatives from every class, model behavior that incoming freshmen should avoid. Cile Pace, her white blouse untucked, slip showing from underneath her dark skirt, was Sloppy Sal. I followed soon after as Flighty Fran, a scatterbrain trailing papers and questions: "Have you seen my book?" "Where's my English class?" "Is there a test today?" Floozy Flo, in tight clothes, all made up, provided another cautionary example, as did Amorous Ann, who was supposed to show how awful it was to hang on boys in the hallways, though with a cute upperclassman helping her play her role, she may have sent a mixed message. There was no question, however, that the type to emulate was Ideal Girl, who appeared last, neat, poised, and calm. As the *Gusher* explained in its report on our skit, she "is always in uniform, studies until she knows her lessons, and is friendly with all."

The do's and don'ts for school hours were clear, thanks to Mrs. Scifers, and so were the rules for out-of-school behavior, although no one spelled them out so explicitly. As my best friend in high school, Mary Grant, remembers it, the list of what was forbidden and permitted boiled down to three things: "No drugs, no sex, and plenty of kissing."

The first rule wasn't much of a challenge, because drugs such as marijuana, cocaine, and heroin simply weren't part of our experience. Maybe if you'd searched hard in the Sandbar, you could have found something to get high on, but if so, we didn't know about it. We gave drugs so little thought that when *The Man with the Golden Arm*, a movie about heroin addiction, came out, we thought of it mainly as a source of great music. At Junior Follies, an entertainment put on by the junior class each year, the best dancers in the class of 1959—Ron Lewis, Mel Brouillette, Diane Chase, and Karen Brewer—performed to the *Golden Arm* music dressed as French Apache dancers, as though the movie had been set in Montmartre rather than Chicago.

Alcohol—a drug, although we didn't think of it that way—was available, but mostly to boys as they approached senior year and could talk older friends into buying liquor for them. Girls experimented, but usually in harmless ways. When we heard you could get high by dissolving two aspirins in a Coke, we tried that a few times, to no noticeable effect. In our senior year, one of my friends acquired a bottle of cherry vodka, brought it to a slumber party, and we mixed it with Coca-Cola, imagining that the result would be something like a cherry Coke. In reality, the mixture was so disgusting we couldn't drink it.

The school had assemblies with speakers and movies to warn of the dangers of drinking and driving, but it happened anyway, and there were accidents. The class of 1958, a year ahead of ours, lost five young men in two tragic car wrecks. One of them was my friend Mary's older brother, Denny Grant, a dark-haired, dreamy-eyed senior who could charm the birds out of the trees. After a football game in Douglas, a town sixty miles away, he hitched a ride with a carload of friends, and on the road to Casper, their car, traveling more than 100 miles an hour, slammed into the back end of a truck loaded with pipe. Weeping students gathered in sad knots in school hallways in the days following the accident, trying to comprehend a fact we had known but never really believed: death can come in youth as well as age. I had dated Denny for several months when I was a freshman and he a sophomore, and a few weeks after he was killed, his mother sent me a prayer card from his funeral at St. Anthony's and a few things she'd found among his possessions—a discount movie coupon issued when I was a freshman, pictures that he'd torn out of the newspaper when we were dating. Coming across an envelope of these things as I write this book, I think about the many, many years he missed.

Mary inherited Denny's 1948 candy-apple-green Ford, pinstriped in white and upholstered in white leather, and every morning for the rest of our time at NCHS, she drove from her house on North Kimball all the way to Westridge to pick me up for school. Some days, particularly if it was a day when we didn't have to wear uniforms, she would arrive to get me wearing white gloves—shorties, we called them, because they ended at the wrist. Nobody else at NCHS showed up in white gloves, but that didn't matter to Mary, who was confident the shorties were a great fashion statement, whether anyone else was wearing them or not. Dark-haired with dark, almond-shaped eyes, she picked me up on one uniform holiday wearing the gloves with a pink-and-white-striped polished-cotton dress, looking exactly like a *Seventeen* cover girl.

All these years later, she e-mails me her observations on our high school years from San Francisco State University, where she works in administration. "No sex and plenty of kissing," her take on the '50s, captures the idea that for all the restraints imposed upon us, we had a very good time. Indeed, it was probably because of the restraints that C Hill, a place where couples parked after movies and dances, was something we laughed about. Since nothing very serious was likely to occur there, we didn't take it very seriously. In one April Fool's issue of the *Gusher*, student editors suggested that the area "be blacktopped and zoned into parking places." Nearby was a photograph, reputedly of C Hill, but actually a junkyard, showing the supposed problem—so many parked cars that the front bumpers of some rest atop the rear bumpers of others. Another proposal that *Gusher* editors advanced was to prohibit foot traffic on C Hill, a suggestion aimed at certain boys who thought nothing funnier than to sneak up behind a parked car and bounce it up and down or, if they happened to have a few firecrackers, to stuff them up the tailpipe.

The prohibition on premarital sex wasn't always obeyed, but it was a limit that we all knew about, a line that girls crossed at their peril in these years before the birth control pill. Our mothers were the chief enforcers. We knew that if we got pregnant, they would kill us—or at least, that's how we expressed the reaction we anticipated. What we really meant, I think, is that if we got pregnant, we would break their hearts.

Guilt, not information, was the main weapon our mothers wielded, and it's almost impossible to imagine how naïve we were. I got the "how do babies get in there" talk when I came home in grade school with a joke that I didn't understand (and can no longer remember) but that my classmates found hilarious, and so I figured my parents would. It inspired my mother to tell me about birds, bees, and people, but in a way so bare-boned that for many months, I thought that sex was something you had once in your life to start your baby machine in motion. Once it started rolling, you could call up as many babies as you wanted. A helpful sixth-grader straightened me out, telling me that once wasn't enough. You had to have sex every time you wanted a baby, a useful piece of knowledge even before you got started down the baby road, she told me, since it allowed you to look at any married couple, count their children, and figure out how many times they had done it. A friend who went down the same misinformation byway tells me that she was actually embarrassed to look at married couples with large families, since the evidence was there for all to see that they had had sex repeatedly.

There was one sex education class—for girls only—in sixth or seventh grade, and that was the end of it. As we advanced through high school, we figured things out, but with very little help from parents and teachers. The adult consensus, I believe, was that we didn't need to know very much to live by the rule, which was don't do it before you're married. And for the most part, we didn't.

I recently came across a speech that sociologist David Riesman delivered in Chicago in 1958, the year we were juniors, which makes me wonder if the habits of our small town lagged behind behavior in other places. In his speech, Riesman worried that middle-class youngsters were becoming increasingly permissive in their behavior, losing their inhibitions as they abandoned a "traditional orientation towards the future." But at Natrona County High School, particularly among girls, the opposite was true. In our late-settled part of the country, many of us were the first females in our families even to consider going to college. We had an orientation toward the future that our mothers and grandmothers had not had—and an additional reason not to get pregnant. And although there was a double standard, with girls paying a much higher price for premarital sex than boys, the situation was not black and white. Boys as well as girls knew that parenthood would likely end their plans for college.

Looked at from one angle, the restrictions we lived with were a fence, a boundary, but viewed from another perspective, they were the opposite, a way of setting us free from our biology so that we could go on with education and contemplate careers. In an age of birth control pills and legalized abortion, there are other ways to achieve this end, but it is not clear to me or to classmates I've talked to that today's young people are necessarily better off. "I worry about my grandchildren," says Bernie See-baum, who now lives in Douglas, Wyoming, and a few days later, another classmate echoed him exactly. To those of us who came of age in the 1950s, today's culture, bombarding young people from every side with messages about sex, seems destructive, a push to grow up too soon, a threat to youthful stability and well-being. We also realize that, as much as we might wish it, there's no going back. We cannot give our grandchildren the gift that we had: time to mature, years to develop judgment.

But as good as the rules of the '50s were for most of us, they were not good for everyone. Assuming as they did that boy-girl romance would be a centerpiece of high school life, they were hard on late blossomers and on kids who were gay—as we know, all these years later, some of our schoolmates were. That possibility never even occurred to most of us then. It was a measure of our naïveté that for decades, an NCHS organization called Big Sisters sponsored an event called the Co-ed Ball that involved senior girls asking freshman girls to a dance and going to pick up their dates dressed as boys. In 1955, my freshman year, the ball was billed as an old-fashioned barn dance. As the *Casper Tribune-Herald* reported it in the vocabulary of the times, "The older girls, dressed in male attire, country-style, squired the freshman girls gay in cottons." The Co-ed Ball was held annually for more than three decades without anyone making jokes about it, at least as far as I can tell. It ended my sophomore year, not because anyone thought there was anything untoward about the seniors cross-dressing—who even knew that term?—but because, as Barbara Scifers explained to me recently, the number of freshmen exceeded the number of seniors, and "there were too many freshman girls crying because they didn't have dates."

The rules of the 1950s benefited most, but not all, and they were hardest on girls who got pregnant. They were expected to get married, as women had been for untold generations, but they were also expected to drop out of school, a harsh requirement in an era in which education through high school and beyond was increasingly held up as an ideal. For a high school girl in the 1950s, a pregnancy threatened everything. It had consequences that any adult would have had trouble managing, which makes all the more impressive the steadiness and strength girls I knew well brought to this crisis in their lives.

Vicky Lagos and I became friends when I was in kindergarten, she in first grade, and her family moved to Casper, where her father, like mine, went to work at the Bureau of Reclamation. My parents spent many evenings with the Lagoses—Pearl, pretty and warm, and Pete, universally thought of as the nicest guy you'd ever want to meet. Born in Wyoming of Greek immigrant parents, he had no airs, no pretense, and a remarkably positive outlook on life.

Vicky became a lovely, slender teenager, with dark pixie hair. She was respected by her peers, who elected her to Girls' League Council and Canteen Council, and loved by Bill Ford, her longtime steady boyfriend. In their senior year, the Lagoses announced that Vicky and Bill would marry on Sunday, February 9, 1958, but in the early hours of the morning before the wedding, as Bill and three friends were driving home from his bachelor party, their car ran into a barrow pit, then plunged into a ravine, killing all four.

Even in the midst of mourning, Bill's father tried thinking of ways for Vicky and Bill to be married, a proxy wedding, perhaps, whereby someone would stand in for Bill and take the marriage vows for him, but such a thing wasn't possible. Since school administrators had a history of looking the other way as long as pregnancies weren't obvious, Vicky went back to school, attending classes until a few weeks before graduation, when someone, apparently indignant that rules were being violated, complained to school officials, setting an investigation under way that would not have been out of place in a Nathaniel Hawthorne novel. At one point, Vicky remembers, school authorities came to her house to see if her pregnancy showed. It didn't, but they asked her to leave NCHS anyway, prompting students to begin a petition drive in her defense, which in turn forced a school board vote, but only two board members supported her. She had to leave school, the board decided, and while she could receive a diploma, she could not sit on the stage with her classmates at graduation.

Through all of this, Vicky carried herself with amazing dignity and composure. When I told her recently that I had discovered in an old *Gusher* that her classmates had named her "most poised girl" at the end of the year, she credited her mother and Bill's for giving her "confidence and love to go on with life." On graduation night, when her classmates saw her entering a side door to the auditorium to take a seat in the audience, they applauded.

Vicky had her baby, and in a few years, with continued love and support from her family and Bill's, moved with her little girl to California, where she fell in love with a young Navy lieutenant. They married, he went on to have a successful career in law, and Vicky has California grandchildren now. With Natrona County High School almost fifty years in the past, she is comfortable with my telling her story, and I'm grateful for that, since it gives me a chance to acknowledge the lesson she taught so many of us so early about courage and grace.

Barbara Riley's is another story that has stayed with me over the years. In late summer, following the year we were both freshmen, Barbara, a bright and pretty girl with abundant brown curls, married my cousin Ron Lockwood, who had just graduated from NCHS, and their son Mike was born the following spring. Two years later, they divorced, and Ron joined the Army, where he would have a nearly thirty-year career. But even after their divorce, Barbara reminded me recently, she was part of Lybyer family dinners, which, as my grandmother grew older, were often held at the Lockwood house. "Maxine told me that I would always be her daughter-in-law," Barbara says, and so, after eating ourselves silly, she and I would stand side by side at the sink, working our way through piles of dishes.

The year before she entered Natrona County High, Barbara, a student at St. Anthony's Catholic school, had been elected May Queen by her classmates. From model Catholic girl to pregnant teen to fifteen-year-old mother was a precipitous fall, made all the more so by rules that prohibited not only expectant mothers but mothers from attending our high school. By the time the rules changed our senior year, allowing mothers to go to school, Barbara had earned enough correspondence credits that she didn't need the second semester in order to graduate. Her life had been upended by marriage, motherhood, and divorce, but she was eligible for her diploma ahead of her classmates and graduated along with the rest of us.

There were some rough times after that, including a second marriage and divorce and some years in San Francisco when Haight-Ashbury was at its peak, but no matter what else was going on in her life, Barbara worked hard. She had learned touch-system typing from a correspondence course and, with a type-writer her sister had given her, earned money producing master's theses and legal briefs. She soon realized there was no mystery to what the people who'd written these documents were doing. She could do it if she dedicated herself, and so, by taking a course here and a course there, she managed to put a B.A. degree together, then earned an M.A. in public administration with an emphasis on criminal justice. She retired recently after working thirty-five years in the criminal justice system.

When she was at the beginning of her career and working with troubled teens, she often cited her own experience to encourage them not to give up. "I've had teenagers tell me there's no sense trying, they're in too deep," she says, "and I tell them that I was once fifteen and pregnant, and I made my way out." The idea that her story will prove useful to others motivates her still. Before I telephoned her, I asked a mutual friend if she thought Barbara would like to talk to me for this book, and word came back that she would be happy to, with the thought in mind that her story might help someone else.

A practicing Catholic, Barbara has been married for twenty-four years to a musician, a former lead guitarist for the Righteous Brothers. She lives in Nevada but remembers Casper as "a really sweet place, a great place to grow up." When I asked her how she accounts for the refusal to give up that allowed her finally to succeed when failure would have been so easy, she talked about her roots. "I came out of good, hardworking Wyoming stock," she said, from people who taught her about faith, honesty, and respect. She also made an important distinction between the rules we grew up with and the enduring qualities we were taught to admire. "I got pregnant at fifteen," she said, "but I never gave up my values."

CHAPTER SEVENTEEN

LOOKING THROUGH an old scrapbook, I see that by the time I was in high school, I was sometimes identified in the *Casper Morning Star* by my first name—"Lynne Returns from St. Paul Winter Carnival Festivities." This was the result, I suspect, of repetition and exhaustion. My mother got my name in the paper so many times that everybody involved got tired of writing the whole thing down.

It also helped that practically any time two or more people gathered, I was there with my baton. Old news clippings report that I twirled at a Democratic picnic at the North Casper Clubhouse, at a gathering of Women of the Moose, and at a band concert in Washington Park, where I was on the program with Miss Brubaker, a lyric soprano who sang a solo from *Madame Butterfly*. I twirled at the opening of the Dave Johnson Power Plant in Glenrock, performing right after the Koshare Indians from Colorado, and once appeared in a synchronized swimming show, even though I was a nonswimmer. My mother understood completely that I didn't want to get my hair wet and turn my eyes red and swollen and, not liking the idea of my being in the water in any case, regularly wrote excuses to get me out of required swimming classes. The result was that I was hard put to sustain a dog paddle, but you didn't have to be a water nymph to do what I did—twirl energetically aboard a small raft as it was towed from one end of the high school pool to the other.

One evening at the Casper Women's Club house, I followed JoAnne Blower, a girl two years ahead of me who had won national recognition for her dramatic readings. She did a scene in which Joan of Arc prays before her execution, stopping every once in a while to go "ding-dong, ding-dong," indicating bells in a nearby church tower tolling the passage of time. After her last "ding-dong, ding-dong," JoAnne as Joan exited somberly to be burned at the stake, whereupon I leaped onto the stage brandishing two flaming batons.

I twirled one baton, two batons, a hoop baton, and an electric baton, in addition to the fire batons, which were the real crowd pleaser. Probably in violation of a dozen fire laws, I would arrive at a performance with a gallon of white gasoline and a mason jar into which I would pour it and soak the ends of the batons. Before I lit them, I tucked my hair into a bathing cap, not a great look but better than the smell of singed hair. After three or four minutes of throwing the flaming batons into the air and usually catching them, I'd run offstage, where some willing soul held metal tubes into which I slid the batons. Then I capped the tubes, extinguishing the flames.

All summer long, I was in parades, leading the Casper Municipal Band. One year, someone decided I should match my costume to a new number the band was playing, "Hold That Tiger." The result was that I marched down many a Wyoming street wearing a tiger-striped leotard trimmed with gold sequins that my mother made, an outfit that was, in those modest times, considerably more modest than it sounds.

My mother continued to look for ways that I could improve, and in the summer of 1955 sent me to a baton-twirling clinic at

Pepperdine University in California presided over by Bob Roberts, who had impressed Casperites with his ability to twirl and roller skate at the same time. I polished my routine there, but not enough, because that August, Patti Dunston, an athletic girl with a big smile from Cheyenne, took the junior state championship title away from me. She, it turned out, had been taking lessons from Ann-Nita Ekstrom, a Carlisle, Indiana, girl who had won the national twirling championship in 1954. The next summer, I was on a plane to Minneapolis to take lessons from the 1956 national champion, Patte Genin, who was a truly impressive athlete. My mother and I had seen her perform at the St. Paul Winter Carnival, where she appeared with the Schmidt's Indians, a drum and bugle corps that could take the roof off an arena. The corps would march onto the floor, raise the rafters with "From the Land of the Sky-Blue Water," and Patte, wearing a full Indian headdress, would hurl one baton after another into the air and steal the show.

I won the senior state championship in 1956, helped by my lessons with Patte Genin and by the fact that Patti Dunston was still in the junior division. When she moved to the senior division in 1957, she beat me again. I had met my match, although unless you followed these matters with dedication, that probably wasn't apparent. There was always another contest—the Colorado Open in Pueblo, a Western Plains competition in Cheyenne—that I could win, particularly if Patti didn't show up, and if I did prevail, you could bet it would be in the paper. When I was named Queen of the Mile-High Twirling Contest in Denver, it made the front page. When I managed to place seventh in the national competition at the St. Paul Winter Carnival in 1957, that was front-page news, too. My mother saw to it that Governor Milward Simpson sent me a letter of congratulations, and that became a hook for two more newspaper stories.

*In 1954, I was Wyoming's junior champion baton twirler.
The next year, Patti Dunston, far right, beat me.*

*I caught a break in 1956 when Patti stayed in the junior division
and I moved up. Fair board member G. G. Nicolaysen
presents the senior state championship medal.*

My mother worked pretty much on her own to burnish my reputation as a baton twirler, but there were other areas of my teenage life for which she recruited help, particularly after my freshman year, when I began to put on weight, maybe ten or fifteen pounds. I wasn't bothered by the extra pounds, until one day, when I walked to school wearing a mouton coat, a trendy item of apparel in the 1950s. *Mouton* is a fancy word for sheep, and these coats were made of sheepskin that had been processed and sheared in hopes of looking like something expensive. My particular coat had also been dyed navy blue, and I was quite proud of it, and myself, until one of my friends declared that she'd seen me walking down the street and thought I looked like a navy blue bear. When I got home, I stood on the coffee table in our front room, took a good look at myself in the mirror over the couch, and concluded my friend had a point. In tears, I called my mother, who sprang into action, buying a tape measure and a scale and consulting her cousin Willocine, who had put aside her career as a hairdresser to sell Stauffer weight reduction equipment. We went to Willocine's apartment on North Beech to try out the Stauffer machine, which was a kind of cot you lay down upon that rocked you back and forth. After a couple of sessions, we concluded I had lost an inch and a few pounds, so my mother talked Willocine into letting us rent a machine. We set it up in my bedroom, and twice a day, I'd go in and rock for thirty minutes, but unfortunately, neither the inches nor the pounds continued to drop.

Next was a '50s version of a high-protein diet that involved eating hardboiled eggs and grapefruit at every meal. The problem was that the high school cafeteria didn't serve either hardboiled eggs or grapefruit, so my mother brought my grandmother into the plan, arranging for me to eat lunch in her apartment near the high school. I must have cheated on the egg and grape-fruit regimen, because I didn't lose weight, which led us to a '50s version of a liquid diet, a concoction of condensed milk and veg-etable oil, the taste of which improved marginally if you kept it very cold and shook it really hard before you drank it. My grand-mother was part of that scheme as well, as she was of dealing with the result: great swollen places all over my face and neck, probably, the doctor said, an allergic reaction to consuming so much of certain foods. Now I spent my lunch hours in my grandma's apartment, holding hot towels soaked in Epsom salts on my face. My grandmother, wearing rubber gloves, took the towels out of a galvanized tub in which she'd dissolved the Epsom salts in boiling water and passed them to me as soon as they'd cooled enough to put on my skin.

Concluding that my difficulty losing weight must mean my thyroid was running slow, the doctor prescribed diet pills—Dexedrine, probably—and they worked like a charm. I wasn't hungry, and I was extremely energetic, cleaning out every drawer in my room and then in the entire house. I got rid of five pounds fast, but no one involved in my weight-loss effort thought that renewing the prescription was a good idea.

About the time we'd exhausted all remedies, my other grandmother, the formidable Anna Vincent, came to town. She listened to my dieting woes, looked me up and down, and de-clared, "You're not fat. You're young, and you're lovely." I wasn't convinced. I still didn't like the way I looked and would have given anything to lose weight, but her assessment, delivered with her customary authority, took some of the edge off my anxi-eties. If I didn't want to look like a blue bear, I started thinking, maybe the first thing to do was get rid of the mouton coat. And while I was at it, I should put away the skirts with six petticoats underneath. That was another bad look—unless you were Carol Lynley, a model for *Seventeen* magazine whom I admired extravagantly. She even looked good in Bermuda shorts.

In any issue of *Seventeen*, Carol Lynley might appear a dozen times, modeling everything from Peter Pan blouses to Art-carved diamond rings, to Chanel perfume. With gleaming blond hair, blue eyes, and delicate features, she epitomized the wholesome beauty of the '50s—an image that she seems to have wearied of in the '60s, when she posed nude for *Playboy*. But when she was appearing in *Seventeen*, she was the queen of the magazine, enough of a draw that in 1958, the editors ran a long interview with her. She confessed to having trouble with her complexion and her weight, which was reassuring though not entirely believable. She looked just right, and I decided that her eyebrows were a big part of it. Thin and elegant, they deserved to be imitated, and so I attacked my own brows with a pair of tweezers. It is not easy when you undertake a radical brow restructuring to keep both brows the same. It's a little like trying to even up the legs of a table. You trim one down, and it turns out shorter than the others, so you trim them, and pretty soon your table has no legs. And pretty soon I had no eyebrows.

When I think back on the early years of high school, I realize how different life was for boys, who weren't spending much time worrying about how they looked. The top leisure priority for many of them was to get outdoors, out on the prairies with a rifle or on the streams with a rod. My future father-in-law, Richard Cheney, bought his sons, Dick and Bob, a bolt-action .22 that they used to hunt rabbits, usually in the winter or early spring. Dick got his driver's license in the middle of his freshman year, and he and Bob, using the family car, would go along Hat Six Road or out by Bessemer Bend to hunt. They'd bring home what they shot and clean the rabbits, and Marge Cheney would fry them up so the boys could take them to school for lunch.

When Bob got his own rifle—a .22 semiautomatic—Dick got the bolt-action. Sometimes he and his friend Tom Fake would go after rabbits west of town, or if it was fishing season, they might head to Alcova, a lake created by a dam about thirty miles from Casper. They used spinners most of the time, though when the lake froze and they fished through ice, worms were the bait of choice. One summer, Tom, Dick, and two other football players, Brock Hileman and T. J. Claunch, drove forty-five miles to Arminto, Wyoming, where they turned onto a dirt road that took them to the top of the Big Horn Mountains. From the camp they set up on top of the Big Horns, they could follow the middle fork of the Powder River down into a deep canyon that was seldom fished. They stayed out there for a week, the four of them climbing down into the canyon every day and fly-fishing. With a fiberglass rod he'd bought at the hardware store and a half-dozen flies, Dick discovered a sport he would love for a lifetime.

But not every fishing trip was a success. Dick, Tom, and Mike Golden, a football player a year younger, had a memorably miserable day at Boysen Reservoir outside Shoshone. Cold, wet, their creels entirely empty, they went to Joe's Pool Hall on Center Street when they got back to Casper, and while they were shooting a game, somebody brought up the pond that haberdasher Harry Yesness had donated to the city for kids fourteen and under to fish. Dick and Tom were sixteen, but when they heard that Yesness Pond had just been stocked, they decided that after the miserable day they'd had, they deserved to catch something, so they drove out south of Casper and, as the sun was going down, walked into the pond. They cast in, and Tom got a bite. He'd just reeled the fish to shore when a voice came out of the dusk. "Fellas, how old are you?" The game warden who had been staking out the pond took them down to the courthouse, where Justice of the Peace Alice Burridge fined them twenty dollars apiece—and confiscated the fish.

One regular summer adventure was to crawl out onto the spillway of Alcova Dam and ride the water like a giant slide down into the Platte River. This feat came to a bad end a few times when sliders veered too far from the spillway's middle, where there was a buildup of slippery moss, and rode down the concrete, leaving behind a lot of skin.

When somebody came up with a pair of water skis, the guys figured out a way to use them without a boat. One of them would get into an irrigation ditch, put on the skis, and grab onto a rope tied to the back bumper of Joe Meyer's 1950 maroon Plymouth convertible. Joe would gun the car, taking off on the road alongside the canal and pulling the skier behind. It was a blast, though you had to strain to keep going down the center of the canal since the car was pulling you at an angle. If you messed up, you'd hit the bank—unless you let go of the rope really fast.

In the winter, when the roads got icy, Bill Henderson would pull John Mayer, Bernie Seebaum, or Dick Cheney in a snow saucer behind his 1932 Ford roadster with a Cadillac engine inside. Or sometimes they would slip and slide all over the place using the hood of an old Buick turned upside down. Once they dragged the Buick hood up to Casper Mountain and used it as a sled, but that ended when Bob Cheney went over a precipice into a willow-filled canyon. Eventually, and fortunately, Bob made it out, hardly the worse for wear, but the Buick hood, deep in the bushes, was never seen again.

CHAPTER EIGHTEEN

ATHLETES WERE THE center of attention in our small town, feted and fretted over, particularly if they played football. Even junior varsity intramural games were reported in the local paper. "Sparked by the running of Dick Cheney and quarterbacking of T. J. Claunch," reads one of the clippings that Marge Cheney saved from 1956, "the Whites came back with a last second touchdown to take a 14-13 win over the Greens in an intersquad reserve game at NCHS."

Starting in August, players got into their practice gear twice a day and ran up Elm Street past my friend Janet Baker's house to a dusty field west of Casper College that became their base for several hours, while they drilled and scrimmaged and ran sprints up C Hill. On the theory that drinking too much water kept you from getting in shape, the coaches rationed it, and when practice was over, the players running back down Elm Street frequently veered off into yards where lawns were being sprinkled, grabbed hoses, and tried to quench their thirst before being spotted by the coaches.

In 1957, these activities took on intense interest for the whole community. The previous season had been a bad one, with six losses, leading to the resignation of the coach and the elevation to the top slot of Harry "The Horse" Geldien, a former star tailback at the University of Wyoming and a biology teacher at the high school. Two weeks before the first game, the *Casper Morning Star* sent a reporter to the practice field to get the new head coach's assessment. "The boys are looking good, and if their willingness and desire continue, we may have a ball club yet," he told the *Star*. The *Casper Tribune-Herald* announced the first home game of the season in inch-high headlines ("Mustangs Open Grid Slate") and ran a couple of big photos, one of which showed Dick Cheney, a 145-pound junior, who was playing second-string halfback behind senior Lou Laske and first-string linebacker on defense.

On Friday night, playing the Worland Warriors before a near-capacity home crowd, the Casper Mustangs delivered, piling up five touchdowns and burying the Warriors 31 to 13. Football frenzy returned to Casper, and it became more intense the next Friday, when the Mustangs beat the Laramie Plainsmen, and the next, when they whipped the Douglas Bearcats. When they triumphed the following week over the Cheyenne Indians, the players lifted coach Geldien on their shoulders, and citizens of Casper were ecstatic. It was the first time in five years that the Mustangs had beaten their rivals from the state capital.

The following week, a couple of key players were sidelined with flu, but the Mustangs managed to beat the Torrington Trailblazers nonetheless. On Friday, October 11, they walloped the Rock Springs Tigers 26 to 0, with senior guard Ernie Trujillo, who would win his second All-State award for his play during the 1957 season, putting in an especially noteworthy performance.

Townspeople were elated. Sputnik had been circling the earth for more than a week, a huge fireball had been seen streaking across the Wyoming sky, but the Mustangs were in line to become state champs, and that deserved notice. Casper merchants bought two entire pages of the *Casper Tribune-Herald* to run individual pictures of the varsity players, declaring them "Wyoming's finest high school football team." Tom Fake's picture was sponsored by Steve Flowers Store for Men, Joe Meyer's by Berlet's Sporting Goods, and Dick Cheney's by Bi-Rite Pay-Less Drugs.

Then the Asian flu hit in full force. The pandemic of 1957, which was decimating school enrollments across the nation, claimed nearly every member of the Casper squad, forcing Coach Geldien to ask for a cancellation of a nonconference game with Rapid City, South Dakota. The Mustangs made their next scheduled encounter, also nonconference, with Grand Junction, Colorado, but, as the *Casper Morning Star* described it, "A fighting band of Casper Mustangs, weakened by the flu for ten days, ran out of gas in the final twelve minutes of action . . . and dropped a 13-0 verdict to the Grand Junction Tigers."

The next week, when the Mustangs were to meet the Sheridan Broncos, the only other conference team with just a single loss on its season record, the newspapers promoted the event from Monday on, describing the history of the two teams, the health of the Mustangs, the length of their drills, and probable lineups. Extra bleachers were set up in the stadium, nearly enough to accomodate the 4,500 people who turned out on Friday night to watch the game in freezing weather. Casper scored in the first quarter on a pass by Tom Fake caught by Brock Hileman that brought the crowd to its feet. Over in the band section of the bleachers, people grabbed for their mouthpieces, which they'd been keeping warm in their pockets, and jammed them on their horns to play our fight song, "All Hail to Casper High School." Then the snare drums set up a roll as the ball was snapped for T. J. Claunch, who kicked the football through the uprights, putting the score at 7 to 0.

By halftime, when the band gathered at the south end of the

stadium, snow was falling. Our drum major, Oscar Morris, had graduated, and since Mr. Coolbaugh, the band sponsor, hadn't yet found anyone tall and male to take the job, it fell to me to blow the whistle and get the band moving, majorettes first, high-stepping in white wool jackets and long pants and wearing white shako hats with yellow plumes. Next were the flag twirlers, dressed in orange and black, our school colors, then the trombones, trumpets, clarinets, drums, cymbals, saxophones, flutes, sousaphones, all marching double-time into the formations we'd practiced after school: a football, a mustang, the letters NCHS. Under the lights on the high plains of the Rockies, the band played, and the twirlers twirled, ignoring the falling snow.

Seven plays into the second half, the Broncos scored a touchdown and made the extra point, tying the game at 7 to 7. Within a few plays of taking the kickoff, the Mustangs were on the Sheridan two-yard line, but despite their best efforts and our loud cheering, they couldn't get the ball into the end zone then or for the rest of the game. When it was over, the two teams were tied, allowing both to claim to be state champs.

It wasn't quite what fans had been hoping for, but in a town where there'd been a long dry spell without a winner, it was enough. At a packed banquet at the Eagles hall, the Quarterback Club presented a three-foot-high trophy to Harry Geldien, who, by the time he retired from coaching seven years later, would have more winning games on his record than any previous coach. Each varsity player, including halfback Dick Cheney, received a white C—as opposed to the usual orange one—to wear on his black letter sweater, and each was given a small gold football charm that said "State Champ." From now on, there were two ways a boy could ask a girl to go steady. He could offer her his class ring, or, even more irresistibly, he could, if he was one of the varsity players from the 1957 football season, give her the gold football to wear on a chain around her neck.

No group of boys at NCHS had as much attention lavished on them as the football players, but there were other ways to be cool, chief among them to belong to one of the car clubs: the Deacons, the Saints, the Conquerors, the Knights, or the Vaqueros. Some of the guys joined the clubs for purely social reasons, but others fixed up old Fords and Chevys, putting V8 engines from Cadillacs and Chryslers in them. Some chopped and channeled their cars, took all the chrome off hoods, headlights, and trunks, and got spectacular paint jobs, many coats with hand rubbing in between that created jewel-like greens and reds and purples and yellows. Subtly pinstriped and exquisitely upholstered, these cars glowed as they cruised from the A&W west of town to the Brig, a drive-in up East Second Street that had the memorable motto "Don't be a pig at the Brig." The cars made their way through town with music from KATI, a local station, playing on their radios, or sometimes it was KOMA, a top 40 station out of Oklahoma City that you could pick up in Casper at night.

According to car club member John Mayer, it was possible to put 135 miles on the odometer on a single night and never leave the strip leading from the A&W to the Brig. But, as he puts it, "One had occasionally to demonstrate what one's $1,000 in speed parts would do," so cars would blast off on the road between the A&W and Garden Creek Bridge, or maybe there would be a matchup out on the old refinery road. "But the really big 'outlaw' drags," says John Mayer, "were held on the Hat Six Road, and we had some good ones! Until the highway patrol showed up."

Almost all the car club members had jackets involving a lot of leather. A few in the class ahead of ours cultivated ducktails,

On Saturday nights in Casper, it was cool to cruise between the Brig and the A&W.

turned up their shirt collars, and wore their pants low, a style that concerned high school administrators, who worried out loud that a clique was being formed. The guys loved the word and made it their own, calling themselves the Click. They often could be found around lunchtime at the Little Kitchen, a one-room restaurant across the street from the high school. Presided over by an elderly widow named Mary Evans, the Little Kitchen was a place where you could get great hamburgers, play a decrepit jukebox, and smoke.

Some members of the Click cultivated a bad boy image, no doubt about it, but most of the guys in car clubs could pass muster with even the pickiest mother. Eagle Scout Bernie Seebaum, owner of a lavender 1932 Ford roadster, was a Deacon, as were Jerry Moore, who lettered in six sports; John Mayer, one of our class officers; and Dave Nicholas, one of Frances Feris's stars. Ron Lewis, a Conqueror, took part in drama productions, dancing in *The Boyfriend* and *By the Beautiful Sea*. And car club members had a wide variety of futures—rancher, airline pilot, diplomat, and business executive, in the cases of Moore, Mayer, Nicholas, and Lewis. Bob Kechely, a football and basketball player who lived by himself in a trailer after his parents were killed in a car wreck, was in a car club and would become a pediatrician. Bryan Brewer, a few years ahead of us, created a gorgeous car by putting Pontiac taillights and a Kaiser grille on a 1949 Ford convertible and laquering it purple. The interior, remembers Dr. Brewer, currently director of lipoprotein and atherosclerosis research at Washington Hospital Center in Washington, D.C., was yellow leather, pleated and rolled.

To an unusual degree, I think, we grew up with the sense that you could do and be whatever you wanted. Some kids had to work to finance cars, clothes, and social life, but beyond that, as

Ron Lewis, whose father was an oil-field mechanic, puts it, "It didn't make any difference if your dad was a dishwasher at the Henning Hotel or president of a drilling company." And it didn't make any difference if you were a football player; you could also be in band, as was Joe Meyer, who played a hot clarinet. It didn't make any difference if you were editor of the annual; you could also win the Pillsbury Bake-Off for your peach pie recipe, as Paula Berry did. And, at least in the case of Tolliver Swallow, a tall, handsome blond kid who would become an airline pilot, it didn't make any difference if you were a cheerleader, which he was our junior year; you could also be a varsity football player, which he was the year we were seniors.

You could hang around the Little Kitchen if you were in the Click, but you could also eat lunch there if you were Ken Hoff, a varsity swimmer and possibly the cleanest-cut kid ever to graduate from NCHS. Ken admired Mrs. Evans's hamburgers and apple pie, as did Principal Bill Reese, who was frequently seen at the Little Kitchen during the noon hour. Members of the Click liked the two pool halls downtown, Joe's and the Rialto, but so did some student council members, including Tom Fake and Dick Cheney.

Girls had social sororities, four of them: Mustangs, Co-op, Eclat, and Tops, the group I joined. These clubs, complete with rush, bids, and hurt feelings, were anathema to high school administrators, who forbade club sweaters around school or any acknowledgment that the groups existed. In the school newspaper and annuals, you could read about athletic teams and car clubs but not sororities, which was probably as it should have been, though I suspect that most girls who really wanted to be in a club got into one, and it was impossible to typecast the membership. Cheerleaders were sure to be in social clubs, but class officers, National Merit Scholarship finalists, and D.A.R. good citizenship award winners were, too.

If sororities were an impediment to the idea that you could be and do anything you wanted, they were a minor one, partly because the clubs' main activity was so nonexclusive. We put on formal dances, one per club per year, pretty elaborate affairs, with rented buildings, decorations, bands, chaperones, and dance programs that came with their own small pencils for writing down which dance you had with whom. All of this amounted to a considerable up-front investment which we had to recover by selling tickets. We pushed them on every boy in school, each of whom could ask any girl who struck his fancy, so it didn't matter what club you were in or even if you were in a club, you might well end up at the fall formal put on by Tops or the Sweetheart Ball sponsored by Mustangs.

When the dances sponsored by the clubs were added to those put on by the school, there was a formal dance nearly every month of the school year, a good thing in terms of kids having things to do but, if you were a girl, a challenge in terms of finding things to wear. I had talked my grandmother into making me the red crinoline dress I'd dreamed of since grade school and had a green one as well, but when I'd worn both of those, it was time to trade with friends. Anyone paying attention would know that the formal I had on at the Eclat dance was the same one Becky Boyles had worn to the Military Ball a few weeks earlier, but we judged that far superior to wearing the same thing every time.

Denny Grant had been my boyfriend for a while, then Tom Fake, but about halfway through my sophomore year, I found myself without a regular date, which made the approach of every dance an occasion of hope and dread, hope that someone I actually wanted to go out with would ask me and dread that someone

I didn't really want to go with would call first. If that happened and you said yes, you were committed. You couldn't change your mind if someone you liked better asked you later. And a no could be pretty final, too. If you turned down one invitation on the grounds that you were busy that night, it was considered bad form suddenly to be un-busy when you got a call from someone else. Looking through a scrapbook of corsage ribbons, I see that it usually worked out, and I also see that there was one flower that really impressed a girl in mid-century Wyoming. "First orchid!" I wrote beside some silver ribbon from a corsage that Denny Grant brought me in 1956. "The prom, Dick, and a white orchid!" I wrote in 1958—but that's getting ahead of the story.

Boys paid for everything, and a formal dance with tickets and corsages was the most expensive way to go out with a girl. Movie dates were probably next, then Coke dates, and then, cheapest of all, Tuesday night at the Canteen, where the only investment was gas for the car. Sororities met on Tuesday nights, and so, conveniently, did car clubs, and after the meetings, about 7:00 P.M., everyone, whether in sororities, car clubs, or not, headed to the Canteen, a long, narrow building located in the 300 block of South David.

The Canteen had started in 1949 as a community undertaking, with one businessman donating the structure and a number of contractors refurbishing it for free. They paneled it with knotty pine, built a snack bar, and put in a hardwood dance floor. Local merchants donated some chairs, a couch, a ping-pong table, and, most important, a jukebox. You didn't have to put money into it, just punch in your favorite song—"Peggy Sue" if you felt like jitterbugging, "Young Love" for a slow dance. Fully chaperoned, often by teachers from the high school, the Canteen had rules forbidding drinking, smoking, and fighting, and even a

rule to ensure that you didn't go outside and do these things. I
remember Grant Boyles, a lovely man, father of Becky and a
counselor at the high school, making sure that kids who left
didn't come back in that same evening.

I often rode to the Canteen with Darla Howard, a fellow Tops
member who had come to Casper from Oklahoma and had an
ability to charm boys that was extraordinary. Once a male teacher,
trying to get her to stop flirting with a boy in class, told her to
"quit getting Eddie's hormones in an uproar," words for which
he had to apologize, not just because *hormones* was considered a
raw term but also because he had implied that flirting was about
sex, which was definitely not how we thought of it. Laughing
and joking and batting your eyes at a boy was simply a way of
letting him know you were interested in him as a *person*, an authority no less than *Seventeen* magazine assured us. Whether or
not boys saw it this way, they responded with mighty enthusiasm
when Darla gave them that certain look. She had so perfected the
'50s art of being alluring without ever sullying her reputation
that her female friends, of whom there were many, held her
in awe.

Her father was a Baptist minister who took an intellectual
interest in religion, studying Greek and Hebrew in his spare
time. Reverend Howard encouraged his children to keep up with
current events by quizzing them about the happenings of the day
at the dinner table, and he kept up with their lives, understanding what was important to them to such a degree that he gave
Darla what was recognized by all her girlfriends as the best
sixteenth birthday gift ever: a 1940 Hawaiian metallic bronze
Pontiac with a 1952 Pontiac engine inside. The guys who paid
attention to cars didn't think a '52 Pontiac engine was anything
special to have under the hood, but that's probably what Rever-

end Howard intended. We weren't going to be going anywhere very fast, but we would arrive there in style, particularly since the Pontiac came with a pair of fuzzy dice hanging from the rear-view mirror.

As a Baptist, Darla wasn't supposed to dance, a point her mother took quite seriously but that mine did not. She was willing to look the other way when a formal dance rolled around and Darla would arrive at our house, pull one of her piano recital dresses out of a bag, and get fixed up for a date. Darla would have told her mother she was spending the night with me, which was the truth, though not all of it, since it didn't include mention that we would be spending the evening dancing.

I shudder a little now at my mother's willingness to subvert the rules by which the Howards were trying to raise their daughter, but she was simply extending to Darla the same generally indulgent attitude she took toward me. If there were things I really did or didn't want to do, she wouldn't press, though sometimes, I suspect, she was tempted. One high school summer, my father bought a used motorboat that we hauled back and forth to Alcova Lake, and when I decided I wanted to water ski, she didn't say a word—even though she was terrified of water, and I, having talked her into writing excuses to get me out of high school swim classes, couldn't swim. She made sure I was wearing a life preserver, bit her tongue, and, I suspect, averted her eyes.

She also had little sympathy for a rule that said teenage girls shouldn't dance. That was as wrong in her view as a traffic ticket you didn't deserve, and so you ought to ignore the former and fix the latter—as she did one day when Darla was cited for parking her 1940 Hawaiian metallic bronze Pontiac on the sidewalk outside the Canteen.

CHAPTER NINETEEN

O N A JANUARY DAY in 1958, as I was walking out of Bob Lahti's chemistry class, Dick Cheney asked me if I would like to go to the Eclat formal with him. "You're kidding!" I responded, words he took to mean "What? Me go out with you?" But that wasn't it at all. I knew that he'd broken up with the blond cheerleader he had been dating but was not expecting that he'd ask me out. I never saw him when my friends and I were cruising between the A&W and the Brig, and he didn't go to basketball games, where a lot of socializing went on. His absence from the social scene, I'd later learn, was because he worked after school and on weekends, and, truth be told, I don't think he saw the point of circling between one drive-in and another, but here he was, asking me out, this smart, great-looking guy I sat next to in chemistry class, and, of course, I wanted to go, but I was surprised, and so I said, "You're kidding!" Fortunately for me, our children, and our grandchildren, he stayed around long enough for me to explain.

Darla Howard was spending the night with me so that she could go to the dance with Tom Fake, whom she had been seeing for a while, and on Friday night, Tom and Dick picked us up at my house in the Fake family's 1955 Pontiac, and we headed for a log cabin west of town owned by the Izaak Walton League, a conservation organization named after the famed seventeenth-century fisherman. Until recently, I assumed that the League's cabin, like so much in Wyoming, had been torn down, but a friend, assuring me it hadn't, directed me to a trailer camp-ground, where the old cabin now serves as a clubhouse. It's a lovely place still, a large, high-ceilinged room constructed of varnished logs and anchored by a pair of stone fireplaces. There was a band in one corner the night of the Eclat formal, and I danced with Dick Cheney, wearing the red dress my grandmother had made.

When the dance was over, Tom, who was driving, headed for C Hill, not a place I would have expected to go on a first date, but I do not remember protesting. We hadn't been there long when the C Hill pranksters struck, a fact we didn't notice right away—no doubt because they operated with such perfect stealth. There were at least two of them, and they crawled on their elbows until they reached the tires, which they proceeded to deflate, and the Pontiac, slowly but surely, sank toward the frozen prairie.

As the 10:30 curfew my mother had assigned to Darla and me approached and we started down the hill, it didn't take us long to figure out that something was very wrong. After Tom and Dick determined it was the tires, Tom drove very slowly back to town, figuring that he was never going to get the family car again if he showed up at home with ruined wheel rims. By the time we arrived at a gas station on CY Avenue to fill up the tires, it was past 11:00. I ran across CY to a phone booth, called home to explain, and found that my mother, whom I'd expected to be frantic and furious, was strangely serene. Her friends on the police force, I later learned, had kept her informed of our prog-ress throughout the evening.

That she wasn't upset probably also reflected the fact that she liked Dick from first meeting him. He didn't talk a lot, but it wasn't hard to get him involved in a real conversation and feel that he was comfortable with it. He wasn't dying to get out the front door and away from adults as teenage boys, shy to their toes, often were. She extended an invitation to Sunday dinner, which he accepted without hesitation, and he was thoroughly appreciative of her chicken and noodles. And it wasn't long before she discovered how competent he was. She had taken me and a few friends to a basketball tournament in Laramie when a winter storm hit. Afraid of the snowy roads, she asked Dick, who'd gone to Laramie with some of his friends, to drive us home, a task that under terrible conditions on the Medicine Bow Cutoff, a tricky road under any circumstance, he performed with reassuring proficiency. When summer came, my father also discovered he was a capable hand. Backing our secondhand motorboat down the boat ramp at Alcova Lake and getting it into the water occasioned much frustration and more than a little profanity on my father's part, until Dick came along and started helping out. It was also good to have him around when the motor flooded, since he had the patience necessary to get it started again, which my father decidedly did not.

Of course, I thought he was adorable. Asked by the *Gusher* to describe my ideal boy, I described Dick: "5' 10", has a sandy crew cut, gray eyes, and an athletic build." He was also—and I couldn't think of a better word then, and I cannot now—*nice*, alert to the fact that other people had feelings and you should treat them that way, a quality rare enough in the world, let alone among seventeen-year-old males. And he was never boring, though when he insisted on watching old movies on television, I worried about that. *Two Years before the Mast* and *Going My Way* seemed hopelessly dated to me. One night, when he was watching something like *And the Angels Sing*, a musical with Dorothy Lamour, Fred MacMurray, and Betty Hutton, I asked him why he liked old movies, and he shrugged, as if to say he just did, but then added, "You see people performing at their peak, and they don't know it." I suspect it was around this time that I said to myself, "Ah, that's what he's doing when he's not talking. He's thinking."

I also liked his family, which in many ways resembled mine. They lived in a tract house on the east edge of town; we were in one on the west. His mother didn't work whereas mine did, but she had before and intended to again as soon as Susie, a toddler, got a little older. Our fathers were both government employees, mine being a GS-12 for the Bureau of Reclamation, his a GS-12 for the Soil Conservation Service, but there was a major difference in how they thought of their jobs. My father was discontented, while Dick's father, no doubt remembering how his parents lost most of their life savings in the Depression, took great satisfaction in having a job that came with the security of Civil Service.

Dick's family also regularly got through dinner without World War III breaking out, which was definitely different from the way my household functioned. I'd given up thinking there was anything I could do about my parents' fighting and had adapted various tactics to get away from it, such as eating early and claiming I had homework to do in my room. Now I had a new one, which was eating at the Cheneys a lot. Marge would talk your leg off, while Dick's father, Richard, didn't talk much, but the whole experience was pleasant, easy. I still had fine times with my parents, too, occasions when we would joke and laugh, but whenever one occurred, I'd think, "Why can't it always be this way?" because so often it wasn't. My household was a volatile place, while Dick's was more serene, and that, I think, gave him a calmer soul.

In the spring of 1958, Dick surprised me, not for the last time in our lives, by announcing he was running for senior class president. There had been a spirited contest for student body president, in which debate star and car club member David Nicholas had prevailed over half a dozen other candidates. His father until recently had been mayor of Casper, and David, understanding that politics is about more than earnest speeches, had clinched his victory by arranging for a marching band to lead him onstage when it was his turn to address NCHS students. "I saw that and knew it was all over," remembers Tom Fake, who was running against him. When everyone was exhausted from the student body contests, Dick, who had never run for school office before, declared for the senior class president slot—and won easily.

I had his gold football by now, the little charm that said "State Champ," and wore it on a chain around my neck. He brought me home from the Canteen on Tuesdays, took me out on Saturday nights, and was my date for the prom. When annuals came out in the spring, we signed each other's book. Mine from that year is lost, but in his I wrote, "Dick, you are the neatest boy I've ever known."

In late May, he went to Boys State, held at the state fairgrounds in Douglas, Wyoming, and was elected a justice of the supreme court; I went to Girls State in the same place a few weeks later and was elected state treasurer. I don't know how important Girls and Boys State are in New York or California, but in a state with a small population like Wyoming, these gatherings are places where you're likely to meet people who will matter to you for the rest of your life. I met Margaret Webster

1958 football players, left to right, Jesse Palato, T. J. Claunch, Joe Meyer, Tom Fake, Dan Potter, Dick Cheney, John Hockett, Mike Cohee, Chet Boudreaux, and Chuck Satterfield.

In this Girls State picture, Maggie Webster from Cody is on the far right in the front row and I am next to her. I got to be state treasurer by promising to "double your mint."

from Cody there, Maggie Scarlett now, one of my best friends. On talent night at Girls State, she tap-danced, and I twirled the baton, and on the day we visited Cheyenne, we rode the Trailways bus together, all gussied up in suits, hats, heels, and gloves. Maggie had been elected superintendent of public instruction, and because we were both state officers, we got to stand right in the front row when the Girls Staters got their picture taken with Governor Milward Simpson, an event we might have forgotten, had not Milward's son, Senator Alan Simpson, found the photo in his father's papers and sent it to us more than forty years later.

One girl I haven't seen since but will never forget is Nancy Tate, a talented redhead from Sheridan who ran for governor of Girls State, a post she was widely expected to win. When she lost in a primary upset to Muggs Young, a sincere and thoughtful girl from Cody, she almost immediately took up her former rival's cause, campaigning for her with an enthusiasm so generous and genuine that it not only helped propel Muggs to victory in the general election, but it started a lot of us thinking that Nancy, as well as Muggs, ought to go to Girls Nation, and we elected the two of them as our representatives.

At the end of June, Dick went to Northwestern University. The teachers at NCHS had chosen him to attend an engineering and science institute for high school students there, and the Elks Club had given him a scholarship, making the whole thing an honor, I realized, but the program went on for five weeks, and when he left, it seemed it would be forever before he returned. In July, I went to Minneapolis to take baton lessons from Patte Genin, and when she suggested that we travel to a couple of contests in Wisconsin, I realized that once I got as far as Kenosha, Dick was only a short train ride away. Patte, a forward-thinking nineteen-year-old, thought it an excellent idea for me to go see him for a few hours, so he played hooky from the institute and I from baton twirling, and we met in Chicago. I did not tell my parents about the excursion, but had they learned of it and dished out serious punishment, it would still have been well worth it. How many times do you get to be sixteen and wander the green parkland along Lake Michigan with the boy you love?

That fall was a tough one for the football team, which had only eight returning varsity players and only one real veteran: Tom Fake. Beginning in August, Coach Geldien drilled them hard, but when Ray Giffen, a sportswriter for the *Casper Morning Star*, went to watch them block and tackle on a practice field turned brown from lack of rain, he found them "as green as the grass which has disappeared from the terra firma." In early September, the situation grew worse. Stalwart quarterback Tom Fake came down with blood poisoning, missing the first game, which the Mustangs lost to the Worland Warriors, 39 to 6.

Tom was back for the next game—a real thriller, it turned out—against the Laramie Plainsman. With just six minutes left and the Mustangs trailing 9 to 14, Casper end Jerry Moore fell on a Laramie fumble at the Plainsmen's 23-yard line, and half-back Dick Cheney carried the ball the next three plays, finally, as the *Laramie Boomerang* described it, "bouncing over from eight yards out." After the game, the happy Casper players carried Coach Geldien off the field.

But then they lost to Sheridan, managed only to tie Cheyenne, and lost to Torrington, in a game in which Tom Fake suffered a concussion that put him in the hospital. The outlook for the upcoming game against Rock Springs, to be co-captained by Dick Cheney and Tim Karnes, could hardly have been worse.

But it was homecoming, a generally happy time, with the band practicing under the leadership of our snappy new drum

Football co-captains Dick Cheney and Tim Karnes gave me a crown and a bouquet of roses.

The homecoming parade. Dick, wearing his letter sweater, and Dion Johnson are in the front seat.

Homecoming, 1958.

major, Willie Joe Mathis, a slender African American kid who led us through our maneuvers with a ton of style. At the end of the football field, the C Club brought in truckloads of wood for a night-before-the-game bonfire. Over in the gym, Girls' League Council members were figuring out how to anchor a large pole to the center of the floor and string crepe paper from it to create a carousel, the centerpiece for the Football Ball.

And in the auditorium, the Pep Club decorated the stage in orange and black in preparation for crowning the homecoming queen, an event that any girl in the running furiously pretended didn't matter in the least. That was actually a pretty good stance to take, since the whole thing was out of our hands. The football team picked queen and attendants from a group of seniors nominated by the student body, and even if it had occurred to any of us to lobby for ourselves, who would have known how to figure the politics of four dozen high school boys? Except maybe one of them. I've long suspected that Dick's first successful campaign for a candidate besides himself was the Natrona County High School homecoming queen race in 1958.

All these years later and in such enlightened times, I am embarrassed to acknowledge that being high school homecoming queen was fun, but it was, all of it, from being crowned with a rhinestone tiara by Dick, to receiving a bouquet of roses from Tim Karnes, to riding in a convertible in the homecoming parade. And the football game that night against Rock Springs was the team of 1958's best. T. J. Claunch, filling in for Tom Fake, "directed the Mustang winged-T attack spectacularly and showed a good passing arm," wrote sports writer Mac Hazel. Fullback Bill Dryer, a bright, mathematically inclined senior, carried the ball into the end zone for three touchdowns, and lanky Bob Kechely made a fourth. Co-captain Dick Cheney, the top ball carrier for the night, gained 129 yards in twenty carries, and when the game was over, it was Mustangs 25, Rock Springs 14. We had won our senior homecoming game.

It was a nice time in our lives, but it was also a time when many of us began to think about leaving Casper. At the urging of geometry teacher Ione Gibbs, I had applied to Barnard College, and a local Yale alumnus, Tom Stroock, was encouraging Dick and his friend Tom to go to Yale. We were not unusual in having our sights set high. Our friends were applying to Columbia, Harvard, Duke, Bowdoin, Vassar, Stanford—partly to fulfill the expectations of Miss Feris, Miss Shidler, and Mrs. Gibbs, but partly, too, because these places were far away, and we wanted to begin to explore the wider world.

Teachers had made us think about life outside Wyoming, but in my case, so had my family. Once we went to Mexicali, which is across the border from Yuma, Arizona, where my grand-parents lived. It was the only time my parents were outside the country, and hardly a glamorous locale, but somehow the trip inspired my father to think of the spot he'd really like to go: Hawaii. In a Mexicali pottery shop, he bought a two-foot-tall piggy bank in the shape of a bull, and we hauled it back to Casper, where he fed coins into it for a trip to the islands. He never got there, but he made dreaming about distant places seem a pleasant pastime, particularly when they were lush and warm and the weather outside was twenty below.

My mother, organizing her interests around people, thought of Germany, where one of her best friends, Maria Senser, had been born. I can't say she wanted to go there, but she wanted to know about the place where Maria grew up and where the Lybyers had come from. She also wanted me to learn about it and saw to it that I spent time with Maria, who had married a GI and come to

Wyoming to live after World War II. The Sensers would some-times go to Alcova Lake with us, and if we were sitting on a blanket on the shore and I failed to encourage Maria to talk about Germany, my mother would ask the questions and watch me to be sure I was listening to the answers.

My aunt Norma also had someone she wanted me to know, Mako Miller, whose mother was from Tennessee and whose father had been a Japanese diplomat serving in Washington at the time of Pearl Harbor. Deported to Japan, Hidenari Terasaki and his family, including nine-year-old Mako, spent the war there, and afterward, Gwen Terasaki, Mako's mother, wrote *Bridge to the Sun*, a best-selling book about their experiences. Mako, tall, beautiful, and outspoken, had married attorney Mayne Miller and recently moved to Casper with him, prompting Norma to have a coffee to introduce her to people, or, in my case, to intro-duce me to her. She sat me next to Mako on the piano bench so I would be sure to visit with this striking woman who described experiences that weren't in the history books: her father's failed efforts to avert war, her family's moving from one small house to another in Japan to stay out of the path of American bombing raids.

The world was full of places to go and things to do, and my classmates and I also wanted to know more about what we could be. A few of us had some definite ideas in mind. Tom Fake told an interviewer for the *Gusher* that he wanted to go to the Univer-sity of Iowa and become a dentist, and he is a dentist in Iowa today. Lou Sturbois had firmly decided on West Point and a mili-tary life, the path he followed, but most of us had little notion of where we were headed or even of the possibilities we should con-sider. Dick's five weeks at Northwestern, during which he had learned about all the different kinds of engineering, from civil to mechanical to industrial, mainly convinced him that he didn't want to be an engineer. I had decided to major in mathematics, but that wasn't a career. On my seventeenth birthday, I cut out an astrology column, "What's in the Stars for You?" by Stella, which promised fame and fortune, assured me I would be a fine teacher, and encouraged me to save money for a rainy day and marry early. Perhaps it seemed wise at the time, since I carefully pasted it in my scrapbook, but more likely, it reflected my own inconclusive mind.

Years later, when I had settled into writing, I would recall that I had known two writers growing up in Casper. One was Betty Evenson, whom I met one day in the Grant family house on North Kimball Street. A round-faced, grandmotherly woman, she was visiting at the kitchen table with Emily Grant, my friend Mary's mother, who introduced her to me as "a published author." I later found out that Mrs. Evenson published almost exclusively in romance magazines such as *My True Story*, but I was still impressed. Someone out there, outside the borders of Wyoming, paid to publish the words she wrote, quite an amazing thing, particularly since she wrote those words in one of the state's most isolated places. Betty and her husband, Maurice, lived in Hiland, Wyoming, a town sixty miles outside Casper that was really nothing more than the Evensons' combination gas station and sandwich shop, a place they had named the Bright Spot, and it was, a white storefront standing out against the brown prairie, the only sign of human habitation for miles. Sitting in the Bright Spot, coming up with love stories set in places where women had neighbors and libraries and grocery stores nearby, not to mention an abundance of men, was no easy feat. Betty once said that she'd papered her outhouse with rejection slips, but she kept at it and succeeded. It was impossible not to admire her spunk.

One of Betty's best friends was Peggy Simson Curry, a woman

about the same age, though taller, more imposing. A rancher's daughter, she had begun by writing for pulp magazines, but by the time I met her, she had published award-winning short stories and two well-regarded novels, *Fire in the Water* and *So Far from Spring*. In later years, it was her nature poetry I most admired. Pared down, seemingly simple, it captures the stark beauty that a practiced eye finds in the mountains and prairies. She could also turn a bawdy verse, calling in one for various misfortunes to be visited on a man she hated: "Lord, give him loose bowels squatting in the ditch/Before the President of the United States." She had that poem read at the governor's mansion the day she was named Wyoming's poet laureate.

I'm not sure where I first encountered Peg, as everyone called her, but I remember that she was smoking and talking about writing and that the people in the room, three or four of them, were hanging on what she had to say. I wasn't thinking about being a writer, but the moment stuck with me: a Western woman sure of her words and in command of her audience. It was a powerful image, and while I don't know that it affected my life, I wonder if years later, when I began to think about writing as a way to spend my years, it might have nudged me along.

It's possible that I met Peg at the Grants', where Emily gathered some pretty interesting people. A rancher's daughter herself, Emily had attended the state university and paid attention to what was going on in the world. She and her husband, Hugh, an independent trucker, subscribed not only to *Time* but to the *New Yorker*, and Emily loved classical music. Her daughter Mary remembers coming through the front door one day to find her mother "lying on the lime green sofa, wrist on her forehead, listening to the Texaco Opera on our Philco radio with the wind howling outside." After her son Denny was killed, Emily found comfort in Gregorian chants, but when, the summer after we graduated from high school, her twelve-year-old son Billy died during heart surgery, there was no consolation, and the house that had seemed warm and welcoming grew endlessly sad.

But most of the years of our growing up, the Grant home was a place of lively conversation and memorable encounters. One day, I met a teenager there, a girl who seemed ordinary enough until she told me that she had a vocation. It took me a while to figure out that she meant she was entering a convent, a stunning idea to my Protestant mind. It was also amazing to consider that someone my age had a plan for her life, knew exactly what she would be doing for all the days and decades that lay ahead. She was from a Wyoming town much smaller than Casper, and how could she know, I wondered? How could she know before she saw more of the world?

I couldn't map out my life from where I was. I needed to see the elephant, as travelers west used to say, to experience things I'd only heard about and explore possibilities hitherto unknown. I was ready to leave home—though not, I soon realized, ready to part ways with Dick.

CHAPTER TWENTY

I N EARLY MAY 1959, the student council took a trip to Laramie, Wyoming, and after spending some time on the bus with one of his fellow council members, a pretty, dark-haired cheerleader in the class behind us, Dick came up with what he thought was a brilliant idea: we should quit going steady and, in his words, "play the field." I did not respond positively to this suggestion, throwing his gold football at him, throwing a few things against the wall when I got home, and the next morning huddling with my mother, who decided to bring in reinforcements, namely my aunt and my grandmother.

Norma arrived bearing two spring dresses she had made for herself but never worn, gave them to me, and then, deciding they weren't enough, took off the green and yellow flowered one she was wearing so I could try it on. It worked, she decided, except for being too long, so she wore it home, shortened it, and brought it back. Grandma, understanding fully that our strategy was to make me look good and thus make Dick feel really sorry for his wandering eye, volunteered to sew something, but there wasn't time, not for a crucial event coming up, a dance for seniors only, where Dick was likely to appear unescorted, since the cheerleader, a junior, wasn't eligible to attend. Grandma, who never set foot in the town's finer department stores, offered to take me to Kassis, one of the finest, watched while I tried on dresses, and wrote a check for a stunning amount for a black lace sheath that didn't fit in about a dozen different ways but that she was confident she could alter.

Meanwhile, I was very glad to hear from Joe Meyer, who had broken up with the girl he had been dating. In addition to being good-looking, Joe had the best car in town, a 1959 gold Pontiac Catalina convertible. With a split grille and double fin blades in the rear, it was a graduation gift from his grandmother, who lived with the Meyers in their modest house on East Second Street and worshipped the ground her grandson walked on. When Joe proposed going to the Skyline Drive-In on Friday night, I accepted right away. My mother and my aunt were waiting in our front yard when he drove up, but it didn't take much of a conversation to put them at ease. Although hardly lacking in self-assurance, Joe wasn't nearly as full of himself as you would expect a guy with such great wheels to be, and besides, my aunt and my mother may have figured, if I was going to the drive-in with a guy in a glamour car, better that it was a convertible. It was also true that if we wanted Dick Cheney to know that two people could play the field, there was no surer way to accomplish that than by going to the Skyline with Joe and cruising the A&W afterward—which, wearing one of Norma's brand-new dresses, is exactly what I did.

Eddie Stuckenhoff, a sweet redheaded guy, asked if I'd go to the senior dance with him. I'd known Eddie since kindergarten, when his mother regularly asked me over to their house after school. His father, Dr. Stuckenhoff, had removed my tonsils and my appendix and convinced me that being carsick was all in my head. Eddie, who could always be counted on if you were down, had a million friends, of whom I was one, but I think even he was impressed by the black lace sheath after my grandmother got through with it. And so was Dick Cheney, who asked me to dance about halfway through the evening—and not long after that, asked to take me home.

Playing the field, start to finish, had lasted eleven days. I can't testify to congratulatory phone calls among my mother, my grandmother, and my aunt, but I suspect they occurred. And what did they say to one another as they contemplated their handiwork? "He's a nice young man," I imagine one of them commenting, and then another adding, "But with the Lybyer women lined up against him, he never stood a chance."

And so we were together for the prom and graduation and all the events that wrap up a senior year, but very soon we were going to be apart. He had a wonderful scholarship and was going to Yale. I had a great scholarship to Barnard and for a long time held on to the idea of going there. New Haven and New York couldn't be too far apart, I thought, given the way things were all jammed together in that part of the world. But I had also received a fine scholarship to Colorado College, a small liberal arts school in Colorado Springs with many attractions, including the fact that I had actually visited it. I could see myself going to school there, while I'd never laid eyes on Barnard and drew a blank when I tried to imagine the simplest things. How would I get to Morningside Heights? A plane and then what? It was easier for me to think about going to Europe than to New York, and that's what I really wanted to do. For all the money my parents would have to spend to get me back and forth to Barnard, I could get to Europe and beyond. I wasn't sure exactly how such a tradeoff would work, or even if it would, but the thought of it helped me decide to go to Colorado College, and that was going to put me half a continent away from Dick.

We signed each other's yearbook, and judging by what we wrote, we handled the impending separation by ignoring it and

Dick and I went to the prom in both 1958 and 1959, our last year in high school. But it was a close call our senior year, when we broke up—for all of eleven days.

I signed annuals and traded graduation pictures with kids I had known since grade school:

Tom Fake, who became
a dentist in Iowa.

Mary Grant, a university
administrator in San Francisco today.

Karen Brewer,
who became a psychology professor.

Dave Nicholas, who married
Karen, became a lawyer and
diplomat, and died of a heart
attack in Ukraine in 2005.

Joe Meyer, who married Miss Wyoming 1961, became a lawyer, and is now Wyoming state treasurer.

Linda Bowman, who had a career in software development.

Darla Howard, who sent her picture from Phoenix, where she moved our senior year. She lives in Florida today.

Eddie Stuckenhoff, who became a rancher and was killed in an automobile accident in 2001.

My favorite graduation picture. Dick and me, with my mother looking on.

relishing our time in high school. "I can never tell you how glad I am that we are signing annuals and sharing all the other things that signify the end of so much," I began. "This has been the most memorable year of my life. I'll never forget homecoming, mixers, formal dances, you, all the happy times we've known together." I praised his fine qualities and at the end of the page, looked forward, but only a little. "I can hardly wait for Friday night—and the next Friday night—and the next Friday night," I wrote.

He wrote, "It seems like such a short time ago that we were freshmen. I would like to do it all over again, especially the last two years." He reminisced about the same things I did— homecoming, formal dances—and added a few: "all the Tuesday nights at the Canteen" and "the time you came to Chicago from Wisconsin just to see me." He paid me extravagant compliments, wonderful to read yet today, including one so sweetly awkward and politically incorrect that our daughters brought the house down when they read it out loud at our thirty-fifth anniversary party. "Lynne," he wrote, "you have a wonderful personality, you're very pretty, and you're awfully intelligent. Most girls are either pretty and dumb or smart and plain. You have a rare combination of both."

When I think of our seventeen- and eighteen-year-old selves, part of me marvels that we didn't chuck everything, get married, and enroll in Casper College or the University of Wyoming together, as did a few of our friends who fell in love in high school. But some of us felt compelled to leave, not just Dick and I but many of our classmates, including our dear friends Dave Nicholas and Karen Brewer. They, too, were sweethearts at NCHS and went their separate ways, he to Harvard, she to Duke, before getting married several years later.

Did the German and Mormon and English and Scots Irish ancestors who picked up and moved across oceans and continents to change their fate leave a mark on us so that we, too, felt obliged to leave the place where we'd grown up, the place we loved, the place we would always think of as home? Was it the many expectations that their descendants had for us that compelled us to go forth in hopes of fulfilling them?

As we signed each other's yearbook, Dick and I could not have predicted the next few years, much less the decades ahead. We loved each other very much but understood that it was not at all certain we would hold on to each other through distance of miles and years.

But we did, and, as the poet said, that has made all the difference.

EPILOGUE

FOURTEEN YEARS AFTER I graduated from high school and nine years after Dick and I were married, my father called in the middle of the night with awful news. "Lynnie, your mother's dead." She'd gone up to Yesness Pond, taking along the two dachshunds she and my father had acquired after my brother and I left home, and when she didn't return, he went to find her. She, who had worried since childhood about water, had drowned in the pond.

The door to her car was open, items from her purse were scattered around, and although the official conclusion was that her death was an accident, for years I wondered if she had somehow been the victim of foul play. But the more likely explanation is the medicine she was taking for her blood pressure, which she had complained made her dizzy, and a couple of drinks she had around dinnertime. I can imagine one of the dogs leaping from the car when she opened the door and her giving chase—and fainting, falling into the pond. The dogs would have raced around frantically, even returning to the car and shaking her purse, so that a few days later, I would find her checkbook on the floor of the backseat.

My father was devastated. Over the years, my mother had become less tolerant of his temper, more likely to walk out herself when he began to shout, and I suspect that they quarreled before she left, adding a dimension of remorse to his sorrow. In his grief, he began to drink more, and in a few years, my brother called to tell me that he had been hospitalized with cirrhosis. His liver, damaged by years of heavy drinking, was no longer filtering poisons from his body, and he spent his final days sleeping, anesthetized by the toxins. The last time I visited him, he awakened just long enough to acknowledge me. "My little girl," he said, squeezing my hand.

My mother was fifty-four when she died, and my father was sixty, and while there aren't many parts of my story I would change if I could, this is one. I would have them live to their biblical three score and ten—and far beyond. I would have them, deep in old age, sit in the painted metal chairs on the grass in the front yard and watch the stars come out. And I would show them their granddaughters, beautiful women now, and introduce them to their great-grandchildren, smiling and happy. And I would thank them for the precious gift they gave me of unconditional love.

NOTES ON SOURCES

I was helped by many people as I wrote this book and hope that by indicating the wealth and variety of resources available, I might be of help to others interested in researching their lives and the lives of their forebears.

I began my research close to home, at the Goodstein Foundation Library at Casper College, and over several years have posed hundreds of questions to the archivist of the Western History Collection, Kevin Anderson, who, with the aid of Margaret Ann Raida, Ardelle Martin, Edna Garrett, and Twilla Herrick, has always come up with the answers. I have also benefited from the collections of the Natrona County Public Library, ably overseen by Bill Nelson and his fine staff, and the Salt Creek Museum in Midwest, Wyoming, where Pauline Schultz has single-handedly saved thousands of artifacts from the oil-boom days at Salt Creek.

The United States has remarkable national research institutions that are open to the public, including the National Archives and Records Administration, a treasure trove for those interested in genealogy. The Archives has a significant Internet presence, and at www.archives.gov, one can find some records that have been digitized, guides to many others, and information on researching at the National Archives building in Washington,

D. C., or at one of its many regional archives nationwide. On my visits to the Archives in D. C., I have benefitted greatly from the patient and knowledgeable assistance of Jacqueline Budell.

The Library of Congress, one of the world's great research libraries, is an amazing storehouse of the historical information that makes family records come to life. Many of the Library's collections are available online and can be browsed at http://memory.loc.gov/ammem/index.html. Over several years, Beth Davis-Brown and Mary Yarnall have provided assistance at the Library of Congress, and I would like once again to thank them. I am also grateful to the staff in the Newspaper and Current Periodical Reading Room: Teresa Victoriana Sierra, Travis Westly, Charles W. Bean, and Lyle Minter.

The Family History Library in Salt Lake City, Utah, which has been gathering genealogical records for more than a century to assist members of the Church of Jesus Christ of Latter Day Saints, is a remarkable resource, open to the public, for those seeking to identify ancestors. I am especially grateful to the staff of the Family History Library, particularly Elaine Hasleton, for directing me to scholarship on important events in Mormon history. In addition to the Family History Library, the Mormon Church has some four thousand Family History Centers around the world open to the public for research. The Web site http://www.familysearch.org/ provides access to many of the church's family records and a guide for finding and using others.

The beautiful Washington, D. C., Library of the Daughters of the American Revolution, which can be visited for a nominal fee, has books, files, and microfilm records helpful to those doing research on family history and provides access through its computers to a number of important databases. I am grateful to Director Eric Grundset and staff genealogists Twyla Jackino and

Tom Gill for guiding me through the library and pointing me in the direction of my ancestors.

As I have read through hundreds of old genealogies, I have been repeatedly struck by the transformation that personal computers and the Internet have wrought, making it easy to add new information to family histories and, more important, putting researchers in contact with databases and one another. In addition to the Web sites mentioned above, anyone researching family history should look at the USGenWeb Project, www.us genweb.org/index.shtml, a remarkable volunteer effort that has grown over the past ten years so that today it offers free access to a vast store of information organized on a county-by-county basis. Ancestry.com, www.ancestry.com, and Genealogy.com, www.genealogy.com, subscription Web sites that provide access to valuable information such as U.S. census data, also have free features, including message boards that connect people with common research interests. The information being posted at such Web sites is quite remarkable. At Rootsweb.com, http:// boards.rootsweb.com/, where the Ancestry.com message board is located, I found a link to a pension file for one of my Revolutionary War relatives.

Excellent histories that analyze the 1940s and '50s have been useful for putting my experiences in context, including Joseph C. Goulden, *The Best Years 1945–1950* (New York: Atheneum, 1976); David Halberstam, *The Fifties* (New York: Villard Books, 1993); William O'Neill, *American High: The Years of Confidence 1945–1960* (New York: Free Press, 1986); and James T. Patterson, *Grand Expectations: The United States, 1945–1974* (New York: Oxford University Press, 1996).

State and local histories have also been valuable, including Irving Garbutt and Chuck Morrison, *Casper Centennial,*

1889–1989 (Dallas: Curtis Media Corporation, 1990); Walter Jones, *History of the Sand Bar, 1888–1977* (Casper, Wyoming: Mountain States Lithographing, 1981); Edna Gorrell Kukura and Susan Niethammer True, *Casper: A Pictorial History* (Norfolk, Virginia: Donning Company Publishers, 1986); T. A. Larson, *History of Wyoming*, 2nd ed. (Lincoln, Nebraska: University of Nebraska Press, 1978); Alfred James Mokler, *History of Natrona County, Wyoming, 1888–1922* (Chicago: Lakeside Press, 1923); and Writers' Program, *Wyoming: A Guide to Its History, Highways, and People* (New York: Oxford University Press, 1941). I've also found the essays written by the Natrona County High School Class of 1950, *Memories of Casper, 1935–1955* (Casper, Wyoming: Mountain States Lithographing, 2000), charming, evocative, and useful. The photographs of historic Wyoming at www.wyo mingtalesandtrails.com have been an important aid to understanding what the state was like when my grandparents arrived.

Schoolmates have helped with many details, and I'd particularly like to thank Ken Hoff and Mary Ann Garman Hoff, who over the years have assumed responsibility for keeping track of the Natrona County High School Class of 1959 and helped me locate many members. My gratitude for sharing memories to: Linda Bowman, Gary Boyle, Kay Schuman Boyle, Jon Brady, Bryan Brewer, Rick Brown, Darla Howard Burris, Molly Peak Campbell, Steve Campbell, Sue Olds Carr, Bruce Cody, Bill Colgin, Joanne Patterson Colgin, Sheila Doing Cooper, Steve Cross, Barbara Lockwood Durbin-Payne, Tom Fake, Karen Whitlock Farnham, Linda Ladd Fellwock, Becky Boyles Ford, Catherine Gibbs, Mary Grant, Kris Koford, Beverly Bunce Lewis, Ron Lewis, John Mayer, Joe Meyer, Jerry Moore, Karen Brewer Nicholas, Irene Grant Noe, Carol Strasheim Purfurst, Karen Romans Randolph, Abby Bowen Rodda, Jerry Sands, Judy Brown Sands, Bob Schuster, Bernie Seebaum, Mary Thompson South, Curtis Strobeck, Tolly Swallow, Susie True, Jackie Carpenter Valdez, Bonnie Burrill Voorhees, Marilyn McClintock Webb, Vicki Lagos Yancey, and Phyllis Lagos Yeamans.

I regret that I couldn't talk to everyone with whom I grew up. I was lucky to share the '40s and '50s with many wonderful people, each of whom experienced these years uniquely and has his or her own story to tell.

PROLOGUE

City directories have been useful in this section and throughout the book to confirm memories of where people lived and worked. My brother Mark Vincent did me an enormous favor by rescuing Casper directories published by R. L. Polk and Company in the 1940s and 1950s from a discard pile and sending them to me.

Local newspapers have provided much information, such as the account of the burned body found on a road east of town. On July 30, 1946, stories about this "cremation murder" began to appear in the *Casper Tribune-Herald*, which, like thousands of other newspapers, is available on microfilm to the general public in the Newspaper and Current Periodical Reading Room of the Library of Congress in Washington, D.C. Beginning in 1949, Casper had a second paper, the *Casper Morning Star*, which I read in hard copy at the Goodstein Foundation Library at Casper College. In 1965, the two papers merged to become the *Casper Star-Tribune*.

PART ONE

CHAPTER ONE: The memories and keepsakes of family members have been an invaluable resource, starting with the picture albums my mother made and saved. Even somewhat distant relatives shared treasures with me, including my second cousin Earl Gary, who gave me a letter handwritten by my grandmother describing my father's 1941 accident, his injuries, and the dire prediction of doctors that I quote in this chapter. My uncle Dale Vincent is among the relatives who provided me with family stories, including the incident in this chapter about my grandmother Anna and the train conductor.

Newspaper obituaries have been an important source of information about people's lives as well as their deaths, and finding the relevant ones, such as those I used in this chapter for information on the Schryer family (*Casper Tribune-Herald*, March 8, 1940; February 26, 1943; October 19, 1944; and March 8, 1945), was made many times easier not only by the assistance of Kevin Anderson but also by the indexing done by the Natrona County Genealogical Society.

CHAPTER TWO: The Lybyer family is among those fortunate enough to have a comprehensive genealogical publication that lays out forebears. I am indebted to John Lavern Lybarger and Lee Hartshorne Lybarger's, *The Lybarger Descendants* (Delaware, Ohio: Lybarger Memorial Association, 2000), a book that lists and often describes in some detail more than 13,000 descendants of Nicholas Leyberger, who spell their names in several ways. To lessen confusion, I've called all in the first, second, and third generation Leyberger, though I have also come across Lyberger and Lybarger, the latter of which would become the most common spelling. In *Descendants*, the Lybargers make a strong case for Nicholas Leyberger being the first of the family to come to America and in a footnote on p. 35 indicate the family story about his selling his services to pay for his passage. As they note, the story is not definitive, but there is not likely to be evidence that is, since few indenture documents survive from the years when he immigrated. Because historians estimate that about half of eighteenth-century German immigrants indentured themselves to pay for passage, I view the story as tipping the balance and making it more likely than not that Nicholas was indentured. Gottlieb Mittelberger's *Journey to Pennsylvania*, translated and edited by Oscar Handlin and John Clive (Cambridge, Massachusetts: Harvard University Press, 1960), provided important information on eighteenth-century immigrant travel from Germany to the United States and on "redemptioning," the practice of selling oneself into servitude after arriving in America.

The quotations from Nicholas Leyberger, who, like my direct ancestor, Nicholas's uncle Ludwick, was a farmer in Bedford County, Pennsylvania, and a member of the Fourth Company, First Battalion of the Bedford County Militia, come from his pension file, available in the Seimes Microfilm Center at the Daughters of the American Revolution Library in Washington, D.C. After my visit to the D.A.R. Library, I also found Nicholas's pension file online: www.heritagepathways.com/pension/pension .htm. The information about the wolves and other details of the Revolutionary period in southeastern Pennsylvania are from E. Howard Blackburn and William Welfley, *History of Bedford and Somerset Counties Pennsylvania with Genealogical and Personal History*, 3 vols. (New York: Lewis Publishing Company, 1906). Part of the Blackburn and Welfley history is available at www .rootsweb.com/~pasomers/index.htm, a Web site that is part of the USGenWeb Project. Larry D. Smith, *Mother Bedford and the American Revolutionary War* (Apollo, Pennsylvania: Closson Press, 1999), also provides details of the war between settlers and Indians. The story about Ludwick Leyberger is from Donald Fisher Lybarger, *History of the Lybarger Family* (Cleveland, Ohio, 1959), p. 16.

Details about the wartime service and medical history of Andrew Simon Peter Lybyer and his brother Salem Lybyer are drawn from enlistment papers and pension files in the National Archives and Records Administration. I relied on homestead files in the National Archives to determine such matters as when people moved, what structures they built on their homesteads, and what crops they planted and harvested.

Ralph B. Strassburger, *Pennsylvania German Pioneers*, ed. William John Henke (Harristown, Pennsylvania: Pennsylvania German Society, 1934) II, pp. 264 and 268, shows the immigrant Nicholas Leyberger signing oaths by making a mark. In the pension file of the Revolutionary War is a page from a family bible that indicates Nicholas's struggle to write German. Family letters written by Andrew Simon Peter Lybyer show his efforts with English.

Throughout this chapter, I have relied on research done on family history by my aunts Norma Lybyer Brown and Marion Lybyer Byron. Family interviews they helped preserve provided many details of life on the Missouri farm, from the "hard on work" quotation, to the chrysanthemums around the farmhouse, to Kaiser, Andrew's horse. I have quoted from family letters they preserved, one from my grandfather to my grandmother dated March 5, 1913, and one from Malcolm Campbell to my grandfather dated April 30, 1970. I also have quoted from a letter saved by Earl Gary that is from Leonard Lybyer to Myrtle Bader, January 20, 1914. Contemporary observations on early German immigrants are found in Benjamin Rush's *An Account of the Manners of the German Inhabitants of Pennsylvania* (Philadelphia: Samuel P. Town, 1875), a publication available at http://books.google.com.

For the section on life in Salt Creek, I've found Jim Crawford's "Last of the Franco Claim Jumpers," an article that appeared in the *Casper Star-Tribune*, March 15, 1970, to be of great use. It was based on an interview done with my grandfather not long before he died. Useful books include Ed Bille, *Early Days at Salt Creek and Teapot Dome* (Casper, Wyoming: Mountain States Lithographing, 1978); *Tour Guide: Salt Creek Oil Field, Natrona County, Wyoming*, a publication prepared for the Natrona County Historic Preservation Commission by Rosenberg Historical Consultants (Casper, Wyoming: Mountain States Lithographing, 2003); and J. T. Wall, *Life in the Shannon and Salt Creek Oil Field* (Philadelphia: Dorrance, 1973). This last book, p. 71, is the source of the quotation about oil-drilling activity in Salt Creek in 1921. The cheer offered at ball games by Salt Creek grade-schoolers is from a reminiscence by Janet Shidler in Garbutt and Morrison, *Casper Centennial*, p. 110.

Pauline Schultz of the Salt Creek Museum showed me, among other things, photographs of ragtown houses, layouts of company shacks, the Midwest High School annual from the year my mother was a freshman, and a photo of the fifty-foot bank over which my grandfather fell. My cousin Glenn Byron kindly provided photographs from my grandparents' early oil-field days. William Wyckoff, *Creating Colorado* (New Haven, Connecticut: Yale University Press, 1999), helped me understand why my grandparents moved to northwest Colorado during World War I.

The information about the Lee family and the account of John Lough's death are from genealogical information and interviews preserved by my aunts. The story of the near-drowning in Midwest is from the *Midwest Review*, July–August 1930, p. 27. I've heard a different version of this story many times, one in which my grandmother and my aunt were in peril, but I think this contemporary account is more likely to be accurate.

Information on the ownership transfer of 906 South David is

drawn from records at the Natrona County Assessor's Office in Casper. They were copied for me by my niece Trisha Vincent Zeller, who kindly unearthed and verified many facts for me.

CHAPTER THREE: Old radio and TV programs can loose a flood of memories, and the Internet has made it easier to find and order recordings. I listened to *Queen for a Day* for February 14, 1944, and August 10, 1945, on a compact disc.

Norma Brown's family—Carla Brown, Tina Brown Jones, and Ben Brown—shared with me the meticulous family scrapbooks that she created. It was in one of them that I found the note from her teacher. Norma's children also told me family stories, as did Norma and Cork's friends Max and Shirley Brown. I interviewed Bub Lockwood, my aunt Maxine's husband, shortly before his death. Bub and Maxine's daughter, Karen Lockwood Canchola, was also generous with her time and very good at remembering details of the past.

CHAPTER FOUR: I am indebted for information on Wonder Woman's creator to Nick Gillespie, who wrote "William Marston's Secret Identity" in *Reason* magazine's May 2001 issue. The article is available online at http://www.reason.com/news/show/28014.html. The quotations from the *Park Ranger* are from a collection saved and generously shared by Karen Romans Randolph. The Carole Kismaric and Marvin Heiferman book is *Growing Up with Dick and Jane* (New York: Collins Publishers, 1996). The reference to work is on p. 70.

Norma Brown recorded memories of her friendship with Shirley Williams on May 16, 1998, as part of an oral history project conducted by students at East Junior High School in Casper, Wyoming, in honor of Martin Luther King, Jr. The history, called to my attention by Kevin Anderson, is on file at the Casper College Library. I've also drawn information from "Shirley's Café Closed," *Casper Morning Star*, February 17, 1955; "Gray Found Dead," *Casper Star-Tribune*, April 29, 1972; and Jones's *History of the Sand Bar.* R. C. Johnson shared with me her knowledge of Casper's middle-class black population in the '40s and '50s and introduced me to the directories published by the African American community. Pat Hurley Bronsdon explained to me how it happened that we got to watch Arapaho dancers every summer and how she became Plume Woman, an event I remember well.

CHAPTER FIVE: Marion Byron saved my grandfather's patent applications, grants, and the correspondence to which I refer. His interview is in the *Casper Morning Star*, August 11, 1950.

CHAPTER SIX: Information on early Westridge is drawn from "Westridge Subdivision Is Rapidly Nearing Completion Here," *Casper Tribune-Herald*, August 14, 1949. Information on Levittown is from Peter Bacon Hales, "Building Levittown: A Rudimentary Primer," http://tigger.uic.edu/~pbhales/Levittown/building.html. For the Exhumation of the Rockies, see John McPhee, *Rising from the Plains* (New York: Farrar, Straus and Giroux, 1986), pp. 52–54. Fort Caspar history is from Mokler, *History of Natrona County*, and Barbara Fifer, *Wyoming's Historic Forts* (Helena, Montana: Farcountry Press, 2002). The quotation is from Fifer, p. 68. For Sally Rand, see *Casper Tribune-Herald*, August 15 and 16, 1954, and *Casper Morning Star*, August 17, 1954.

CHAPTER SEVEN: I drew information about Eleanor McLaughlin from Dana Van Burgh, "Eleanor Mc," and Loren J. "Buz" Bemis,

"My Grade School Teachers," in Class of 1950, *Memories of Casper*, pp. 33–34 and 117, as well as from Bob David, "Narrative," part of an unpublished manuscript on file at Casper College. The quotations about McKinley School gangs are from this manuscript. I was fortunate enough to be able to interview Anne Marie Spencer. The Frank Merriwell reference is from David Riesman, with Nathan Glazer and Reuel Denny, *The Lonely Crowd* (New Haven, Connecticut: Yale University Press, 1961), p. 101 of 2001 rev. ed. The information about polio in Casper comes from the *Casper Tribune-Herald*, July 11, 1945; August 7 and 13, 1946; August 2, 1949; October 2 and 22, 1951.

CHAPTER EIGHT: Dale Vincent supplied me with much information about his and my father's Mormon forebears, including genealogical records, an interview done with Katurah Vaughn, and Charles Vincent's obituary. Douglas Vincent, a great-grandson of Katurah Vaughn, has with his wife, Donnett, been generous with news clippings, relationship records, and family stories. Marie Vincent, widow of Charles Glen Vincent, who was Katurah's great-grandson, shared much family history with me and put me in touch with Colin Vaughn Morgan, a relative in Wales.

For the story of Katurah Vaughn's journey to Council Bluffs, I am deeply indebted to the work of Ronald Dennis, a scholar at Brigham Young University, who immersed himself in Welsh so that he could translate the writings of Welsh Mormons, including diaries and other records of the first Welsh immigration to Utah of which Katurah Vaughn was part. Dennis's *The Call of Zion: The Story of the First Welsh Mormon Emigration*, Religious Studies Center Specialized Monograph Series 2 (Provo, Utah: Religious Studies Center, Brigham Young University, 1987) is a model of the rich information that painstaking scholarship can

yield. The lyrics to "The Saints' Farewell" are from this mono-
graph, p. 135. The quote about Brother Smith is from p. 46.
For information on the trail westward, I am indebted as well to
Bernard DeVoto, *Across the Wide Missouri* (Boston: Houghton
Mifflin, 1947); Merrill J. Mattes, *The Great Platte River Road*
(Lincoln: Nebraska State Historical Society, 1969); and Wallace
Stegner, *The Gathering of Zion: The Story of the Mormon Trail*
(Lincoln: University of Nebraska Press, 1964). For the color of
Platte River, see James Evans as quoted in Mattes, rev. ed., 1987,
p. 163.

Details about the Mormon War are from Norman F. Furniss,
The Mormon Conflict, 1850–1859 (New Haven, Connecticut: Yale
University Press, 1960); Richard D. Poll and Ralph W. Hansen,
" 'Buchanan's Blunder,' The Utah War, 1857–1858," *Military
Affairs* 25 (1961); Brandon J. Metcalf, "The Nauvoo Legion and
the Prevention of the Utah War," *Utah Historical Quarterly* 72
(2004); and Richard D. Poll, "The Move South," *BYU Studies* 29
(1989). Estimates about polygamy are in Metcalf, pp. 301–2.
"Enslavement of women" is from *New York Times*, March 30,
1857; and "sink of iniquity" is from *National Intelligencer*, April
20, 1857; both are quoted from Furniss, p. 83.

Both Dale Vincent and my brother Leon Vincent shared with
me memories of my grandparents Anna and Lyn. Dale's unpublished history of his family, which he wrote in 1995, has been
particularly helpful, especially with its memories of the years
when my father was growing up. One detail not in that history,
that in 1910 my grandfather "corked flumes" in Telluride, Colorado, comes from federal census records, which are a remarkable
aid to historians. I accessed the census for various years through a
subscription Web site, www.ancestry.com. The quotations from
the early Irish arrival in Casper, Frank O'Mahoney, are from Garbutt and Morrison, *Casper Centennial*, p. 32.

CHAPTER NINE: "Mrs. Casper's Cooking Class," featuring my mother, appeared on March 21, 1952.

CHAPTER TEN: I particularly appreciate Lana Templeton Henman's sharing baton-twirling memories and photographs with me. Bob Roberts's quotation is from the *Casper Morning Star*, August 14, 1953. Details about sponsorship to the national contest are from the *Casper Morning Star*, January 28, 1955. IWBF is from Anna Fels, *Necessary Dreams: Ambition in Women's Changing Lives* (New York: Pantheon Books, 2004), p. 3.

PART TWO

CHAPTER ELEVEN: Throughout her life, my husband's mother, Marge Cheney, kept extensive scrapbooks and photo albums, and I have relied on them for this book. The article on military wives in San Diego, saved by Marge, was in the *San Diego Daily Journal*, August 25, 1944. The Cheney family is fortunate to have a family history done by one of the outstanding genealogical researchers of the late nineteenth and early twentieth centuries, Charles Henry Pope. I have relied on his book, *The Cheney Genealogy* (Boston: Charles H. Pope, 1897), throughout this chapter. I am indebted to Perry Miller's *The New England Mind: The Seventeenth Century* (New York: Macmillan Company, 1939) for its explanation of Puritan faith and worldview. The idea that joining the church would be painful for those who found it difficult to speak in public was suggested by William Rathband, whose views are presented on p. 453 of Miller, Belknap Press 1982 reprint. Quotations about Margaret Cheney are from Pope, pp. 18 and 29. With regard to William Cheney, who lived on Grand Menan Island, I understand that the term *United Empire Loyalist* is commonly applied to those who left the United States after war with Britain began, but as the family chart makes clear, the Cheneys thought of William that way even though he left before the Revolution.

Brad Quinlan and other members of the research branch of the 21st Ohio Re-enactors, including Lollie Haugh, Josh Haugh, Sue Howell, Mark Stibitz and Joan Stibitz, have kindly provided much information about that regiment and Samuel Fletcher Cheney, and I have drawn on the fruits of their labor as I have written this chapter. Information on Samuel Cheney also comes from military, pension, and homestead records in the National Archives. In addition, I am indebted to the following books: Thomas B. Buell, *The Warrior Generals: Combat Leadership in the Civil War* (New York: Crown Publishers, 1997); Richard W. Johnson, *Memoir of Major General George H. Thomas* (Philadelphia: J. B. Lippincott & Co., 1881); Captain S. S. Canfield, *History of the 21st Ohio Volunteer Infantry in the War of the Rebellion* (Toledo, Ohio: Vrooman, Anderson & Bateman, Printers, 1893). Ernest B. Ferguson's article, "Catching Up with 'Old Slow Trot,'" *Smithsonian*, March 2007, was also useful. The quotation from Colonel Miller is from his official report, available at http://hometown.aol.com/stonesriverdan/millersbrigade.html. A transcription of George Squire's letter can be found in the Stones River National Battlefield regimental files. The story of General Thomas's review of the 21st Ohio is from Canfield, pp. 158–59. The quotation from Samuel Cheney about his men having supper and other court-martial details are from his court-martial file in the National Archives. Quotations about Lee's surrender and Lincoln's death are from Canfield, p. 188. The quotation about Samuel Cheney's accident is from a March 4, 1891, affidavit in his pension file at the National Archives. I originally learned of Samuel's becoming part owner of a planing mill from an article in a Defiance paper, Jack Palmer, "Dick Cheney's Family Linked to Defiance," *Crescent-News*, February 17, 2002. Defiance city historian Randy Buchman and research librarian Elaine Walker of the Defiance Public Library provided further details. Rhonda Casler of the Defiance County Records Center helped me find deeds recording Samuel Cheney's purchases and sales of land, as well as documents concerning the assignment of his business to a trustee. Steve VanDemark, General Manager of the *Crescent-News* in Defiance, kindly provided microfilm of the *Defiance Democrat* from the early 1880s. Information on the effect of the 1890 drought on Samuel Cheney's farm is from an affidavit in his pension file. Irene Mollard, whose family lives on land homesteaded by Samuel Cheney, provided me with the sheriff's deed record of the sale of Samuel's Nebraska homestead, as well as photographs of what it looks like today.

Margaret Tyler Cheney's genealogy book is Martha Coleman Johnson, *The Prichard Family* (n.p., 1915). Documents relating to the Richard Cheney who came to Maryland are in the Maryland State Archives, and state archivist Edward C. Papenfuse, Jr., guided me to them and provided a wealth of information. Anne Arundel County archeologist Al Luckenbach and architectural historian Donna Ware showed me Richard Cheney's seventeenth-century homesite. Reverdy Lewin Orrell III shared with me the work he has done on the genealogy of the Maryland Cheneys. The genealogical work of William Addams Reitwiesner has also been useful. See www.wargs.com/political/cheney.html. Many of the details of the life of Richard H. Cheney, my husband's father, come from a series of taped interviews that my daughter Elizabeth Cheney Perry did with him before his death. The number of bank failures in 1931 is from Timothy Egan, *The Worst Hard Time: The Untold Story of Those Who Survived the Great American Dust Bowl* (New York: Houghton Mifflin Company, 2006), p. 95.

CHAPTER TWELVE: Details about Marge Dickey and the Syracuse Bluebirds, including quotations from newspapers, are taken from a scrapbook she kept. She did not often label the clippings she pasted in the scrapbook, but many are from the *Syracuse Journal Democrat*. David Hackett Fischer's book, *Albion's Seed* (New York: Oxford University Press, 1989), is a wonderful explanation of how four different groups from Britain brought their cultures to America. I am indebted in particular to the section on the Scots Irish, a group that Fischer prefers to call border people, and their clans. I am indebted to genealogical information on both the Cheney and McGaugh families provided by Ann Sudom, Doreen Pigeon, and Bill and Sherry Parkinson. Bill, like Marge Cheney, was Laura Nora's grandchild and gave me a copy of the diary she kept. He also provided many details of Dickey's Café, where he worked as a young man. Gene Dickey provided family photographs. Information on young men of Southern sympathies leaving Missouri can be found in Robert Beebe David, *Finn Burnett, Frontiersman* (Glendale, California: Arthur H. Clark Company, 1937), pp. 20–26. Page references are to 2003 Stackpole Books reprint with new introduction. This book was called to my attention by one of Finn Burnett's descendants, Senator Alan Simpson. David Dickey's joke about the carp was recalled in a condolence letter to his family after his death in 1955. Mrs. E. Albin Larson presented it as a story told by her son Vic. Information on the Burr fire is from an unlabeled newspaper clipping saved by Marge Cheney.

CHAPTER THIRTEEN: The John Keats quotation is from *The Crack in the Picture Window* (Boston: Houghton Mifflin Company, 1956), p. xii. *A Treasury of Heroes' Stories* was published in New York by Hart Publishing, 1949.

PART THREE

CHAPTER FOURTEEN: For details on Bill Daniels and Community Television, I am indebted to Stephen Singular, *Relentless: Bill Daniels and the Triumph of Cable TV* (Bill Daniels estate, 2003). The Matt Tinley quotation is on p. 108. I found details of the history of Community TV and the armory display in Betty James, "Equipment to Be Placed on Display" and "TV System Justifies Vision, Confidence of Casper Group," *Casper Tribune-Herald and Star*, January 6, 1954; and "Large Crowds Attending Television Shows Here," *Casper Tribune-Herald and Star*, January 10, 1954. The Gene Schneider quotation is from Stephen Singular, "Before Cable Was Cool," *Cable World* (July 7, 2000), p. 15.

I watched recordings of undated episodes of *I Led Three Lives* and *Your Hit Parade*, as well as *The Honeymooners: The Classic 39 Collection*, programs that ran in 1955 and '56, and *The Honeymooners: Lost Episodes*, boxed set one, sketches from the *The Jackie Gleason Show* in 1953, 1955, and 1956. I also watched undated reruns of *What's My Line?* on the Game Show Network. I have used details and quotations from these sources. Information about Joyce Brothers is from Halberstam, *The Fifties*, p. 648 of 1994 Ballantine Books ed. The quotation about "Love Is a Many-Splendored Thing" is from www.answers.com/topic/love-is-a-many-splendored-thing.

CHAPTER FIFTEEN: The history of Natrona County High School is from the National Register of Historic Places Registration

Form, an undated speech by William Reese on file at Goodstein Foundation Library, and an obituary of Arthur M. Garbutt, *Casper Tribune-Herald*, December 31, 1953.

Frances Feris's autobiography, "'Rough, Stark' Childhood in Wyoming," appeared in *Casper Star-Tribune*, March 12, 1972. Details of the estate are from Irving Garbutt, "Miss Feris Wills Bulk of Estate to Students," an undated article from *Casper Star-Tribune* on file in the Goodstein Foundation Library. On progressive education in the 1950s, see Lawrence A. Cremin, *The Transformation of the School* (New York: Alfred A. Knopf, 1961), pp. 328 ff. Information about Margaret LaViolette is from an undated interview conducted by Angela Sidwell and *Casper Star-Tribune*, January 28, 1969, and February 19, 1985. Information on Kathleen Hemry is from an autobiographical essay in Garbutt and Morrison, *Casper Centennial*, pp. 185–86; Susan Anderson, "Raised in a Sheep-Wagon, Hemry Gave $1 Million before Death at Age 100," *Casper Journal*, April 7, 2004; Brendan Burke, "Kathleen Hemry Dies at 100," *Casper Star-Tribune*, April 3, 2004; Kathleen Hemry, *Kathleen's Book: An Album of Early Pioneer Wyoming in Word and Picture* (Casper, Wyoming: Mountain States Lithographing, 1989). Quotations about galloping on the prairie and being Irish by name are from Garbutt and Morrison. The quotation about the U-Haul is from *Kathleen's Book*, p. 130. Information on Margaret Shidler is from interviews with friends and relatives, Jim and Carole Franklin, Kathy Pons, Chuck Jones, and Marvine Shidler, as well as with her students Ken Hoff, Joe Meyer, and Bob Schuster. Information on Ione Gibbs is from an interview with her daughter, Catherine Gibbs Shaw, and from an obituary in the *Casper Star-Tribune*, December 12, 2001. I interviewed Bob Lahti and Don Weishaar's widow.

The news carrier report of a flying object is from *Casper Tribune-Herald*, November 7, 1957; Vanover Bush, October 15,

1957. The Rickover quotation is from Cremin, *The Transformation*, p. 347. History of the Carnegie Library is from "Helping Hand of Carnegie Gave Natrona County Original Library," *Casper Tribune-Herald and Star*, November 24, 1957.

CHAPTER SIXTEEN: Details about Barbara Scifers's life come from an interview with her, as well as from Delta Kappa Gamma Society, *Let Your Light Shine: Pioneer Women Educators of Wyoming, Volume III* (Sheridan, Wyoming: Wyoming Print Shop, 1965), pp. 180–81; "Leland Floyd Scifers," *Casper Star-Tribune*, March 11, 2003; and "Philanthropist Scifers Earns Award," *Casper Star-Tribune*, August 20, 2006. Quotations from the *Gusher* are from May 18, 1956, and April 1, 1958. David Riesman's speech, delivered at the University of Chicago in February 1958, appeared in expanded form in *Marriage and Family Living* 21 (August 1959). A report on the Co-ed Ball is in *Casper Star-Tribune*, October 23, 1955.

CHAPTER SEVENTEEN: The Carol Lynley interview is "Read Her Thoughts," *Seventeen*, May 1958.

CHAPTER EIGHTEEN: Quotations about football are from clippings saved by Marge Cheney: *Casper Tribune-Herald*, October 18, 1956; September 6, 1957; and October 15, 1957; also *Casper Morning Star*, August 20, 1957, and October 26, 1957. *Seventeen* magazine addressed flirting in "Sex and Your Emotions," July 1957.

CHAPTER NINETEEN: Quotation from the *Gusher*, October 31, 1958. Quotations about football from clippings saved by Marge Cheney: *Casper Morning Star*, August 15, 1958; *Laramie Boomer-*

ang, September 13, 1958; *Casper Tribune-Herald*, October 13, 1958. Details about Betty Evenson are from her autobiography, *Fifty Years at the Bright Spot* (Casper, Wyoming: Mountain States Lithographing, n.d), and from Mary Alice Gunderson's introduction to *Landmarked: Stories of Peggy Simson Curry* (Glendo, Wyoming: High Plains Press, 1992). Peggy Simson Curry's poem is also quoted from this introduction, p. xxxiii. Details about Emily Grant are from her autobiography, *Trails of the 7L* (Casper, Wyoming: Mountain States Lithographing, 2000).

PHOTO CREDITS

Courtesy of the author: pp. 12, 15 all, 18 both, 31 bottom, 41, 52 top, 68 both, 75 bottom and right, 87 bottom, 109 bottom, 123 top, 134, 138, 146 all, 153, 156 both, 164 both, 175, 176 both, 241 bottom, 264 bottom right, 277 bottom, 280

Courtesy of Lloyd Bowman: frontispiece

Courtesy of the Brown family: pp. 75 top left, 87 top

Courtesy of Darla Howard Burris: p. 279 bottom left

Courtesy of the Byron family: pp. 24 bottom right, 31 top

Courtesy of Casper College: p. 221

Courtesy of Casper Public Safety Department: p. 116 bottom

Courtesy of *Casper Star Tribune*: pp. 52 bottom, 116 top, 123 bottom, 241 top, 267 both

Courtesy of Earl Gary: p. 24 top and bottom left

Courtesy of Natrona County High School: pp. 204, 214 both, 215 both, 218 all, 252 both, 277 top, 278 all, 279 top left and right and bottom right

Courtesy of Jess Palato: p. 264 top

Courtesy of Alan Simpson: p. 264 bottom left

Courtesy of Anne Marie Spencer: p. 91 both

Courtesy of Douglas and Donnett Vincent: p. 109 top

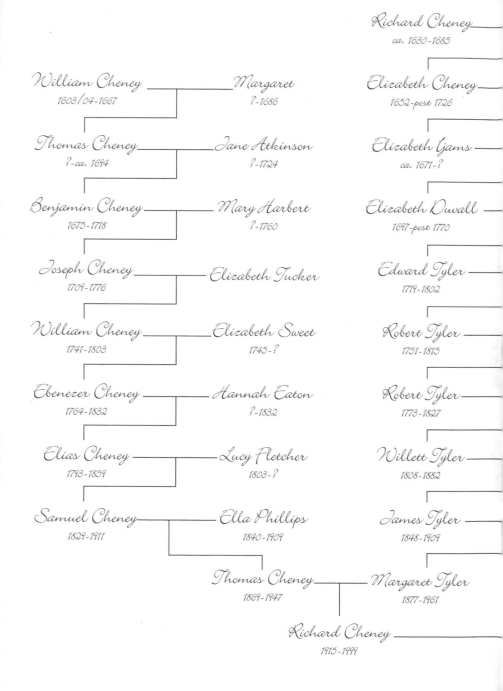

Richard Cheney
ca. 1630-1685

William Cheney
1603/04-1667

Margaret
?-1686

Elizabeth Cheney
1652-post 1726

Thomas Cheney
?-ca. 1694

Jane Atkinson
?-1724

Elizabeth Gams
ca. 1671-?

Benjamin Cheney
1675-1718

Mary Harbert
?-1760

Elizabeth Duvall
1697-post 1770

Joseph Cheney
1709-1776

Elizabeth Tucker

Edward Tyler
1719-1802

William Cheney
1741-1803

Elizabeth Sweet
1745-?

Robert Tyler
1751-1815

Ebenezer Cheney
1764-1832

Hannah Eaton
?-1832

Robert Tyler
1773-1827

Elias Cheney
1793-1859

Lucy Fletcher
1803-?

Willett Tyler
1808-1882

Samuel Cheney
1829-1911

Ella Phillips
1840-1909

James Tyler
1848-1909

Thomas Cheney
1869-1947

Margaret Tyler
1877-1961

Richard Cheney
1915-1999